# HOW TO COLLECT & RESTORE CARS

BY MIKE MURPHY & DAVID B. WEEMS

MODERN AUTOMOTIVE SERIES

TAB BOOKS Inc.

BLUE RIDGE SUMMIT, PA. 17214

FIRST EDITION

SECOND PRINTING

Printed in the United States of America

Reproduction or publication of the content in any manner, without express permission of the publisher, is prohibited. No liability is assumed with respect to the use of the information herein.

Copyright © 1981 by TAB BOOKS Inc.

Library of Congress Cataloging in Publication Data

Murphy, Mike & Weems, David B.
    How to collect and restore cars.

    Includes index.
    1. Automobiles—Restoration. 2. Automobiles—Collectors and collecting. I. Weems, David B., joint author. II. Title.
TL152.2.M87    629.28'722    80-28687
ISBN 0-8306-9624-5
ISBN 0-8306-2067-2 (pbk.)

Cover photo of a 1927 Chevrolet "Woody Wagon" courtesy of Frank Gudaitis.

**Other TAB books by David B. Weems:**

1064 *How To Design, Build, And Test Complete Speaker Systems*
1234 *21 Custom Speaker Enclosure Projects You Can Build*
1334 *30 Projects To Improve Your Stereo System*
1364 *Designing, Building & Testing Your Own Speaker System with projects*

# Preface

The old orange tractor had an engine that looked strange and yet familiar, with its gray block and a bright blue valve cover. Yes, it was a Ford 200-cubic-inch 6-cylinder car engine. And the tractor's original close-spaced front wheels had been replaced by a more useful wide track front end, based on a front axle from an old pick-up truck.

When I saw the unusual tractor, it aroused my curiosity. After investigating, I learned that the tractor had been abandoned because of the high cost of repair parts for old farm equipment. But it had been converted into a useful piece of machinery by a mechanic who operated an oak board garage on an Ozark road. His name was Mike Murphy.

I later learned that such conversions are routine for Mike. He has had a varied career in automotive mechanics that includes two tours of Sea Bee service in Viet Nam, five years working in a large garage, and seven years running his own shop, besides teaching auto mechanics in a community college.

This book draws heavily on Mike's practical experience at restoring old cars. We mention many short cuts, but we also tell the disadvantages of those short cuts. Above all, we show the low-cost way to do any job, from buying a suitable car to saving money on paint.

As a bonus, we added a concept that can drastically cut the cost of owning a car for commuting service or even general family use. As you will see, the potential savings from this concept alone can add up to thousands of dollars over several years time. It's in the last chapter. Don't miss it.

David B. Weems

# Contents

**1 Why an Old Car?**     9
Restoring Vs. Hot Rodding—Buy Them While They Are Down—History Can Be Fun—Car Clubs—Shows and Swap Meets—Related Hobbies—The Ultimate in Practical Restoration—One Man's Olds—Bad Luck and Good—From Hobby to Business

**2 What Kind of Car?**     25
Classes of Cars—Body Models—Trucks—Car Choice: Personal Factors to Consider—Contrary Opinion and Car Collecting—Some Out-of-Favor Models—Chance and the Car Collector

**3 Antique Cars**     41
High Wheeler Automobiles—Steam and Electric—Brass Era Cars—Later Antiques: The Ford T—Antique Chevrolets—Willys-Knight

**4 Classic Cars**     57
What is a Classic?—Packard—The Mystery of the Chains—Stutz—Mercer—Duesenberg—Cadillac—Lincoln—Wills Sainte Claire

**5 Production Cars**     71
Production Cars Vs. Antiques—Plymouth—The Production Fords—Mercury—Chevrolet Production Cars—Other Production Cars—Late Production Cars

**6 Foreign Cars**     85
Volkswagen—Renault—MG—Other Foreign Cars

**7 Getting a Car**     99
How to Find a Car—Car Clubs Again—Public Sales—Publications—Dealers—The REO in the Shed—A Second Look—Is the Price Right?—Legal Considerations—Moving Your Car—Trailers—Trucks for Car Hauling—Finding Parts

| 8 | **Workshop and Tools** | 121 |

Workshop—Lighting—Shop Fixtures—Shop Tools for General Use—Electrical System Tools—Tools for Engine Work—Tools for Body Work—Welding Equipment

| 9 | **Strip Down** | 139 |

Preparation for Disassembly—Strip Down Procedure—Engine—Interior Strip Down—Body Removal—Final Strip Down

| 10 | **Engine Restoration** | 153 |

Kinds of Engines—Valve Arrangements—Materials Used in Engines—Engine Diagnosis—Cleaning Engines—Frozen Engines—Disassembly Procedure—Cylinder Damage—Ring Installation—Bearings in Old Engines—Valves—Hydraulic Valve Lifters—Gaskets—Gasket Installation—Engine Swaps

| 11 | **Fuel Systems** | 187 |

Gas Tank—Gas Lines—Vacuum Tanks—Fuel Pumps—Carburetors—Fuels and Efficiency

| 12 | **Electrical Systems** | 199 |

Some Basics—Troubleshooting—Troubleshooting with Meters—How to Find Shorts—Battery—Cables—Generators—Voltage Regulation—Starters—Lights—Dash Gauge Problems—Primary Ignition Circuit—High Tension Wiring Problems

| 13 | **Cooling Systems** | 231 |

Thermostat—Coolants—Hoses—Fan Belts—Water Pump—Radiator—Leak Detection—Cracks in Head or Block—Other Heating Problems—Temperature Gauges—Air-Cooled Engines

| 14 | **The Power Train** | 149 |

Clutch and Flywheel—Clutch Removal—Transmission—Transmission Trouble Diagnosis—Drive Shaft and Universal Joints—Differential—Differential and Rear Axle Diagnosis—Rear End Removal

| 15 | **Other Chassis Components** | 265 |

Front End Design—Front End Inspection—Replacement of Kingpins and Bushings—Steering Linkage—How to Make a Press Fit—Servicing Rear Leaf Springs—Shock Absorbers—Mechanical Brakes—Hydraulic Brakes—Brake Lining Replacement—Tires for Old Cars—Lubrication for Old Cars

| 16 | **Body Restoration** | 285 |

A Special Problem with Body Bolts—Wood Work—Door and Glass Repair—Body and Frame Alignment—Hammering Out Dents—Replacing Sheet Metal—Using a Grinder—Using Body Filler—Sanding—Masking—Safety Precautions—Buying Paint—Painting—Interior—Door Panels—Seats—Headliner—Panel Dials

## 17 How to Get a Work Car Cheap  307
The Old Car Getaway—Mike's Story—Engine Disassembly—New Rings—Body Condition—A Trip to the Salvage Yard—Sheet Metal Work—Grinding and Filling—The Rest of the Body—Sanding—Another Trip to the Salvage Yard—Interior Metal—Painting—Wheels and Tires—Upholstery

## 18 An Encouraging Word  227

**Appendix   National Car Clubs And Publications**  331

**Index**  333

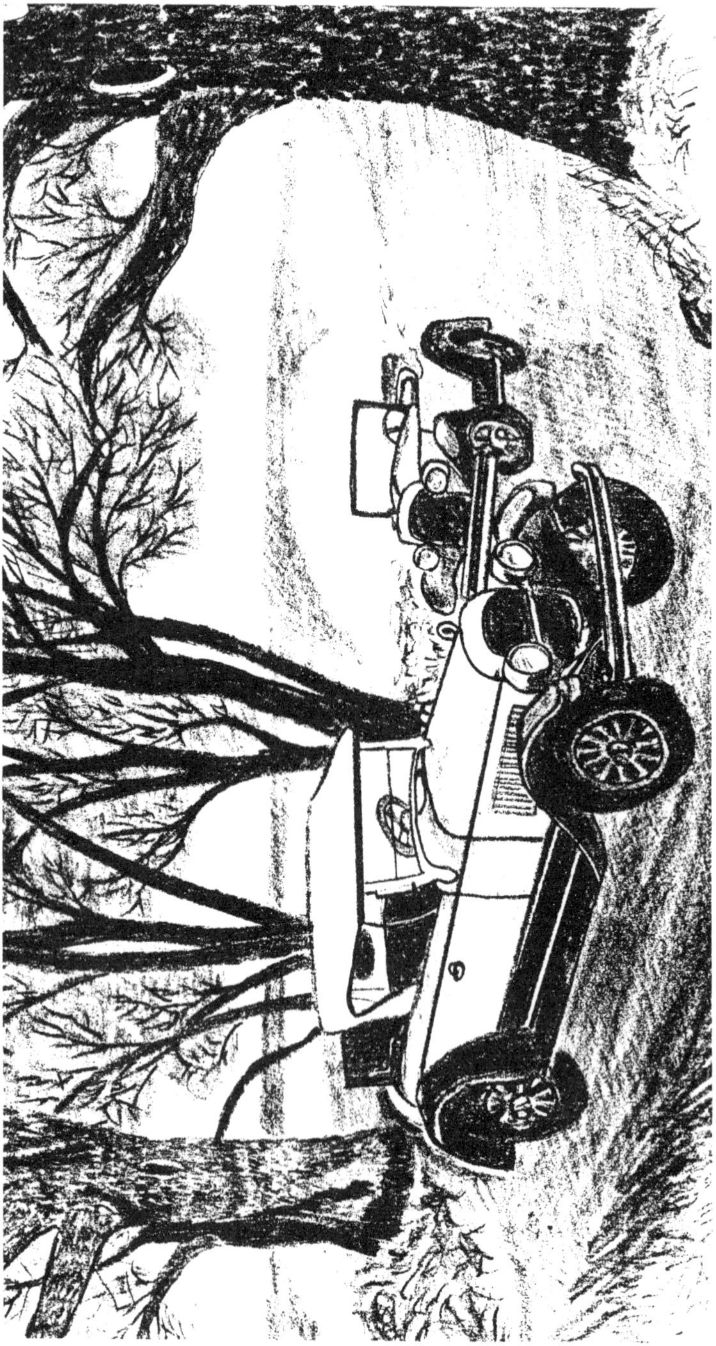

# Chapter 1
# Why an Old Car?

At first look, car collecting might appear to be the most impractical of hobbies, the last fling of rich old men trying to relive their youth. But if you visit any old car show, you will find some people exhibiting cars built before they were born (Fig. 1-1). And it's easy to see that most of them are *not* rich. There is obviously more to car collecting than meets the eye of the casual observer.

When you examine the hobby from every angle, as we will in this book, you may be surprised to find that car collecting can be one of the most *practical* of hobbies. How many hobbies provide you with a hedge against inflation? No one can predict the future, but we will show you how an astute buyer of used cars during the past generation could have multiplied his money by up to *twenty times* the original investment, even if he had done no restoration on the cars he bought. And we'll suggest some likely choices of cars now selling at give-away prices that could become tomorrow's high-priced treasures.

Even if you are a car owner who has no interest in collector's items, there is an aspect of car restoration that can staunch a yearly hemorrhage of funds from your bank account. You can apply this special kind of restoration if you have an average or better ability to use hand tools and can invest a few hundred dollars. We will give you the figures on one such restoration plus the step-by-step procedure used on it. But this interesting hobby has many aspects, and we will examine each of them.

To many people, cars are symbols. When you buy a new car, your friends will notice it as long as you leave the price sticker in

Fig. 1-1. This beautifully restored 1933 REO Flying Cloud shows why an old car.

the window. Its beneficial effect on your image is that of avoiding undue negative attention, of becoming one of the crowd. If you arrive at the ten-year reunion of your old school class driving a down-at-the-fenders car that was built the year you graduated, it's unlikely that your old classmates will figure you for an eccentric millionaire. But suppose you show up in a nicely restored car made during the 1950s or earlier? Instead of *losing* status by driving an old car, you *gain*. Moreover, people will probably see you as someone interesting and distinctive, someone worth knowing.

**RESTORING VS. HOT RODDING**

Whole generations of young American males (and some females) have joined the car tinkering game via hot rodding. Some hot rodders argue that theirs is the greater challenge because they do original things with their cars while restorers are copycats who follow factory specifications. We'll grant that hot rodding presents challenges, but so does restoring. Sometimes the restorer's challenge requires a different kind of skill—such as assuming the role of a private eye to locate a rare part and the wiles of a diplomat to persuade the owner of the part to sell it. Hot rodders say that they can drive their converted buggies anywhere but that restored cars have to be stored and brought out only for special events. So, they say, hot rodding is more practical. But is it? One of the authors of this book used to be a sometime hot rodder. Mike Murphy found that when he finished a new hot rod, he often had invested more than the vehicle was worth, and it began to depreciate the day it was completed, just like a new car. *Restored* cars, on the other hand, make good investments. It's a hobby that can actually pay for itself. And over several years there's a good chance it can preserve your money against the erosion of inflation.

Recently we got a first hand look at how prices on collector cars have appreciated in the last 25 years. We were unpacking some items that had been wrapped in newspapers a generation ago. The newspaper was the *Los Angeles Times,* dated October 7, 1955. By chance one sheet carried ads for automobiles, arranged in alphabetical order. The ads for domestic cars started with Buick and ended somewhere in Cadillac. Here are some of the prices listed:

| Car | Kind of Ad | Stated Condition | Price |
|---|---|---|---|
| 1949 Buick | Dealer | Immaculate | $395.00 |
| 1949 Buick Convertible | Dealer | Beautiful All leather interior Thick carpeting | $499.00 |
| 1942 Cadillac Club Coupe | Private party | Exceptionally clean | $345.00 |
| 1950 Cadillac 62 Sedan | Dealer | Fully equipped. Priced $100 high but worth it. | $1575.00 |

If you could go back to 1955 for one day, would it pay you to buy any of these cars? According to our investigations of prices in 1980, you couldn't have gone wrong on any of them. The best choice would have been the 1949 Buick convertible, now worth about twenty times the price quoted then. Even the poorest choice, the 1950 Caddy, would now be worth about three times its former value.

But what if they weren't really as good as the ads suggested? Even if we grant that the sellers may have been *highly* enthusiastic in their claims, and if we estimate that each car would now bring only about 50% of the top price for its model, the cars would still be worth an average of *four times* what they cost in 1955. How many other investments would have done that well?

One obvious reason for the poorer investment performance of the 1950 Cadillac was its much higher initial cost as compared to the other cars. This shows that if you want maximum appreciation from your old car investment, you should buy after the car is old enough to lose value as a used car but *before* it is old enough to become desirable to collectors.

## BUY THEM WHILE THEY ARE DOWN

You can get into car collecting and cut car costs at the same time if you will observe one single rule about car prices. A new car loses value rapidly for the first five years, and then somewhat more slowly. After about fifteen years, its price levels off just above salvage rates. Then, as the model grows scarce, it begins to rise.

Dick Powell, a carpet layer, bought a 1952 Pontiac Chieftain sedan with wide whitewall tires—a good car for its age—for $75 in Oakland, California in November, 1966. He drove the car for eleven years. During that time he had some typical repair costs: $75 in 1968 to get the transmission fixed; $50 for a valve job; $15 for brake bands that he installed himself in 1970; $60 for paint in 1974. In all he invested about $300 in the old Pontiac.

Dick found the car so reliable that he drove it on a vacation trip from Blythe, California to Fredonia, Kansas in July, 1967. Then, in 1973, he used it to move from California to the Midwest. He continued driving it until December, 1977 when he retired it because the old flathead straight-8 was using too much oil.

Dick still has the car. After eleven years of service the old car is worth more than it was when he bought it. By overhauling the engine he could probably sell it for about $1000; with full restoration, the car could be worth considerably more than the $2200 or so that it cost somebody in 1952.

Sometimes timing and luck can enable you to make a good buy in an old car that will ensure a later profit. One man we know bought a 1931 Dodge Sedan in 1966 for $200. The car was original, with all the original equipment, but was unrestored. When the new owner found that the car was in good running condition, he used it as a work car, keeping it maintained but doing no restoration work on it other than to replace rubber items, including brake cylinder cups. The car had been painted with a brush and showed brush marks, but he did no body work or painting. In 1971 he sold the car for $750. Try to do *that* with a late model car.

Here is how one expert on investing in collectibles views restored cars as investments. Richard Rush, Connoisseur for the Wall Street Transcript, was recently interviewed on the television program *Wall Street Week*. Louis Rukeyser, the host of the show, mentioned in his introductory remarks that some objects had appreciated considerably during the decade of the 1970s. One category he mentioned was classic cars. Some of these, he said, were worth eight times as much at the end of the decade as at the beginning. Later Rukeyser asked Rush what he would choose for a Christmas gift for someone if he were to choose from among the many kinds of collectibles discussed on the program. Without hesitation Rush suggested classic cars. The specific cars he chose were a Rolls Royce Silver Cloud III at $25,000, a 1976 Cadillac El Dorado convertible at $8,000, and 1965 Mustang at $2500. These, of course, would be cars already restored or in excellent condition.

No one can say what kind of prices a certain model of car will bring during the next generation, but if history is any guide, the old car you restore today will lose *no* value *regardless* of economic conditions. And it could keep you ahead of inflation. That, at least, is what some financial experts are saying.

Hot rodders will often admit that restored cars are good investments. In fact, they sometimes put down collectors by saying that all a collector needs is money. That is, he can go out and buy a car completely restored and gain status among old car buffs. That *is* true, but most of us don't have that kind of cash lying around. And at current interest rates it wouldn't make much sense to borrow it. In this book we'll show you how to restore a car without having to mortgage everything you own. The secret is to find an old car at a reasonable price for its condition, then do much of the restoration work yourself. Exactly how much of the restoration you will do depends on your interest, skills, and available money. And there are all degrees of restoration. If you have to settle for a cheap old car, a basket case, you may find that you don't have nearly all the parts to end up with the kind of show car that goes for big money. For such a situation, you can fix up a poor man's antique. It won't be 100% to factory specs, and it could raise a few eyebrows among the purists, but it will be a fun project. And that's what car collecting *should* be.

## HISTORY CAN BE FUN

Along with the fun, you'll find that you will gain an insight into the history of this country. It is almost inevitable that you will try to dig out some information about your car and the year it was made. From there you will go to the cars of the same make preceding yours because you will probably want to know when certain features were first offered. A Ford collector, for example, can usually tell you that the last Model T was made in 1927 and that if Henry Ford had had his way, it would probably still be produced today. He can also tell you how quickly Ford put the Model A into production once failing sales forced Henry to make the change.

And, again, how the initially popular Model A fell behind the competition in 1931, which led to the first flathead V-8 engine in 1932. That engine is the one that carried Ford through the remaining Depression years, catching the imagination of hot rodders and becoming so well known that Bing Crosby made a hit record with a song about a tenderfoot cowboy who rode the range in a Ford V-8.

One characteristic of old car buffs that you may notice is that many of them are strongly prejudiced about the virtues of the cars they favor. A collector will tell you that while modern cars, excluding imports, are all of a kind, the old car makers held strong opinions about how to make a good car, and their designs showed their opinions. He will mention such unusual features as extra valves, wooden frames, steam engines, electric drive, and many others.

## CAR CLUBS

Whatever the brand of car that you decide to restore, there is probably a car club devoted to it. By joining the club, you can get original equipment specifications, the names and addresses of dealers who can supply parts, and other useful information. In addition to special interest clubs, there are other clubs with a wider range of interest. These clubs may be dedicated to promoting activities in a certain class of old cars, such as classics or antiques.

Here is an example of another kind of advantage you may get by joining a car club. A Midwestern club bought a spot welder. When they paid for it, the dealer told them there would be a series of free lessons provided to show the members how to use it. The club members scheduled the next few meetings at the homes of each member so that each one could use the welder on his car under the supervision of a qualified teacher.

Another useful club technique is to schedule, say, an upholstery meeting at the home of a member who knows how to upholster a car's interior when that member is planning to do some work. Members can help with the job and learn whatever skill is being practiced by doing it along with an expert.

Some clubs have a membership that is geographically dispersed over the nation; others have memberships that are restricted to a certain region, state, or city. You can find a list of car clubs in the appendix of this book.

## SHOWS AND SWAP MEETS

No matter where you live, there is probably an annual show within easy driving distance of your home. Car clubs usually sponsor the shows along with a swap meet, where collectors can exchange information, parts, or even whole cars. If you are even slightly interested in old cars, a trip to a local car show is the logical step for initiation into this fascinating hobby. Car clubs welcome visitors, even those who have no cars of their own.

Some shows and swap meets are so large that they attract collectors from all parts of the country. If you live in the Eastern part of the United States, you may want to visit the Hershey, Pennsylvania meet in October. Westerners can find a big one at Reno, Nevada each June. And for Midwestern collectors, an annual meet is held each year at Petit Jean, Arkansas, site of a large car museum. Any car club in your area can give you the exact date of these meets for the current year, along with information on other swap meets or car shows.

## RELATED HOBBIES

Lack of skill or money should not keep you from restoring a car, as we will show, but you may feel that you don't want to start with a plunge into a major restoration. In that case you can limit your participation in the hobby to such pursuits as collecting old license plates, car ads, nameplates, emblems, hub caps, spark plugs, radiator caps, or any other kind of auto accessory that shows distinction. Even old service station signs, glass items from old gas pumps, and other such equipment make interesting collections. Some collectors have used such items to furnish a room in their home, finding imaginative new uses for them. You can join another collector and help restore a car to gain skill in doing body work, woodwork, upholstery, or mechanical repair. Some people even collect period clothing to match the era of the cars they like. Then they show up at car shows wearing the appropriate outfit, feeling that they are a part of the show even if they have no car.

Collecting special parts, such as nameplates or radiator caps, is a practical alternative to car restoration if you have no current storage space for a car. It can serve as an entry into the larger hobby of car reworking. If you approach the hobby gradually, collecting items only when they are available at reasonable prices, you will probably derive a profit from it a few years down the pike. Or you can use the parts as trading bait to get rare parts in case you decide to restore a car in the future.

## THE ULTIMATE IN PRACTICAL RESTORATION

No one can predict what a certain car model will be worth several years after you collect and restore it. Going by past history we can guess that its value will more than keep up with inflation, but guarantees for the future are good only if you have a crystal ball. (Ours is broken.) But there is one *sure* way you can profit greatly from car restoration: fix up a car you can use.

To see why, consider the typical American pattern of car ownership. You buy a new car, drive it a few years, then trade it for another new car. If this is what you are doing, you will wake up some day to the realization that you own a $100,000 car. The biggest cost in your transportation budget is probably car depreciation. The rate of depreciation varies, but it is determined by how often you trade cars, how many miles you drive per year, and, to some extent, on the model you choose. Few people know how much depreciation they suffer, even though they may keep records on each car trade. To get an idea, write down the total price of the last car you bought. Then take the car to a dealer and see how much cash you can get for the car. Notice that this figure will be lower than what you will be offered on a trade. You might get more for the car by selling it yourself, but you should subtract from that price all selling costs. The only possible error in finding depreciation this way is that if you traded another car for the current model you own, you really don't know how much the car cost you.

When you try to figure depreciation this way, don't forget to add in the financing costs for your new car. Simply total the monthly payments and add that figure to your down payment. Surprised? Now you know why the average citizen of this country has a hard time getting from paycheck to paycheck.

*But*, you say, your car is getting old. The engine needs an overhaul, the upholstery is ragged, and the body is showing rust. If this is your situation, and you have another car for interim use, you can enter the hobby of car restoration in the most practical way. You can restore a car that you already own.

Or suppose you need an extra car in the family. Find a car old enough to be cheap but recent enough to make parts easy to get. Restore this car to any condition you desire, from drivable to like new, and then use it for whatever purpose you choose. This is one way to cut your car costs to a small fraction of that for the average driver. We'll show you the step by step method used to rework one junker in Chapter 17.

Although this is a book on car restoration, we would be the first to admit that there are all degrees of restoration. Some purists insist on nothing but the exact factory specifications on each part or material used in the car. A car so completed will meet the requirements for a show car and can have great value. But many restorers take a more relaxed attitude, stressing the *fun* aspect of old cars. In still other cases, certain restorers prefer to do only the engine work, or body work, then sell the car to someone who specializes in the part of the job left undone.

## ONE MAN'S OLDS

Here is how one car turned out. Mike found the car in a rural salvage yard about 1970. Picture this: a 1936 Oldsmobile sitting flat on the ground because it has no wheels. The hood is up, probably left up years before when someone removed the air cleaner from the carburetor. The salvage yard owner says that the owner abandoned the car during World War II because he couldn't get tires for it. Twenty-five years is a generation for humans, eons in the life of a car. And even more if that time is spent in an open field, part of it with the hood up.

Considering the condition of the car, the proprietor of the yard offered to sell it at a bottom salvage price, $20. Mike told John, a friend, about the car, and John was interested. They returned to see it, and John talked the man down to $15. To move the car, John installed 14" wheels and tires. He found that the fatter-than-original tires rubbed the body and frame when he tried to turn too sharply, but the wheels permitted them to move the car. They put a chain on it and started to drag it out of the salvage yard. That was when they found that the brakes didn't work. The clutch didn't work either—the disk had rusted to the flywheel, but they could get the car in or out of gear when it was stopped.

Pulling a car with no brakes is a dangerous business, so John and Mike decided to try to break the clutch loose and then use the engine as a brake. They gave the car several hard jerks, then stopped to inspect it. Instead of breaking the clutch loose, they had broken the engine mounts and moved the engine to one side of its compartment. Mike found a jack, and they jacked the engine back into its proper location. They left the jack there to hold the engine in place and dragged the car onto a dirt road. They also removed the hood so Mike could keep an eye on the engine. As they dragged it along the road, they broke the clutch free. Now they could proceed, using the clutch to brake the car.

They started rolling toward John's home, and approached a railroad track. John, in the forward car, hit his brakes, lashing the brake lights. Mike released the clutch in the old car, expecting the stuck engine to lock the rear wheels. Instead, he watched incredulously as the fan began to turn. The engine was free. It offered some resistance for braking but much less than they had anticipated, so they drove the rest of the way at low speeds, keeping to back roads and streets. On the way they stopped and removed the spark plugs, then poured oil into each cylinder. They continued, leaving the car in gear now, so the engine would turn over as they drove. Mike noticed that the oil pressure gauge was working.

After helping place the car in John's backyard, Mike left to do some errands. He returned later in the afternoon, thinking he might help John remove parts for a stripdown. As he walked around John's house, he heard the sound of an engine running. Then, for the second time that day, he got a pleasant and almost unbelievable surprise. The old 1936 Olds, after sitting in a field for 25 years, was *running*. But the car wasn't exactly original now. A coffee can with a hose attached to it supplied the fuel. The gas tank had rusted through and would have to be patched or replaced. Another problem—the water pump spurted water as it ran.

John gave a quick report to Mike on his adventures getting the car running, including the reason that the engine was able to run after twenty-five years in the weather. When he started to pour some gasoline into the air intake of the carburetor to see if the engine would run, he saw that it was blocked. He removed the carburetor and found that the air horn was sealed by a mud dauber's nest. Apparently the mud daubers had done their work shortly after the air cleaner was removed, and before the first rain.

John and Mike assessed the condition of the whole car and came up with the conclusion that it was amazingly good mechanically, but needed extensive body work. Much of the body was supported by wood, and the wood was rotten. Some of the doors sagged so badly they had to be wired shut. After fixing the gas tank and finding another water pump, John used the car to pull a boat trailer to a lake a few miles away. This was a convenience for him because his small imported car didn't have enough power for that job. Later, he sold the car to a policeman in his city. It had become an excellent candidate for complete restoration.

**BAD LUCK AND GOOD**

If you restore old cars, you will have various kinds of adventures. Some deals on derelicts work out well; others can be disappointing—or worse. The more experience you get, and the more thorough your inspection of any car you buy, the better your chances of a successful deal and restoration.

James, a friend of Mike's, once failed to look closely enough at a gift car. The owners told him that he could have their old 1957

Chevrolet for towing it away. It had no engine or transmission, but with 4 wheels and usable tires, towing would be easy.

Or so James thought.

Mike and James went to get the car after work one day. They put a chain on it and connected the chain to Mike's pickup. When Mike pulled the car onto the road and picked up a little speed, he saw James in the rear view mirror, waving his arms. Mike stopped.

"It's making a terrible noise. Must be a wheel bearing."

Mike went around the car, feeling each wheel to see if any of the brake drums were hot. They weren't. He told James not to worry and started on. Once again he could see James waving. Same problem.

The car had no engine, no transmission, and the wheels were all right. What could be wrong?

"Must be the rear end," Mike said, and crawled under the car.

He reached up to feel the differential case. *It wasn't there.* The ends of the axle housings stuck out at each other, but the differential had been scavenged. Every time the car got up a little speed, the axles would rotate and hit various parts of the body. Mike returned to his pickup and moved forward—*slowly*. They had planned to deliver the car to James' home in an hour or so. At sundown they stopped and wired on some lights. They got home after midnight. Moral: *Know what you are getting, even if it's free*.

Sometimes the delay is with people. Mike once saw a 1945 Chevy pickup in a back yard and asked if it was for sale. The owner said no. Then he told Mike how he had put a rebuilt engine in it in 1958 and had driven it very little since then.

After a half hour of conversation, the old man stopped and said, "People are always asking me to sell that old truck and I always say no. But I'll let you have it for $35."

Mike reached for his wallet, but the old man put him off.

"No. I told you about the rebuilt engine. I want to change the oil and have it run for you."

"That's all right; I believe you," Mike said.

Finally the old man agreed to let Mike pay for the oil and change it. Mike got some oil and returned to change it. The old man looked out the window at him occasionally. Then when Mike was ready to try the engine, he came out. The fuel pump was leaking, so Mike had the old man hold a pop bottle of gas and pour a little into the carburetor to start the engine. The engine fired, ran a minute, then stopped.

The old man said, "All right. It hit on all six and didn't knock. You can take it now."

Some of the surprises you get while collecting cars can be *good* ones.

## FROM HOBBY TO BUSINESS

If you ever travel through Missouri on U. S. Highway 71, you might notice a line of old cars at a converted truck stop just north of the town of Diamond. Stop and look around, but if a young man or a young woman appear, don't ask for their parents. Ron and Jeanie Riediger, both 22 years old, are the owners of this antique car business. Almost every car or car part on the lot was manufactured before the Riedigers were born. The typical visitor to the lot is likely to be middle-aged, or older, and wants to examine a car like the one his parents once owned. When the visitors learn that Ron and Jeanie are the proprietors, they ask how two people so young became interested in old cars.

Ron grew up in Minnesota where he helped his father run a service station. He added to his natural skill in mechanics by a year in a Texas college where he took some vo-tech courses. While in Texas he met Jeanie, a girl who was going to college in Oklahoma. They soon married and settled in Missouri where Ron went to work driving a truck for his father-in-law.

When Ron bought his first old car it was just a hobby to him (and madness to some of his friends and relatives). But Ron was hooked enough to buy another, then another and another until he had more than he needed. He started selling a few cars and it gradually became a business. He has sold about 50 cars and has 50 more on his lot, but the business isn't well enough established yet for Ron and Jeanie to make a living from it.

In addition to traveling highway 71 from Missouri to Minnesota for cars and parts, Ron has gone as far as Pasadena, California where he bought some parts at a swap meet in the Rose Bowl. But he finds most of his specimens by combing an area within a 60 mile radius of his car lot. One of his most exciting finds was a 1932 Franklin, parked in the brush on an Ozark hillside (Fig. 1-2). The car needs a complete body rebuilding job, with much wood working to be done. But when you consider that only about 1900 of that model were manufactured 50 years ago, it has to be worth the time and expense of restoration.

Ron (Fig. 1-3) finds many of his parts stored away in old barns, garages, or at sales. He sometimes buys a truck load of parts

Fig. 1-2. About 1900 Franklins were made in 1932, so even this dilapidated specimen is worth restoring.

without really knowing exactly what he is getting. Someday he will do an inventory, but for now his energies and resources are concentrated in collecting. Meanwhile, if you need a grille for a 1934 Ford or an ammeter for a 1939 Lincoln, call Ron.

Fig. 1-3. Ron Riediger turned an old car hobby into a business.

Ron's story shows just one of several ways some collectors have converted the hobby to a business. One man we know runs a limousine service. After ordering a Bentley and a Rolls from England, when prices were lower, he got a chauffeur's suit and affected a British accent. His prices start at $30 an hour, but considering the instant status his service confers, customers think it's a bargain. For one evening, from the time he holds the door for you and your guests until it is time to say, "Home, James," you are a millionaire.

We're not suggesting that everyone should go into car collecting to make money, just showing that it *can* be done—especially if one applies a shot of personal ingenuity. Maybe those who say that car collecting is an impractical hobby are the ones who are cold-blooded and sensible about it.

Or maybe they just lack imagination.

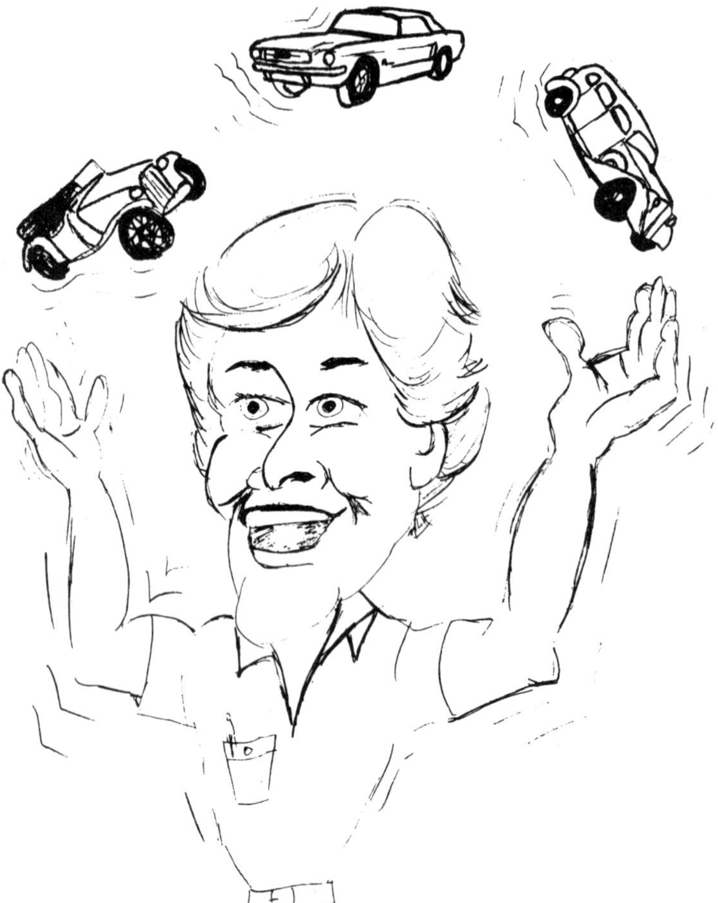

# Chapter 2
# What Kind of Car?

There are many factors to consider when you start to narrow your choice among the almost unlimited models of cars that have been produced since the automotive age began. Consider the various facets of restoration: cost, time, skills, space, degree of challenge, and what you will do with the car after it is restored. To put these various considerations in proper focus, you must consider the question: *What is my purpose in restoring the car?*

There are several legitimate reasons for car restoration, but one should come to your mind immediately: *fun*. If you think you'll have fun doing it, go ahead and choose a car. But if fun isn't one of your motives, do some hard thinking about whether the project is worthwhile for you.

The fun should be a by-product of the restoration work, but there is more than one kind of fun with restoring cars. Mike was introduced to one kind of fun by a friend who owned a 1931 Dodge sedan. Mike, his friend, and their wives liked to go to garage sales, so they often took the old Dodge. The expression of unbelieving surprise on people's faces when they drove up to a garage or yard sale in the Dodge was enough to make their day.

Some people go into car restoration purely for the profit. This is often a mistake. There's nothing wrong with the desire for profit, except that it may be unrealistic. In the typical restoration you will earn lower wages working on a car than you now earn at your regular job. Unless, of course, you find a fantastic buy in an old car in relatively good condition. To be realistic, consider any financial gain from car restoration as a long term goal, something you can realize only after holding the restored car for a number of years. There is one kind of restoration, described later in this book, that can save you thousands of dollars, but that is a different matter.

There are other personal factors to consider, but first, let's review the various classes of vintage cars and the kinds of car bodies and their names.

## CLASSES OF CARS

There is usually rough general agreement on how to classify a specific car, but different car clubs sometimes assign a particular model to different categories. Vintage cars can be divided into three main divisions: *antique, classic*, and *production* cars. We will later explore each class in some detail and look at the history of some representative cars, but for now, here is how each class is defined.

An *antique* (Fig. 2-1) is generally regarded as any car produced before 1930. This class is often subdivided into more limited categories, such as high wheeler, brass era, steam, electric, and gas vehicles with 1 cylinder, 2 and 3 cylinders, 4 cylinders, and more than 4 cylinders. The class is often further broken down to provide a separate class for Ford T and A Models, and these categories are often subdivided by time. For example, Ford T Models are often segregated by placing those with brass radiators in a separate group, sometimes two groups. Another possible line of demarcation can be made by separating cars with 2-wheel brakes from those with 4-wheel brakes. Finally, the classifications above apply only to cars; a special class is assigned to commercial vehicles, fire trucks, and racing cars. Even if you don't intend to show a car, you should be familiar with the specific rules for classification at any show you plan to attend.

One characteristic of antiques that the restorer should note is the amount of wood used in the body and sometimes even in the frame. The earliest cars had bodies that were built almost entirely from wood. Second growth ash was long used for the frames in certain cars because it was light and strong. In fact, manufacturers claimed that their wood frames were stronger than steel frames of the same weight. Even those cars made before 1930 that had steel chassis frames often had the upper bodies framed in wood. The shift away from wood was a gradual one and was not completed until manufacturers were well into the class we now call production cars, roughly the mid to late 1930s.

You will notice later that the description of *classic* applies to many cars that were built before 1930. In this case the term classic

Fig. 2-1. This 1924 Chevy is a typical antique.

takes precedence over the name antique. To be a classic, the car must have been almost universally considered a fine car when it was built. Because such cars were always relatively expensive, classic cars were made in lower production runs than other cars and are therefore rare today (Fig. 2-2).

To get a picture of the classic car par excellence, consider a Rolls Royce. Note that when we mention Rolls Royce, we don't

Fig. 2-2. Classic cars are longer, lower, and more expensive than other cars of their era.

have to specify a certain model. With many makes that qualify for classic status, one must look for a special few years when the brand name was especially esteemed or find a car with a custom body rather than a body built by the company that made the chassis. But with Rolls, as with a select few other makers such as Alfa Romeo, Bentley, Bugatti, Duesenberg, Hispano Suiza, Mercer, and Stutz, just the brand name is enough. If you buy into this exclusive group of cars, you will need plenty of cash or an oil well in Texas for collateral.

In addition to the ultra-highbrow classics, such as those mentioned above, there are many other good cars. Some of these are more likely to be found in a condition that will bring the price down to a reasonable level. You won't be likely to discover a Rolls rusting away in a back pasture, but you just *might* find an old Packard there, and many Packard models are listed as classics. In fact, Packard probably produced a larger number of classic cars than any other manufacturer in the world. Give that a thought, and if your heart is set on a classic, you might start looking for one of the good years. With Packard, the relative esteem given a particular car is more a difference of models than years. One must be aware that the company introduced a cheaper line of cars late in the Depression years. Those low-priced models don't rate as classics, regardless of how you might feel about their mechanical reliability or general quality.

The classic category is often subdivided into classes specifically named by time of manufacture. The time periods, for example, can run through a couple of years or more, such as 1930-31, 1932-33, and so on.

The class of cars called *production cars* is expanded year by year because it includes cars that were made after 1930 but are at least 25 years old. In 1980, for example, the production class included cars made from 1930 to 1955. But it would *not* include any classic car built during those years. As a rule of thumb, if the car is a major American brand (except Cadillac, Lincoln and certain Packards) and was made during the Great Depression or after World War II, it is a production car (Fig. 2-3). This class also includes lesser-known low to medium-priced makes. Production cars are often divided into sub-groups as to year of manufacture, similar to classic car years. Ford made so many cars during those years, cars with unusual features for a low-priced car such as the V-8 engine, that Ford is often assigned to a class of its own.

Fig. 2-3. Abandoned production cars are easy to find.

In considering which class of car you will restore, consider whether you will use it regularly. If you plan to drive it to work, for example, you will get better service from a production car than an antique. Cars made after the mid-1930s, on the average, do better at highway speeds than cars made before that time. Another reason for choosing a production car—it will cost less to buy and less to insure. You might have second thoughts about driving a 1930 Duesenberg any more than would be required to show it. But a postwar Ford or Chevy could be quite useful.

One point to consider is that the number of cars that find favor with collectors is expanding rapidly. Ten years ago the interest was mainly in pre-World War II cars. For several reasons postwar cars are now attractive, even some models made during the 1960s. As inflation drives up restoration costs, it drives many collectors to choose cars that are in reasonably good condition. It is easier to find late production cars that need little or no body work. Also, younger collectors find the cars of their youth interesting. And the later cars usually require a lower initial investment.

## BODY MODELS

In addition to choosing a make and model, what kind of body will your car have? Many cars are described incorrectly because either the manufacturer or the state in which the car was registered made a mistake. Here are some of the more common body types, and a few uncommon ones, and a description of each.

**Coupe:** An enclosed body with a single cross seat. Some large coupes have an extra seat and a quarter window. The larger coupes, with a rear seat, are often called *club coupes*.

**Roadster:** An open body with a fold-down top and a single cross seat. Usually have curtains for side windows.

**Phaeton:** An open body with two cross seats, a fold-down top and a fold-down windshield. This body style is often quite valuable.

**Touring Car:** Similar to a phaeton but longer, and has curtains for side windows.

**Sport Coupe:** Similar to coupe but with a rumble seat in the rear deck.

**Cabriolet:** Similar to sport coupe but with a convertible top.

**Coach:** An enclosed five-passenger two-door, with access to the rear seat by individual fold-down front seats.

**Sedan:** An enclosed six- or seven-passenger four-door. Large sedans sometimes have two extra jump seats. Sedans often have quarter windows.

**Convertible Sedan:** Similar to sedan but with a convertible top.

**Landau:** Similar to a short sedan but with a folding rear quarter.

**Imperial Sedan:** A sedan with a chauffeur's compartment and a glass partition separating it from the rear compartment.

**Town Car:** Similar to imperial sedan but with an open chauffeur's compartment.

**Two-Door Hardtop:** Steel roof unsupported by door post. Otherwise similar to coach. This body first appeared in the late 1940s.

**Four-Door Hardtop:** Similar to two-door hardtop but with four doors. Appeared about 1955.

## TRUCKS

If you like parades, almost any vintage car will get you invitations to drive in parades for all kinds of occasions from the Fourth of July to Christmas. But if you have an old truck, you may be in even greater demand.

One man, who wanted a pickup truck that could be used daily but who didn't want a common make like Ford or Chevy, found a 1952 Studebaker and restored it. He chose the Studebaker because it is modern enough to be useful and small enough to give good gas mileage. It also has the advantage that it is different from the horde of ordinary pickups in his small town. The same man wanted a large truck for parades, so he located an old Indiana truck, made in the

1920s. The old truck is an eye stopper, but the vacuum tank fuel system isn't as reliable as he would like for constant use.

If you are considering adding an old truck to your car collection, check the small-town fire departments in your area to see if any of them have old fire trucks that they are planning to replace. Most small towns don't have the space to store the old truck when they purchase a more modern one. An obsolete fire truck has several advantages over the typical well-worn truck used for commercial purposes. Fire trucks are almost always spotlessly clean—after all, those firemen have to do *something* while waiting for a fire call. They are well maintained mechanically too, often showing extremely low mileage for their age. And *nothing* adds more to any parade than a fire truck. Strike up the band!

## CAR CHOICE: PERSONAL FACTORS TO CONSIDER

Probably the first personal factor to consider is how much money you can invest in the hobby. That, again, depends somewhat on your purpose in restoring the car. Do you want it just to have a project for rainy weekends, or is it to be a long-term investment? Or will you use the car regularly? Obviously, if you expect to get some transportation from it you can afford to put more in it. On the other hand, a used car will probably be cheaper than one bought strictly for restoration. If you will drive the car regularly you will surely want a production car or even a later model.

As a long-term investment, the classic cars are probably the best choice. Any top classic will be expensive to buy and restore, but such a car will almost certainly continue to appreciate in value. The number of such cars in existence is limited, and they are no longer manufactured—at least not in America.

Another point to consider is the size of your family or other group that you will want to transport in your car. If you never expect to have more than one companion with you, a coupe will be fine. But look ahead on this: a few years down the road, you may be more encumbered with family than now, and children like to ride in parades. Another aspect of body type to consider is the demand for your car if you ever want to sell. Sport models often bring more interest and a higher price than the typical sedan. And remember, convertibles are no longer manufactured in the U. S., so even a relatively late American convertible could eventually become valuable.

Before you make a final choice, ask yourself this: What are my skills? If you like to work with wood and have plenty of patience, you might enjoy making the carefully fitted dove-tail joints necessary to renew the framework of an antique body. But if you dislike woodwork, avoid basket-case antiques. Later cars require a higher degree of metal working skill. Early production cars had bodies with parts bolted together; on later models they are welded. Even if you don't plan to do extensive metal work, you can get a car with a sound body and do the paint preparation work yourself.

When you have narrowed your choice down to a certain make or type of car, try to find a restored specimen to examine. If you see an appealing car that you can afford, go ahead. It should be an affair of the heart as well as of the wallet.

## CONTRARY OPINION AND CAR COLLECTING

In the investment world, there is a school of thought known as *contrary opinion* and followed by some of the most astute investors and money managers. The contrarian approach to making investment decisions is to *avoid the crowd*. According to contrary opinion, you should *buy* what other people are *selling* and *sell* what they are *buying*. These canny investors do the financial equivalent of buying snow shovels in the spring.

What has contrary opinion to do with car collecting? It just could offer you a way to get into car collecting on a shoe string. Look around you and see which cars are being offered for sale at the biggest discounts. Then ask yourself if those cars have even an average (or better) chance to become a collector's item. As an almost obvious example, you now can find large luxury cars in addition to certain "muscle cars" offered at distress prices. Large cars with even minor damage are going to salvage yards. In time, this constant attrition will reduce the number of cars with a reputation for heavy fuel consumption. If this trend goes far enough, and trends have a habit of going beyond all reason, these cars could grow in appeal to collectors.

As an example of how big cars have gone through earlier periods of low demand, consider the World War II era. At that time many luxury cars were available at bargain prices because of tire and gas rationing. One of the authors of this book can remember seeing a 1931 Duesenberg in top condition offered for $800. Offered, but no buyers. It was soon after the war, and people who remembered the gas rationing said, "Who needs a big old car?" Does history repeat itself?

## SOME OUT-OF-FAVOR MODELS

If big cars represent one kind of out-of-favor vehicle, cars with innovative design which fail in the marketplace are another good prospect for the contrarian car collector. Time after time in automotive history such cars have declined in esteem until they reached a point where they could hardly be sold at any price. And time after time such cars have become collectors' items. When a car is first discontinued, people are worried about getting parts. Then, as the car becomes rare, demand for it rises. A fairly recent example of this kind of transformation from discontinued and unwanted to a desirable model is the Chevrolet Corvair, especially the 1962-64 Corvair Monza Spyder.

We will go out on a limb and choose some cars that could be winners someday. When you read Table 2-1, remember, we have no crystal ball. If a top flight baseball player gets one hit in three, he is a candidate for the batting championship of his league, and we'll settle for that average. Just because you see a certain model mentioned here is *no* guarantee it will ever demand a premium. Control that urge to buy until you find a bargain.

## 1961-63 Pontiac Tempest

This is one of those cars with unusual engineering features. In 1961 Pontiac used half of a V-8 engine to offer a 4-cylinder engine that would compete with the sixes and small V-8s of other compact cars. The early Tempests also had a flexible drive shaft, which provided a flat floor, and independent rear suspension. Some automotive writers greeted these introductions with acclaim, but most customers apparently sided with critics who said the car offered nothing more than expensive novelties. The 4-cylinder engine performed satisfactorily, but people who bought it in expectation of high gasoline mileage were usually disappointed.

Some say that the Tempest (Fig. 2-4) was too exotic for American tastes of the times, with a design more in keeping with European engineering practice than that of Detroit iron. The few remaining cars are sometimes now offered for sale at salvage prices. But collectors are beginning to get interested. The most desirable models are the convertibles which were made in 1962 and 1963. Don't expect to find a good one of these that is still cheap. At the present time, the Tempest V-8's sell for more than the 4-cylinder models. This situation may continue, but since a 4-cylinder car was an unusual item on the American scene in the early 1960s, we'll bet that the four will get its share of recognition in due time.

If you have a choice in Tempests made in different years, choose the 1961 model. You should be able to find one of these in

Table 2-1. Some Cars Which Are Available At Low Prices Now.
Some Of These Are Sure To Become Desirable Collector Items In The Future.

| MAKE | MODEL | YEARS |
|---|---|---|
| Buick | Special with aluminum engine | 1961-63 |
| Cadillac | Any that sells cheap | All recent |
| Chrysler | Imperial, New Yorker | All recent |
| Ford | Lincoln | All recent |
| Oldsmobile | F-85 with aluminum engine | 1961-63 |
| Pontiac | Tempest | 1961-63 |

average to poor condition, but easily restorable, for $100 to $300. It could be worth much more in another ten years.

## 1961-63 Buick Special or Olds F-85

The early 1960s were a time when General Motors made several radical departures from tradition. The Corvair was GM's most radical achievement—a car which turned out to be *too* radical for the times. The Buick Specials and Olds F-85s were much more conventional, but they included an engine that some automotive experts greeted as the prototype of what would be a major trend, the aluminum V-8. This engine coupled good fuel economy with superb balance. The typical American car has always been front-end heavy, a condition that produces understeer and virtually necessitates power steering for easy handling. The Buick Special had the smoothness of a V-8 but the economy and lighter weight of a six. The Buick-designed aluminum V-8 was so well accepted in

Fig. 2-4. The often reviled 1961 Pontiac Tempest. So long down, it looks like up.

engineering circles that there was talk of using it in the MG sports car. At least a few of these cars were built, which sports car enthusiasts described as a fantastic success, but for some reason production never got started.

Like every other new concept, the aluminum V-8 had its share of disadvantages. For one, it was intolerant of undue heating. If you broke a water hose in traffic, the only prudent action was to stop and wait for a wrecker. When new, the engine had a peculiar habit that quickly infuriated owners. If you left the car out in sub-zero weather, there was a good chance that the battery would refuse to turn over the engine. The aluminum evidently contracted against the steel liners, squeezing them against the pistons. Another disadvantage was related to those mentioned above: mechanics universally hate aluminum.

The car itself suffered a bit from faddish styling. The wrinkled sides of the early Buick Specials left many potential customers cold. But driving it was something else. Its power, good balance, and smooth ride easily beat out the competition that other compact cars of those years offered. And the optional 15" wheels were easy on tires.

These cars will never be classics, but they were better cars than most people realized. We should mention the possibility of bias here, since one of us owned a 1961 Buick Special and considered it to be the best all around car he ever had, even though it used oil at 90,000 miles. They are cheap now, but as their ranks thin, they will surely gain status.

### 1960-70 Muscle Cars - Fallen Stars

Memories of a dead language:
"I think the tires got a little hot on that last run."
"How's the dry ice doing on the intake?"
"The engine sounds loose. Better push start, just before the next run."

If this jargon sounds strange, you weren't around the drag strip staging lanes of the 1960s. There will always be a few muscle cars, for entertainment if nothing else, but when gasoline cost approaches the price of an hour's work, as some experts predict, *how many?* This kind of car is being replaced today, along with the language. Some people who remember those days say the salvage rate on cars with big engines is alarming. In fact, one former aficionado calls their march to the junkyard a trail of tears.

As a car collector, how does this fall from glory for the muscle cars affect you? If you believe in contrary opinion, you can gamble that these cars may someday again win esteem. Consider one possibilty, the Chrysler cars of the mid-1960s.

After 1962 Chrysler became king of the strip. To further enhance its position, Chrysler revived and updated its old Hemi engine in 1964. Richard Petty chose one of these with a 4-barrel and 410 horsepower to up the 1963 Chevy record by 10 mph to 176 mph. But the same virtues that made them kings then has now made them dogs. Some of the hot car image may have helped drive Chrysler down the road toward its financial crisis. One aspect of the muscle car picture that you should consider is this: they aren't making them anymore.

### Muscle Cars Beginning To Move

While some muscle cars are hard to sell at any price, others are worth more now than a few years ago. These are beginning to be recognized by collectors and so you have less risk that they will become worthless. But, having passed their point of lowest demand, the percentage gain you can expect for these is probably less than for cars that are still out of favor. Remember that when you buy a car that no one wants, you get the biggest possible bargain—or you get a white elephant. There is some safety in following the trend, rather than anticipating it. But you will have to pay for the security you get by waiting.

A list of cars that are already recognized as desirable models by collectors must include convertibles, even late models. So when you look over the list in Table 2-2, remember that convertibles are especially desirable.

As an example of the cars that have begun to grow in favor, consider the Olds Toronado. This car was GM's mid-1960s experiment with front wheel drive. Some automotive enthusiasts greeted the 1966 Toronado with a prediction that it was the wave of the future. But other large front wheel drive cars never appeared (except the Cadillac Eldorado). This alone makes the early Toronado a likely collector's item.

### 1960-75 Large Luxury Cars

Here, we believe, could be the real sleepers. Clean specimens of Cadillac, Lincoln or Chrysler Imperial cars are now going at give-away prices compared to what they cost when new (Fig. 2-5). We recently stopped at a salvage yard where a 1973 Cadillac Sedan DeVille was brought in. The car was loaded with extras and the engine ran like a new one. Unfortunately for that Caddy, the left rear fender had been smashed and there was some minor trunk area

Table 2-2. Some Cars Of Recent
Manufacture Which Are Already In Demand By Collectors.

| MAKE | MODEL | YEARS |
| --- | --- | --- |
| Bricklin | All | All |
| Chevrolet | All | 1955-57 |
|  | Corvair Spyder | All |
|  | SS Convertible | 1963-64 |
|  | Corvette | 1963 |
| Ford | Crown Victoria | 1955-56 |
|  | Thunderbird | 1955-57 |
|  | Mustang | 1965-66 |
| Oldsmobile | Toronado | 1966-69 |
| Pontiac | The Judge | 1968 |
|  | GTO | 1964-69 |
| Studebaker | Silver Hawk | All |
|  | Golden Hawk | All |
|  | Avanti | All |

damage. Otherwise it was a clean car. It was there because the body repair would cost more than the car was worth. We asked for a price on it, and the salvage yard owner said he needed the transmission—it had already been promised. When pressed further he said he would sell the car and find another transmission, but he'd want $600. We wandered around the salvage yard for a half

Fig. 2-5. When spotless Cadillacs go begging, it may be time to buy.

hour, thinking about the Cadillac. When we returned to the work area, a mechanic had already removed the hood, radiator, and air conditioner compressor. Another big car bit the dust.

Large cars with big engines, such as this one, may be the last of a kind. Right now no one thinks of them as collectors' items because you can find them for sale on almost every block in your city. Many years may have to go by before they are rare, but if you have storage space, it could pay you to buy a clean one now and put it away. It just might take care of you in your old age.

## CHANCE AND THE CAR COLLECTOR

Regardless of the care you choose to collect, chance sometimes takes over and decides for you. Mike once made a trip with a friend named Joe to get a 1953 Buick which Joe had bought at an auction. The sale had been held by a salvage yard with a rule that all cars must be moved by Sunday. Mike and Joe made the trip on Sunday, driving a pickup truck and taking along a tow bar, extra wheels, tires, and various tools which they thought could be helpful. When they started to move the car, they found that someone had removed the wheel bearings.

They toured the neighborhood looking for a parts store, but the town was closed up tight. The salvage yard was cleared except for a few cars that were to be moved that day. Finally, Joe went to the owner of the yard to see if he could rent space to keep the Buick there until wheel bearings could be found. No way. But the owner did have a 1953 Packard convertible that he would trade for the Buick. Of course, Joe would have to pay some boot. At the time it seemed like a bad deal, having to trade under duress. But when Joe's wife saw the Packard, she loved it. Joe decided he liked it too, so he became a Packard collector and now has a backyard *full* of Packard cars. In time, the 1953 Packard convertible has become worth much more than the Buick he bought at the sale.

When you select your car, be alert to any alternative that presents itself. It could be a better choice than the car you are seeking.

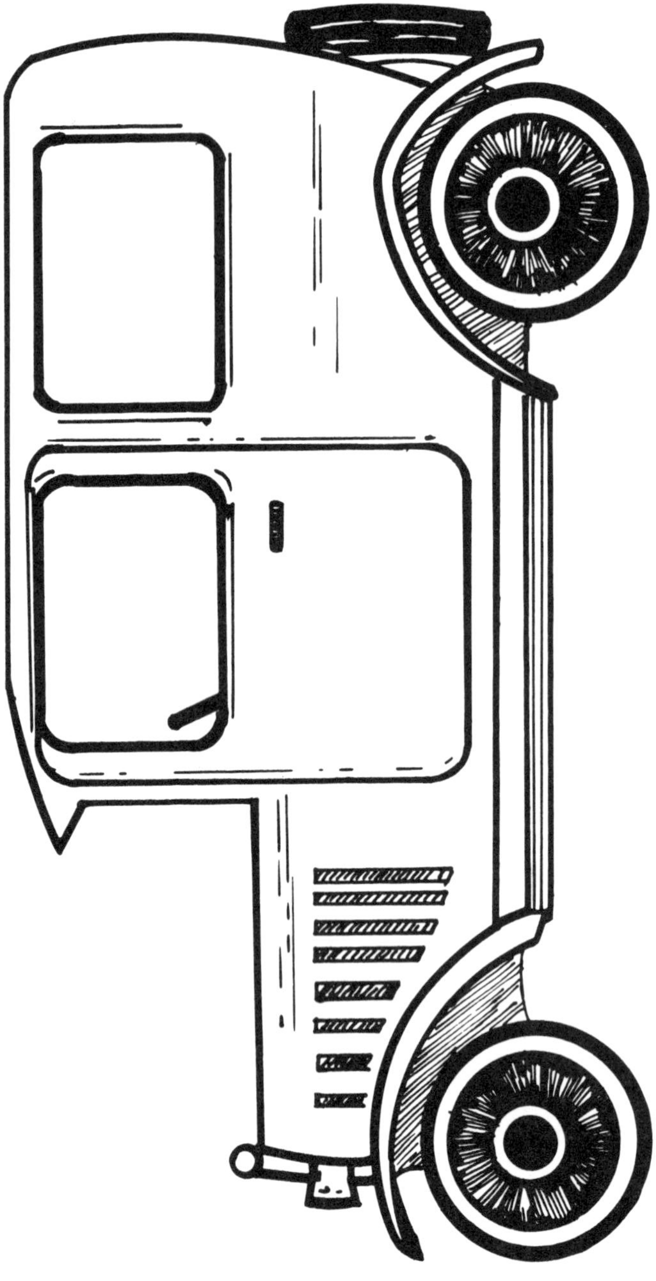

# Chapter 3
# Antique Cars

Anyone with an old car to sell will likely advertise it as an antique, but car clubs generally recognize only those cars made before 1930 as worthy of the name. Some states recognize all cars older than, say 25 or 35 years old as antiques, but this official designation is valid only for licensing purposes. By registering your car as an antique with your State Department of Motor Vehicles you can obtain a license for a reduced fee, but only if you limit your use of the car as prescribed by the license. The usual restriction is that you can drive the car in parades, shows, and to be repaired, but not much more than that.

One of the reasons for making 1930 as the breaking point in car classification is that changes in manufacturing methods were adopted by the makers about that time. Before 1930 more wood was used in cars—wood in the body, the wheel spokes (Fig. 3-1), and even in the chassis frame. Much of the wood work was done by skilled craftsmen who were later phased out of car factories as stamped steel parts could be turned out at lower cost. So while the cars of the 1930s became less distinctive than those of a decade earlier, they were usually more durable in body as well as in chassis. Less inspired perhaps, but more practical. This is one of the reasons, in addition to age, that makes the earlier cars (Fig. 3-2) more valuable. The old wood-framed bodies rotted down after years of abandonment to the weather (Figs. 3-3, 3-4). It started with a leaky top, then progressed at a faster and faster rate until the body caved in.

Although we may complain about the lack of durability in the old wood-framed bodies, restoring them may be easier than the job

Fig. 3-1. Wood spokes are a sure sign of an antique.

of future collectors who choose to work on an old 1980s model. Plastic doesn't rot, but time and temperature change may take their toll, even if the plastic parts escape getting hit by another car or a baseball. Replacing broken plastic parts could be a nightmare, unless some enterprising parts people develop a low-cost way to cast plastic in any desired shape.

    A small percentage of cars that were retired many years ago were stored in sheds and are still in fairly good condition. With persistence and a lot of luck you might be able to find one. There are some ways to make short cuts in the search, which we will show later, but they usually require more money. Whatever method you use, some kinds of antiques are much easier to find and restore than others. For *easier* you can also substitute the word *cheaper*. Here is a rundown on the different kinds of antiques, but it's unlikely that you will find one in either of the first three special categories.

## HIGH WHEELER AUTOMOBILES

These cars show their kinship to the old horse-drawn vehicles of rural America at the dawn of the automobile age. They date from the earliest horseless carriages of the late 1800s to about 1910-15. As the name suggests, their distinguishing characteristic is their high, narrow, buggy-like wheels. This class of antique car is more closely related to the wagon or buggy than to a true automobile. For example, the first self-propelled vehicles had both front wheels mounted on a single axle with the axle pivoted at its center. All that was missing was the singletree and shaft arrangement for a draft horse! When you consider that most early cars were built by horse and buggy factories, the similarity in design isn't surprising.

Here is how one high wheeler was developed and how it was quickly changed to a more advanced design. In 1895 two young men in Lansing, Michigan decided to build a horseless carriage. One of them, Ransom E. Olds, was the son of a manufacturer of stationary gasoline engines, and Frank Clark, the other, had access to his father's carriage works. Olds and Clark combined an Olds engine with a Clark carriage to produce the first Oldsmobile.

Later, in 1897, the Olds Motor Vehicle Company was incorporated in Lansing. It was the first automobile company in Michigan. It produced four vehicles the first year, but Lansing

Fig. 3-2. Some antiques, such as this 1917 Dodge, have no bumpers.

Fig. 3-3. Wood was used extensively in antique bodies.

wasn't ready for the horseless carriage, so Olds moved to Detroit. There he started a second, larger company. Later, after a fire destroyed much of the Detroit plant, Olds moved his plant back to Lansing.

Although he had started with a primitive machine, Olds quickly recognized that a vehicle powered by a gasoline engine had different design requirements than a wagon or buggy. Within a few years he abandoned the original design, although some manufacturers continued antiquated high wheelers for another decade or more. The high wheelers that continued in production probably appealed to farmers, who thought the high wheels offered certain advantages on country roads. Some of the last specimens of this type were offered in the pages of the Sears catalogs. The 1912 catalog, for example, showed high wheeler vehicles with tillers, or "Johnson Bars," instead of the steering wheels which had been adopted by most car makers by then.

For car collectors, the high wheelers are something to see on an occasional trip to a car museum. The chances of finding a restorable one now is rather remote. Another reason to leave these cars to museums: you wouldn't want to drive one very far. They are historically interesting but crudely made and extremely unreliable.

## STEAM AND ELECTRIC

We now hear talk of the possibilities of electric cars during the next decade or so, but most drivers now consider either steam or electric cars as novelties. It is hard to believe that such cars were once the norm and internal combustion cars were the freaks. In 1900 the break-down was: steamers, 40%; electric cars, 38%; internal combustion machines, 22%. In 1899 for the first time a man had traveled at a speed of more than a mile a minute in a road vehicle, and that was in an electric car built by a Belgian named Jenatzy. A few years later a steam car would make racing history. Then steam and electric cars would gradually fade away.

Again, your chances of finding an unrestored steam or electric car at a reasonable price are about the same as finding a bar of gold on sale at a flea market. But the Stanley Steamer was one of the most famous cars of its time. More than 100 different kinds of steam cars were built, from the early Dudgeon Steam of 1857 to the Reading Steamer of 1960. Most of these cars were produced in small numbers for a year or two only.

Like other cars with unusual features, the steam cars suffered from prejudice against their propulsion system. But some old-timers still talk about the steady, smooth power of steam cars in a day when many cars had to make a run at any incline higher than a railroad crossing. Steam engines were so powerful and flexible they needed no transmission. In fact, it was a Stanley Steamer that brought the Daytona Beach speed record back to America in 1906 after European cars had ruled the beach for several years. Fred Marriott drove his Stanley at 127.56 miles per hour that year to break the record of 109.75 held by Mercedes. The next year, Marriott drove another Stanley racer to a considerably higher

Fig. 3-4. A basket case, useful only if you love challenge.

speed but crashed when he hit a bumpy stretch on the sand. In those years the Stanley was an almost sure winner at races and hill climbing events, but the Stanley brothers lost interest in racing after the 1907 crash at Daytona.

In addition to restoring vintage steam cars, some collectors have obtained old steam engines and installed them in production cars. Then they sit quietly at stoplights, waiting for someone to challenge them. Drivers of muscle cars with their roaring engines are sometimes mystified by the innocent looking old car that shoots past with no more than a gentle whoosh. The Stanley Steamer could accelerate from 0 to 50 miles per hour in just over 9 seconds. And this with a 2-cylinder/engine that had a displacement of a little more than 200 cubic inches, about the same as the smaller Ford 6-cylinder engine used in the Mustang and Maverick cars. While the Stanley engine was only a fraction of the size of the gasoline-powered race car rivals, it had a similar weight because of the required boiler.

Newspaper accounts of the Stanley's exploits in races and hill climbs were often played down or even distorted. Some steam car partisans claimed that the inaccurate reporting was part of a conspiracy to discredit the steam engine as a viable alternative to the internal combustion engine. But there were some valid reasons for the decline of the steam car. The Stanley Steamer was of relatively simple design compared to the White Steamer, but driving one required considerable attention to the boiler and engine. To start the machine, a firing iron had to be removed and heated red hot, then screwed in place again to heat the vaporizer. Then one could light the pilot and, finally, the main burner. From a cold engine it could take up to a half hour to get up steam. Another disadvantage of the Stanley was water consumption by the boiler. The range of the various models, without refilling the water tank, was listed as 20 to 50 miles. Hard water caused problems by producing scale. And although the car had great acceleration, the quick get-away was possible chiefly because while it was stationary the car could get up steam for the jackrabbit start. Unfortunately, the steam build-up couldn't be well maintained, so the Stanley was best at short races or hills.

As mentioned earlier, the Stanley Steamer was the most popular and successful steam car, staying in production from 1897 to 1924. It was relatively simple in the engine department but, if you included the boiler, which of course was necessary, a steam car could be a plumber's nightmare.

The Stanley was the most popular steam car, but the Doble Steamer was the most advanced model. Abner Doble dropped out of school at M.I.T. to pursue his dream of building a successful steamer. About the time of World War I, he sold a design to a Detroit engineering firm, which manufactured the Doble-Detroit steam car for a short time. Then in 1921, Doble, his father, and three brothers started the Doble Steam Motors company in California. They were apparently perfectionists, taking three years to refine their car. The extent of their success can be judged by one fact alone: Howard Hughes owned Doble Steamers.

The Doble added a unique page to the history of the automobile. It had an advanced chassis design that permitted flat, high-speed cornering. At a time when most cars were front end heavy, it had 52% of the weight on the rear wheels, 48% on the front. It had an electrical system to power a turbine that forced air and fuel through a venturi tube at high velocity where it was ignited by a spark plug. The burning fuel went through the coils of a tube 576 feet long, but occupying less than 2 cubic feet of space. This boiler was tested for leaks at tremendous pressures, and Doble was so confident of it that the company offered a 100,000 mile guarantee on it. This steam unit was located at the front of the car, with the 4-cylinder engine built into the rear axle. Steam drove the pistons from each side, so each stroke was a power stroke instead of the 4-cycle internal combustion engine's one in four. This gave the 4-cylinder Doble the smoothness of a 16-cylinder engine. To top it off, the steam was collected and returned to the front radiator, or condenser, so that the water could be reused. Unlike the simpler Stanley, the Doble could be fired up in a half-minute, and it would cruise for hundreds of miles without a refill of water.

Stanleys were noted for their smoking engines, but the Doble ran almost smoke-free. The burner of the Doble cut in and out automatically to maintain almost constant steam pressure. When the fire was out, one got the effect of tremendous silent power; as the pressure dropped you could hear a low muffled roar from the burner. The lack of the pulsing explosions of an internal combustion engine added to the effect of effortlessly smooth power.

Before you rush out to look for a Doble, consider this: the price of a new coupe or sedan 50 years ago was $11,200. That perhaps tells why few were made; less than 50 E-Series Doble are believed to have been made from 1924 to 1932. The company was high on innovation and quality but less adept at financial survival, so the Depression marked the end of the most advanced steam car ever made.

The Doble is one of those cars that would surely fit into more than one category. It was undeniably a steam car, but it was also a classic. In this case its rating as a classic would take precedence over the incidental fact that it also had a steam engine propulsion system.

The early steam and, especially, the electric cars had one significant advantage over the internal combustion machines: they were quieter. In fact, the sponsors of a race in Chicago in 1895 awarded the Gold Medal to an electric car on that basis even though it failed to finish the race. The race had been postponed several times, and when it was finally run, in November, a snowstorm caused most of the drivers of electric cars to withdraw. They knew that their batteries were not up to pushing a snowplow. Two electrics completed and one, the Electrobat, completed 18 miles before its batteries ran down. It got the award. But the problem that caused it to stall—a limited driving range—still plagues would-be inventors of electric cars.

As mentioned earlier, at the turn of the century the electric car outsold the gas autos by about 2 to 1; a few years later that ratio increased. But even at its zenith the electric had some questionable habits. One of these seems to be a general characteristic of all battery-powered devices, a characteristic brought home to us while writing this book. Mike went to his shop one February morning and found the shop much colder than usual. While waiting for it to warm up, he picked up a battery-powered tape recorder and began dictating some information for the chapter on workshop and tools. Later, when we tried to play it back, we thought someone must have been fooling with the tape recorder, possibly recording the chipmunks. Careful listening proved that the chipmunk on the tape was talking about workshops and tools. The low temperature in the shop had reduced chemical action in the batteries, causing the tape motor to turn at a subnormal speed. Then when played back in a warm room, the motor ran at the standard speed, delivering sentences as if they were shot out of a machine gun and at a pitch far up the frequency scale from Mike's normal tones. An electric car that could be driven for more than 30 miles on a charge would go a creeping 10 miles when the temperature was 40°. Even in the best of weather, battery discharge was a constant threat. One suspects that the next command after "Home, James," was likely to be, "To the charger, James."

Electrics were also much more expensive than the typical gas car. And the initial cost wasn't the end of it. Batteries went bad, and you can imagine how much you might have to pay for a set of batteries large enough to power a car. (In 1979 General Motors announced an improvement in battery technology, a zinc-nickel oxide battery that will last for about 30,000 miles. That's about 3 years of use for the average driver, but the development was considered newsworthy enough to be reported in the news media as a great breakthrough).

An easy way to judge the success of any car is to see how many years it was produced. Like the steamers, there were many brands of electric cars but only a few that lasted for more than a year or two. Some of the more durable were the Anderson Electric 1907-19, the Baker Electric 1899-1915, and the Baker R & L Electric 1915-20, the Detroit Electric 1906-23 and 1930, the Milburn Electric 1910-24, and Rauch & Lang Electric 1920-24, and the Waverly Electric 1898-1917. Very few electric cars were built after about 1920.

## BRASS ERA CARS

During the early years of this century car manufacturers made extensive use of brass parts. You can quickly identify brass era cars by examining such parts as the headlamps, other lamps, horns, dash or windshield trim and radiators. Early Ford Model T's, up to about 1916, made extensive use of brass parts. Various car makers used brass to a different degree in their cars, but if a car has a brass radiator, it is almost sure to be classed as a brass era car.

After the Oldsmobile evolved beyond the high wheeler stage, it became the typical early brass era car. R. E. Olds saw the advantages of standardization of parts as a means of increased production and lower costs. His car became the first one that could be said to have reached mass production, selling in the thousands during the years 1902 to 1905. The popularity of the car was demonstrated by the 1905 song, "In My Merry Oldsmobile."

During the early years of this century the Oldsmobile was easily recognized by the profile of its front end, the curved dash runabout that resembled the front of a sleigh. Replicas of the 1903 Olds runabout are often seen in parades now.

In 1908, W. C. Durant put together a combination of companies to form a union that he called General Motors. Among the corporations that he bought were Buick and Olds. Oldsmobile production was then shifted to large, closed, more expensive cars. Production, which had already lagged that of the early years of the century, remained at a little more than 1,000 cars a year until 1915. Olds later started another company, but, having sold the rights to the Olds name to General Motors, he put his initials together this time to make up the name of the new car. He called it the REO.

Again, as in the case of high wheel, steam and electric cars, your chances of finding a restorable brass era car at an affordable price is less than inspiring. And, beware of replicas.

## LATER ANTIQUES: THE FORD T

If you seriously want to restore an antique car, your chances are better with the cars of the 1920s. The most common make is, of course, Ford. There are several reasons why you see so many restored Model T's and Model A's. The obvious one is the number of those cars that were produced. More than 15,000,000 Model T's were sold during its model run from 1909 to 1927. Such production improves the odds that somebody in your part of the U.S. put one away many years ago and that it still sits there, forgotten. Some Model T buffs say it needn't be so many years as you might think, because, they say, the T was more durable than many of the more expensive machines of their time. One reason: their simplicity. When you drove a T, you didn't have to worry about the complicated vacuum tank that brought the fuel forward on more advanced cars; instead you avoided hills too steep to permit the simple gravity feed to work. The engine was lubricated by a splash system (no oil pump) and cooled by thermosiphon which required no water pump.

In judging the Model T's design, one should compare it to the competition in 1908 when it was designed rather than almost 20 years later when it was abandoned. Only a few years before, nearly all cars had transverse engines with open chain drive systems. Henry Ford had built such a car in his first "Model A" in 1903. He believed that a low-priced practical car was needed, but his financial backers urged him to build a car for the rich. He complied with his Model K, which had a 6-cylinder engine. The engine was badly unbalanced and Henry Ford dropped it, then gave his opinion that 6-cylinder engines were inherently poorly balanced. Ford also believed that the secret of producing a people's car was to make one basic design and stick to it through thick and thin, thus saving the tremendous development costs necessary to constantly bring out new models. In this he was proved correct; the first T's sold for close to $1000, but after a few years the price had dropped to below $400 and later to below $300. Ford's concept was right in regard to price, but his refusal to alter the basic design led to its ultimate decline.

The Ford was unusual in 1908 by having the cylinders cast in a single block instead of in separate pieces, by its integral upper crankcase, and its simplicity of controls. Instead of having to learn to use a clutch and a gearshift lever, or to double clutch to avoid gear clashing, a Ford owner manipulated the gears with his feet and the gas with a hand lever. The metals used in the engine and drive train were first class for their time, which may help explain the popularity and durability of the car.

Compared to cars today, the electrical system was weird. It was a magneto system, with the magneto on the flywheel where 16 magnets were attached, in a radial pattern, which induced current in 16 stationary field coils. Instead of the high voltage distributor of modern cars, there was a low voltage timer and a separate tremblor coil for each cylinder. The timer was the source of considerable trouble unless frequently cleaned and oiled, so backfiring was a common sound from Model T engines.

When you got into the driver's seat, you found three pedals: the clutch, reverse pedal, and the brake. Pushing the clutch pedal all the way to the floor tightened the band on the low gear of the planetary transmission, putting the car into low gear. Releasing the pedal shifted to a direct drive high gear. Two speeds. To crank the engine, which you had to do if you wanted to start it on level ground, you pulled back the emergency brake to activate the clutch and throw the car out of gear. When the oil was cold, the engine was hard to crank and the transmission had a tendency to make the car creep forward. If the emergency brake lever was worn, or the notches that held it, the car could jump into high gear and take off. Model T Fords and their owners were the butt of endless jokes. But the car had so much character that people loved it even when it was at its tempermental worst. Two reasons: its low price and its ability to run on and on with makeshift repairs.

When someone mentions the modification of Fords in pursuits such as hot-rodding, the image of a 1950s teenager working on a flathead V-8 comes to mind. Actually, Ford modification began long before the introduction of the V-8, during the days of the Model T. Some of the changes were made for reasons of utility, such as the two-speed rear axles added to early Ford trucks. Other alterations were aimed at producing the kind of behavior esteemed by hot rodders. One famous modification was made by, believe it or not, the Chevrolet brothers. Their tail twisting for the T included such innovations as overhead valves, higher compression ratios, and even overhead camshafts.

While Ford refused to change the basic design of the T, a whole industry devoted to making accessories for hopped-up Fords grew up during the T's lifetime. Some of these accessories gave the engine higher compression, making it hotter in more ways than one. To control the temperature, an add-on water pump was available. And a heavier chrankshaft with five main bearings handled the increased thrust of the improved engine.

But the goodies for the T were not restricted to the engine compartment. There were brake sets, extra speed transmissions, and even different bodies. The body change often made the T into a racy runabout. These sporty shells sometimes came in a prefab bolt-on kit, sometimes as a set of sheet metal patterns for the backyard modifier. They were echoed much later by the kits people applied to the VW.

In 1923 Ford sold over 2,000,000 T's, its high water mark. At that time Ford was selling more cars than all other makes *combined*, but Henry's stubborn refusal to alter the T's basic design made it vulnerable to cars with up-to-date refinements. By 1927 it was obvious, even to Henry Ford, that something must be done to meet the competition. Ford scrapped the T and went ahead to design, test, and market a new model in less than a year. The new car, the Model A (Fig. 3-5), was an instant success. But though it gained the short term initiative for Ford, its reign was short compared to that of the T. Automotive design was moving forward by great leaps, pushing Ford ahead, too. The public wanted a smoother power plant, and, because Henry was opposed in principle to a 6-cylinder engine, Ford made the first flathead V-8's in 1932. And by that time the company was committed to a practice that Henry had fought most of his life—the annual model change.

## ANTIQUE CHEVROLETS

Ford's main rival, the Chevrolet, went into production in 1912 as a luxury car priced at more than $2000. Later the company was acquired by General Motors, and the Model 490 was offered to compete with Ford's Model T. The name was suggested by its price of $490, but jokesters claimed that the real significance of the title was that you could drive the car four days and then you had to work on it for ninety. Chevys were reputed to have a grabby clutch that could eat up drive train parts, particularly rear axles, in short order. Some collectors insist that early 4-cylinder Chevys are rare now because most of them didn't even survive the 1920s while T Model Fords rolled on and on.

Chevy 4-cylinder engines were more complicated than Fords of similar vintage. The Chevys had a vacuum tank to bring the fuel forward, an oil pump that was located outside the engine, and open push rods. The oil pump was mounted behind the generator and coaxially with it so that an extended shaft from the generator armature could drive it. If you should happen to find an old Chevy, you will likely have to replace the oil pump because the original ones were made of poor metal that disintegrates with time.

One interesting feature of the early Chevy fours was an oil can mounted on the firewall. The purpose of the can was to provide oil for the tappets. Each morning, before you started the car, you were supposed to squirt some oil into the holes in the top of the valve cover. After the initial oiling the tappets would receive adequate oiling from the engine.

In 1921 Ford was outselling Chevrolet by about 13 to 1 and it looked as if General Motors might have to drop the Chevy line. But after a reorganization of the company, the Chevy became consistently more competitive until in 1927 it outsold the Model T for the first time. In fact, the final sales figures for the year showed that Chevy, in one great leap, had outproduced Ford by about 2 to 1. At that point, Henry Ford recognized that Chevrolet's continual modifications had paid off against his concept of an unchanging basic car at a low price. The late 1920s were boom times and so price became somewhat less important to many buyers. Chevrolet went to a 6-cylinder engine in 1929, and although they sold

Fig. 3-5. A 1930 Model A Ford restored to like new condition.

1,238,605 cars that year, more than in 1927, Ford's Model A production was almost 2,000,000.

## WILLYS-KNIGHT

The Willys-Knight ads of the 1920s boast of long wear and quiet running for its sleeve valve engine. No pounding valves, the ads said, no grinding, no hammering push-rods, and no clashing cams. Those ads seem almost mysterious today and the reader begins to wonder, what kind of engine was this? And what happened to it? Was it unsuccessful mechanically? Or did it die purely because it was too expensive?

John Willys, a car dealer, took over the failing Overland company of Toledo, Ohio in 1908 and renamed it the Willys-Overland Company. Then he bought the Pope-Toledo factory so he could increase production to meet demand. Although Willys-Overland produced vehicles from the formation of the compnay in 1908 until after World War II, the span of the Willys-Knight car was shorter. The addition of the Knight name came after the company adopted the sleeve valve engine patented by Charles Knight.

Willys wasn't the first company to employ the Knight engine, nor the last. Knight's engine went by the appealing title of the "Silent Knight," which made it suitable for automobiles of class, even those chosen by royalty. In 1909 the English Daimler company chose the Knight engine to power its big expensive cars. In 1910 King George V purchased a fleet of sleeve-valve Daimlers for the royal family. They were used for 14 years before they were exchanged for a new stable of Knight-powered Daimlers.

To reduce the noise from pushrod-actuated poppet valves, Knight designed an engine with sliding sleeves operated by small connecting rods. When ports in the sleeves were aligned, fuel could flow in through the ports or exhaust gases forced out. It was claimed that sleeve valve engines improved with use with almost no repair costs. In search of first-hand experience with one of these engines, we found a man, now past 70, whose girl friend in the 1920s had owned a Willys-Knight.

"It was a sweet running car," he says.

Did the engine require any unusual care?

"We always carried a couple of quarts of oil with us. It used a lot of oil until she had put about 15,000 miles on the car. After that it wasn't so bad. Smoked a lot at first. *Clouds* of blue smoke."

Willys-Knight wasn't the only American company to make use of their countryman's invention. Knight-powered cars were built by others, including Stearns-Knight, also headed by John Willys, and Handley-Knight.

Although Willys-Knight made much of the engine's ability to improve with use, it quickly deteriorated if left idle. The heavy oil usage made the engine carbon badly, and it would seize if stored. When the car was started again, often by pushing, the engine was usually damaged. The large surface area of the sleeves and the gummy condition of many Knight engines make seizure likely on any old car that has been abandoned. Loosening such an engine is a major challenge and requires the use of a great amount of solvent as well as patience.

There were, of course, many brand names in the days that antiques were produced that are no longer in production. Such names as Essex, Maxwell, Durant, Hupmobile, Jewett, Oakland, REO, Star, Windsor, and about 3000 other makes. Many of those makes that disappeared deserved their oblivion, but in some cases they were victims of the Depression or of poor financial control rather than of bad engineering. If you find an old car that was discontinued many years ago at a decent price, you *may* have a jewel; you will *certainly* have a challenge.

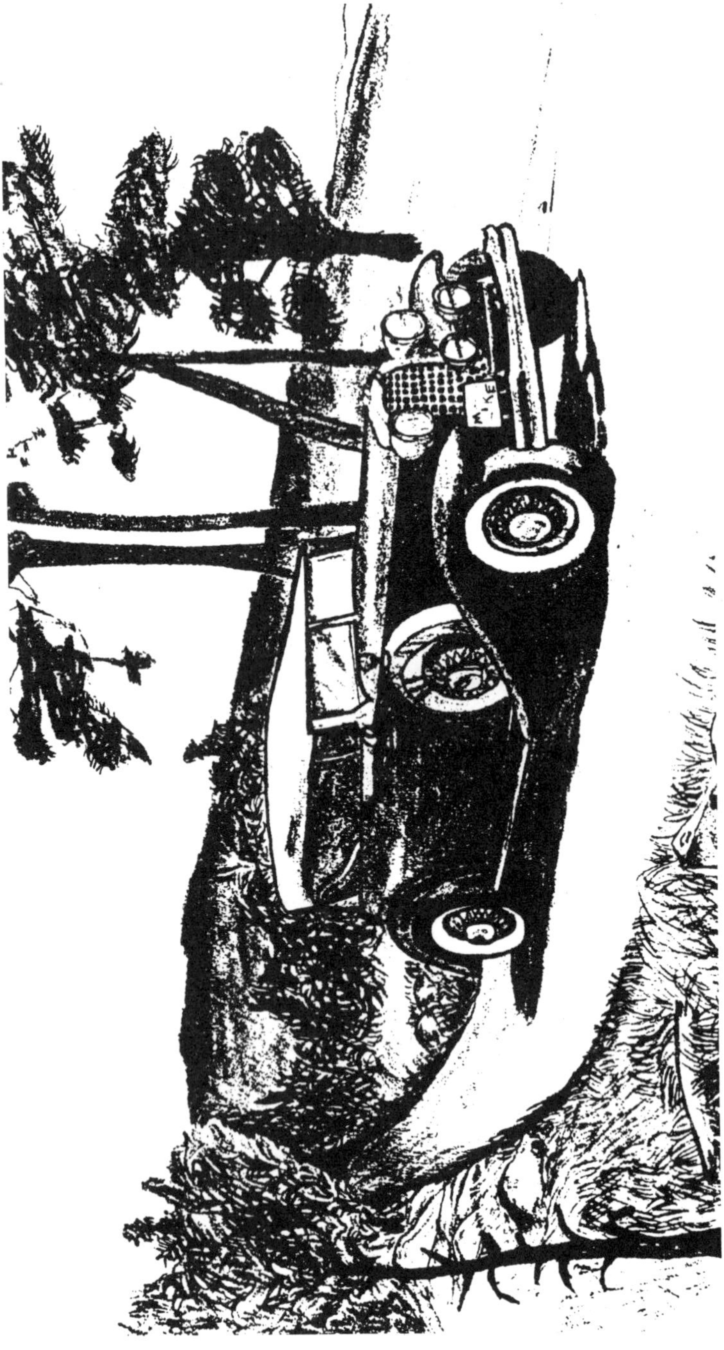
MIKE

# Chapter 4
# Classic Cars

Classic cars, like great works of art, become more valuable with passing time. To be a classic *now*, the car must have been something special when it was new. Or, as one collector says, "If you want to invest in a car that will sell for big money someday, go for class. If it was a dog when it was new, it will *always* be a dog to the smart money."

The ideal classic car is one that combined superior engineering and design with high craftsmanship during construction. But while a powerful engine and mechanical reliability are important, the most distinguishing feature of cars that have come to be known as classics is that they must have *style*. The great cars of the past are good looking, but their styling is essentially rather simple. For example, the exaggerated tail fins of the cars built during the late 1950s are distinctive, but *not* the kind of styling that gains acceptance with classic car fans.

## WHAT IS A CLASSIC?

The typical classic car is long and low. It has a roomy interior, a long wheelbase, and looks expensive. Its long hood suggests a powerful engine, partly because the era during which the great classics were built was one during which the straight-8 engine was the most esteemed power plant. A few late classics have V-type engines, but these are sometimes V-12 or V-16 engines that are also rather long.

The supreme example of a classic car will have a custom body. Although some cars with stock factory bodies rate as classic, most of the top classics have bodies that were designed and built by body specialists. Such cars were never meant to be high production models. Like rare coins, these cars' inherent quality and desirability is enhanced by their scarcity.

The great classics are the cars that were built without regard to cost. In some cases a certain model of a generally well made brand earned the reputation of classic; in other cases simply the name of the make is sufficient for universal recognition. Of cars in current production one name comes immediately to the surface: Rolls Royce. You will find it listed in any compilation of classic cars without any mention of specific models. In addition to such names as Rolls, Stutz, Mercer, Alfa Romeo, Bugatti or Duesenberg, there are other makes that contain a goodly number of classics among their various models. An example of the latter group is Packard.

Many of the great classics were victims of the world-wide depression of the 1930s. Their makers knew how to build fine cars to uncompromising standards of excellence, but they didn't know how or refused to cut corners and reduce costs during hard times. After World War II, the world of the old classic cars was gone forever. At that time you could buy a fine used classic car for prices as low as $500 to $1000. Those bargains represented the buys of a lifetime for people living then.

A look at pictures of the earliest cars shows that they were no more than warmed-over buggy designs. Gradually the cars of the early 1900s developed a shape of their own, but the shape was usually an ugly one. Then in the mid-1920s, some designers came up with cars that looked like a car and yet suggested class at first sight. The improvement in car style owed much to certain custom body builders. These custom designers sometimes conferred the status of classic to a few models of an otherwise average-to-good car of undistinguished style.

Unrestored classic cars can still be found, but they are rare. Your best odds on finding a classic car is to look for a classic model of the auto maker that built more classic cars than any other, Packard. In fact, except for the low-priced models introduced in the late 1930s, Packards were long considered to be one of the finest cars in America.

### PACKARD

The Packard brothers, James and William, built their first car in the closing months of the 19th century. Their machine was an oddball for the times because it had no tiller to guide it. Instead, it had a rotary mechanism that we know today as the steering wheel.

A few years later they patented an H-slot gearshift. They dropped their early name of Ohio Automobile Company and became the Packard Motor Car Company. In 1913 Packard adopted a pressure-fed oiling system, and in 1915 it built the first 12-cylinder car in America, the "twin-six." During World War I this engine was developed further into the Liberty engine that powered warplanes. Then, in 1919, a Packard racing car set a new mile record at Daytona. Ralph DePalma drove a car with the familiar Packard radiator and its 12-cylinder engine to a speed of 149.87 miles per hour. The performance of the Packard was greeted with enthusiasm by Americans because foreign cars had dominated Daytona since the Stanley Steamers quit racing. The celebration was especially sweet because the Packard had smashed the record held by a car built in Germany, the enemy in the recent war.

In the 1920s Packard retired from interest in racing and began to emphasize style and luxury, calling its product "the restful car." The distinctive shape of the radiator (Fig. 4-1) and the recessed hexagon on the hubcaps, adopted in 1904, became as famous as the Packard name and slogan, "Ask the man who owns one." In the mid-20s Packard's advertising cited the fact that when six round-the-world fliers were given a motor car, five of them chose

Fig. 4-1. The most distinguishing feature of the Packard car was the radiator shape.

Packard. Presumably their experience with the Liberty engine influenced that choice. And, Packard's ads suggested, just by choosing a Packard, one could show evidence of taste and judgment. After all, at that time a majority of a highly select group of public figures who were expected to exercise good judgement in thier work—members of the Supreme Court—owned Packards. In another 1925 ad, Packard reported that a survey in 51 U. S. cities showed that during the preceding 5 years only 2 out of every 100 Packard Six cars sold had been replaced. The same ad suggested that to be welcomed by a Packard dealer, you should be able to buy a Packard out of income and without disturbing your capital. This was one of many ploys used by the makers of fine cars to gain status for the purchaser. When one considers that the price of a Packard Eight 7-Passenger Sedan F. O. B Detroit at that time was $5000, and remember those were 1925 dollars, it is remarkable that Packard sold as many as 50,000 cars during the best years of that decade.

The obvious reason for Packard's popularity, considering the price, was quality. But another grew out of the company's styling policy, which was to maintain the well-known Packard identification features and to make only small styling changes. A 1925 Packard, the ads said, would not be out-of-date in 1935. Then Packard qualified the statement a bit, saying it wouldn't unless Packard could succeed where others had failed, to improve on the Packard styling. In a day when there were significant gaps between the quality of low-priced cars and expensive cars, the Packard image was more important to many than owning a new car. The ideal of many conservative car buyers was to purchase a fine car and keep it indefinitely. Packard catered to such motorists.

In 1923 Packard offered 4-wheel brakes and a straight 8 side valve engine. This engine, with numerous refinements, was used for many years. The chassis had an unusual oiling system, an oil reservoir with a pump to permit the driver to lube the car's 45 oiled joints with a pull of the pump plunger. This sytem was used until the late 1930s.

During the Depression years Packard produced two divergent lines of cars, one for connoisseurs, the other for the less affluent buyers. The first departure was the introduction in 1932 of a new V-12 engine. This was a highly respected power plant, but it gave poor gas mileage, even for a large car. The second big development was a low-priced series of cars, the 110 series with 6-cylinder engines and the 120 series, powered by 8-cylinder engines. These models helped Packard sell over 100,000 cars in 1937, double the number they sold in the late 1920s (Fig. 4-2). Low-priced Packards such as the 110 and 120 cars are not considered classics, but after Packard ceased production, all Packards became interesting to collectors.

Although there is no such thing as an uninteresting Packard car for collectors, as for every brand of car there are certain models that collectors find *irresistable*. For Packard, the most desirable models were made about 1930 and later. As a rule of thumb, any Packard made between 1929 and 1933 that has a convertible top is a car that will be an exciting car for anyone who likes old cars. Boatrail racers are rare and expensive. Packards with bodies by custom builders such as Dietrich, LeBaron and Rollston would be on any select list. And Packard V-12's are always prized.

In the late 1930's a new series of Darrin-designed cars appeared in the Packard line. These Packard Darrins, with the Super 8 engine, are among the most desired and expensive of all Packards.

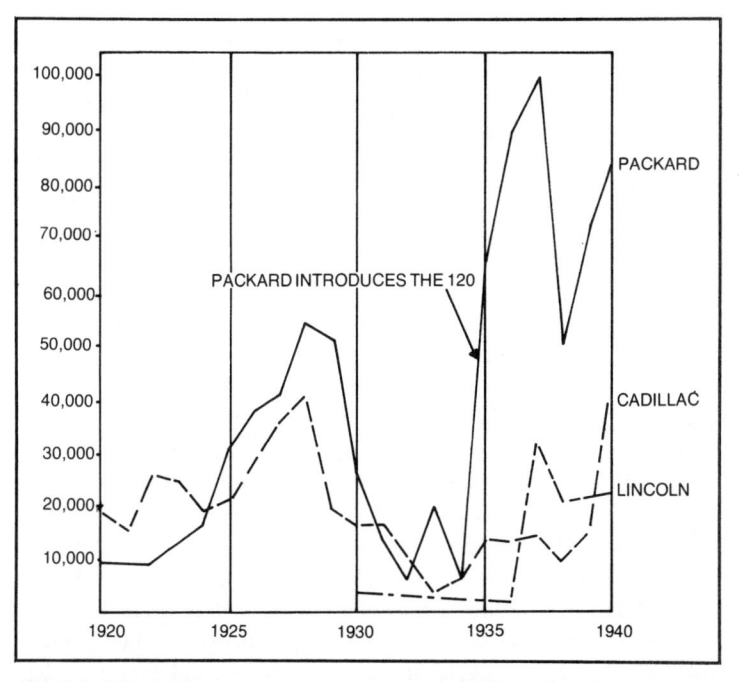

Fig. 4-2. Production rate on some classic cars. Surge in Packard during the mid-1930s was due to the introduction of the successful but non-classic models 110 and 120.

## THE MYSTERY OF THE CHAINS

One old man who used to haul new cars remembers an unusual experience he had once with 1955 Packards. He loaded his car carrier semi with new Packards and chained them down. Then he boomed the chains, using a lever to put tension on each chain and lock it down. He had barely finished the job when he heard a chain snap, then another one. He watched in disbelief as the chains on each car broke in rapid succession. After a career of hauling cars he was completely mystified by the breaking chains.

The driver knew that he couldn't haul the cars unless he could tie them down, so he had to find someone who could explain why the 1955 Packard resisted chains. When he learned what had caused the strange behavior, he found that Packard had a new suspension system for 1955. Packard advertised it as the Torsion-Level Ride (in some ads they called it a "levelizer"). The Packard suspension had two sets of torsion bars, long bars for springing and short bars which maintained the body at constant height. A sensor was connected to the long bars so that when they flexed, the sensor sent a signal through a switch to an electric motor that tightened the short bars to resist the movement of the body. This feature made these cars popular with bootleggers because it was impossible to tell how heavily the car was loaded.

When the driver learned what had caused the Packards to pop their chains, he made a simple change that ended the problem. He disconnected the batteries on the cars and boomed them down again. This time they stayed put.

During its late production years Packard was often the most expensive American car. For example, in 1953 you could buy the most expensive Cadillac for under $6000, but you could pay more than $7000 for some Packards. One reason for this difference was GM's habit of subsidizing the Cadillac through massive sales of their lower-priced cars. During those late production years Packard also had the widest range of prices of any American car. The same year mentioned above, 1953, you could buy some Packard cars for less than $3000. But if that seems low priced by today's standards, remember that inflation has changed the pricing structure of new cars by considerably more than 100% since then. Only Lincoln and Cadillac had a higher starting price than Packard. And you could buy one of the big three low-priced cars that year for under $2000. In comparing those prices to current figures, you would have to add at least $100 for taxes and transportation charges.

Whatever you may think of Packard styling or other features, the make has one big advantage for collectors. It offers your best chance of finding a classic car.

## STUTZ

When car collectors discuss American-made classics, the name Stutz always turns up. Harry C. Stutz worked for several companies as an engineer before starting his own company in 1911. While working for another company in 1905, he designed the American Underslung, a car so unusual for the times that the company adopted the name of Stutz's design for its own. The Underslung was an early sports car with large-diameter wood-spoked wheels and a low center of gravity. These features gave it a somewhat similar appearance to the wire-wheeled M.G.'s of the 1940s.

While Stutz was working for the American Underslung Company, several men associated with the automobile industry decided to build a testing ground for cars at Indianapolis. The location was a logical one because many companies were then located in and around Indianapolis. The track was started in 1909 and completed before the end of 1910. A series of races had been held there, starting in 1909, but someone got the idea of holding a 500-mile endurance race and the first one was scheduled for May 30, 1911. Stutz left his job at American to start his own company and built a car to enter in that race. There were 40 entries in the race, most of them from well-known car makers, but only 22 made it across the finish line. One of these was the single Stutz entry, which placed 11th. Unlike most of the other cars, the Stutz required no tinkering with the engine during the race. Following the race, Stutz chose an advertising slogan based on his car's performance at Indianapolis, "The Car That Made Good in a Day."

The original Stutz car had a 4-cylinder T-head engine with extremely large crankshaft bearings, 3½ inches long, and a combined transmission and differential at the rear. Stutz continued development on this theme and, in 1914, introduced a car that soon became a legend, the Stutz Bearcat. The Bearcat offered a choice of the 4-cylinder or a 6-cylinder engine and a top speed of at least 75 miles per hour. The visual design was simple, the roadster showing two bucket seats, a cylindrical gas tank behind the seats, and a luggage trunk behind that. At first glance one could not escape noticing the long post that held the steering wheel and the outboard control levers.

The Stutz cars entered many races and often won, which added to their reputation and to the demand for them. Stutz built a larger factory, then, in 1919, sold out and started a new company, the HCS Motor Car Company. He built HCS cars for a half dozen years before going into semi-retirement.

The old Stutz company continued to build cars of exceptional quality under its new management. In 1926 it introduced the "Vertical 8," an overhead camshaft engine that borrowed some features from European racing cars. Stutz cars were built lower to the ground than competing makes, their low stance permitted by an underslung worm rear end.

In the late 1920s Stutz again entered racing with a vengeance, winning a string of victories in 1927 and a year later challenging European sports cars in the Le Mans race. During the late 1920s that circuit was dominated by the English Bentleys, made by the company that was later absorbed by Rolls Royce. In the 1928 race, a Stutz Blackhawk temporarily took the lead from Bentley, but the final victory went to the British car. The Blackhawk's second place finish was the nearest thing to a Le Mans win for an American car until almost 40 years later.

In 1931 Stutz refined their 8-cylinder engine further with the DV32, a model number that designated 32 valves, 4 per cylinder. Because the 16-valve model was called the DV16, some auto writers have carelessly assumed that Stutz was producing a 16-cylinder car to meet the 12's and 16's of competitive makes. The arrival of the DV32 coincided with the re-introduction of the Stutz Bearcat and Super Bearcat. Those cars were guaranteed to have a top speed of over 100 miles per hour.

Regardless of the high quality and superior performance of Stutz cars, the company was a victim of the same villain as many another make, the Great Depression. Following that time, and World War II, the cars that survived began to look more alike as the market for truly distinctive cars of high quality evaporated.

## MERCER

Although the Stutz is probably the most famous early American sports car, the Mercer Raceabout was once held in similar esteem. The Mercer company was formed by a group of men from two families, the Roeblings and the Dusers. Their Mercer car, which pre-dated the Stutz by a couple of years, first had a T-head 4-cylinder engine that was changed to an L-head engine in 1915. The Raceabout was a highly successful car, both in winning races and in sales. The small company employed less than 500 workers and were never able to keep up with demand.

Three Roeblings were involved in starting the company, and one was lost on the Titanic. After the other two died in 1917 and 1918, the company was sold by the heirs. The new company tried to expand, buying out the Locomobile company, but a postwar depression in the early 1920s put it out of business. Mercer cars are, of course, extremely rare and expensive.

## DUESENBERG

A third sports car that arrived on the scene later than the Stutz and Mercer became the most expensive car ever built in America. Powered by a straight 8 engine with an overhead camshaft and with hydraulic brakes, the Duesenberg Model A was a jump ahead of the competition in 1921. A Duesenberg race car, using two 8-cylinder engines, set a new Daytona record of 156.04 mph. Duesenberg race cars were also successful at the Indy 500, winning first place in 1924, 1925, and 1927.

The original company made better progress in engineering than in financial matters and so it was bought out in 1926 by the president of the Auburn company, E. L. Cord. Under his direction the Duesenberg brothers continued to run the chassis manufacturing division, farming out the body work to custom builders.

The new company designed the Model J, which appeared on the market in 1928 at prices from $8500 up, chassis only. The prices alone explain why the Duesenbergs were not popular cars. One model went by the name "Twenty Grand," with good reason.

Although Duesenbergs were in considerable demand by wealthy playboys and by Hollywood stars such as Clark Gable and Gary Cooper, the car was another victim of the Depression when its parent company, Auburn Cord, went into liquidation in 1937.

## CADILLAC

The classics mentioned thus far all had in-line engines, which in the 1920s were considered more desirable than V-types. But a few classic cars had early V-8 designs. Outstanding examples were the Cadillac, Lincoln, and Wills Sainte Claire. Cadillac introduced a V-8 engine in 1914, the first one in American production cars. It had also been the first car to offer a starter, in 1912. One of the reasons that Cadillac has survived numerous depressions, wars, and other changes in American society, is that it became part of General Motors in 1908. During the years when the market for fine cars was too small to make such cars profitable, losses in the

Cadillac division were erased by profits in Chevrolet and other lower-priced cars.

Although some collectors consider any Cadillac a classic, the preferred models were built after 1925. General Motors purchased Fleetwood Body Corporation in 1926 and assigned it the job of building custom bodies for Cadillacs. Then, in 1930, Cadillac introduced their V-16 and V-12 engines. The timing of this move was both good and bad. It put Cadillac ahead in the race to produce multi-cylinder smooth engines, but with the Depression coming on, sales were probably lower than anticipated. The long-range effect was to squeeze out competing makes that didn't have the General Motors financial strength behind them.

As the 1930s passed, Cadillac began to limit the production of V-16 cars to special orders. In 1938 the company introduced a new V-16 with a square bore/stroke ratio, $3¼ \times 3¼$, and dropped the V-12. Emphasis was put on production of up-to-date V-8 engines, and by 1941 the V-16 was also dropped. Cadillac had by then become the most successful high-priced car.

The most desirable Cadillacs were built during the 1928-35 era, especially those with V-12 and V-16 engines. The hard times of the early 1930s prevented heavy production of these cars, insuring their high value to future collectors.

## LINCOLN

The Lincoln Motor Company was founded in 1920 by Henry M. Leland, who had been associated with Cadillac in earlier years. The engines for the early Lincolns were works of art, with inner parts machined instead of left rough. Another unusual feature of the engine was the way the connecting rods fit onto the crankshaft. Instead of a side-by-side arrangement with the cylinders staggered to permit the offset as in conventional V-8 engines, the Lincoln rods were of the fork and blade type. The big end of one rod was forked so that it could straddle the narrower blade of the other rod.

Although Leland insisted on a beautifully-made chassis, the car itself looked undistinguished with its high roof and box-shaped body. The company was unsuccessful, probably because of styling and the post-war depression. Ford, who wanted a prestige car, moved in. Edsel Ford took over the management of Lincoln and continued production of the chassis used by Leland, but with a chain of styling changes. The cars gradually began to look longer and lower, in keeping with the styling trend on other prestige cars of the times (Fig. 4-3).

Lincoln styling evolved over almost two decades until it culminated in the strikingly different 1940 Lincoln Continental, a car that was destined to become a classic by styling alone. Edsel Ford is generally credited with having the inspiration for such a car. Thus the Lincoln, having begun life as a car that had mechanical class but no style, emerged in the last years before World War II as one with classic styling but unexceptional mechanical design.

There is some disagreement about which Lincolns qualify as classics, but most collectors omit the Lincoln Zephyrs of the 1930s from the list of classic Lincolns. The most valuable Lincolns are those made from about 1928 to the mid-1930s, especially those with 12-cylinder engines and convertible tops. Lincolns with custom bodies by such builders as Murphy, Rollston, and Le Baron invariably sell for large sums. The Lincoln Continental is one of the most desirable and probably last model of classic cars made in America. The original series was continued after World War II until 1948.

## WILLS SAINTE CLAIRE

As H. M. Leland had left Cadillac to Build the Lincoln, C. H. Wills left Ford in 1919 to make the Wills Sainte Claire car. The Wills Sainte Claire, like the Lincoln, had a V-8 engine, but where the Lincoln engine featured high craftsmanship on a tested design, the Wills car adopted an advanced overhead camshaft engine. But

Fig. 4-3. A typical classic, the 1926 Lincoln Sport Roadster with body by Locke.

Fig. 4-4. The air-cooled Franklin rates as a classic because of strict quality control by H.H. Franklin.

it, too, boasted of fork and blade connecting rods. The Wills Sainte Claire was smaller and lighter than competing fine cars. Its most recognizable feature was the dished disc wheel design. The name persisted until the mid-1920s when Wills added a 6-cylinder overhead camshaft engine to the stable. The price of the cars, starting at about $3000 during the later years, were not the highest but were high considering the size and weight of the car. Despite their reputation of high quality, they went out of production in 1927.

The cars described here show a representative sample of some American cars that are considered classics. Other American cars as well as many foreign cars fit the classification. The following brand names include at least a few models that could be called classics: Auburn, Cord, Chrysler, Cunningham, Doble, Franklin (Fig. 4-4), Dupont, Kissel, Locomobile, Marmon, Peerless, Pierce-Arrow, REO, and Ruxton. As the time span since the great classic cars were made grows greater, the chances are that the remaining specimens will command an ever-increasing price from collectors.

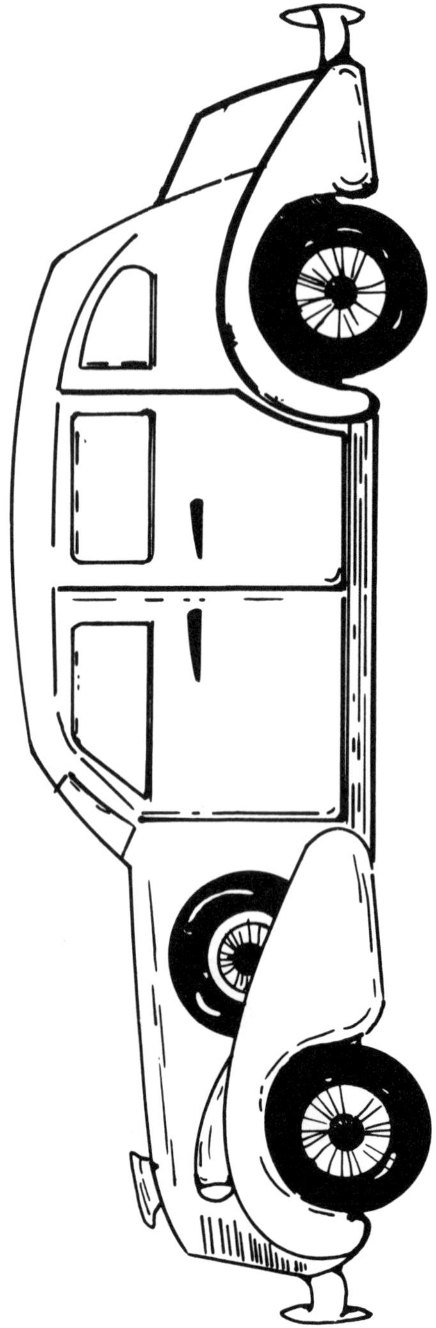

# Chapter 5
# Production Cars

The class of cars called production cars, built from 1930 to 25 years ago, include the greatest number of available cars for restoration. More cars and parts are sold and traded in this category than in any other. Your chances of finding an unrestored car of this vintage is excellent, and the price will often be reasonable. But there are great variations in availability because of differences in original production figures. For example, the Ford Motor Company produced about 940,000 Ford V-8's in 1935, while fewer than 20,000 Willys and under 10,000 Hupmobiles were made. During the 1930s, the big production cars were Ford, Chevrolet and Plymouth. The Ford-Chevrolet battle had been going on for a long time, but Plymouth, a relatively new entry in the low-priced field, scored big gains during the early 1930s as shown in Fig. 5-1.

You might think that a 1935 Willys car in good condition would be a valuable find, since relatively few of them were made. But if you compared the average price of a 1935 Willys and a 1935 Ford, the production leader for that year, you'd get a surprise. The Ford is almost always the more valuable car. Apparently the rule that holds here is that a car that was in demand when it was new will still be in demand four or five decades later. The original production figure evidently has a big effect on the prices of restored cars only when the production figure was very low. This suggests that you don't have to give much attention to production figures unless you are interested in a car that was extremely rare even when it was new.

## PRODUCTION CARS VS. ANTIQUES

Most cars made before 1930 look like a box on wheels, although some of the classic cars of the late 1920s had good styling. The first production cars began to show small changes away from the box, even with low-priced models. For example, the fenders of antiques formed a half circle in profile, but fenders on the early production cars were swept back. Drum headlights gave way to bullet-shaped lights, and highly styled hood ornaments replaced the flat temperature gauges on the radiator caps of the 1920s. The large diameter wheels of the antiques were replaced with smaller wheels, usually the 16" size. The spare tire, which was usually carried behind the trunk on the cars of the 1920s, moved up to the side of the hood. The trunk itself underwent a significant change. Antique car trunks were separate boxes, made much like rectangular-sided steamer trunks, held on by straps. In the early years of production cars the trunk became an integral part of the car, larger and built into the body.

The window glass of cars has gone through several changes since the day of the antique car, both in area and shape. Closed cars

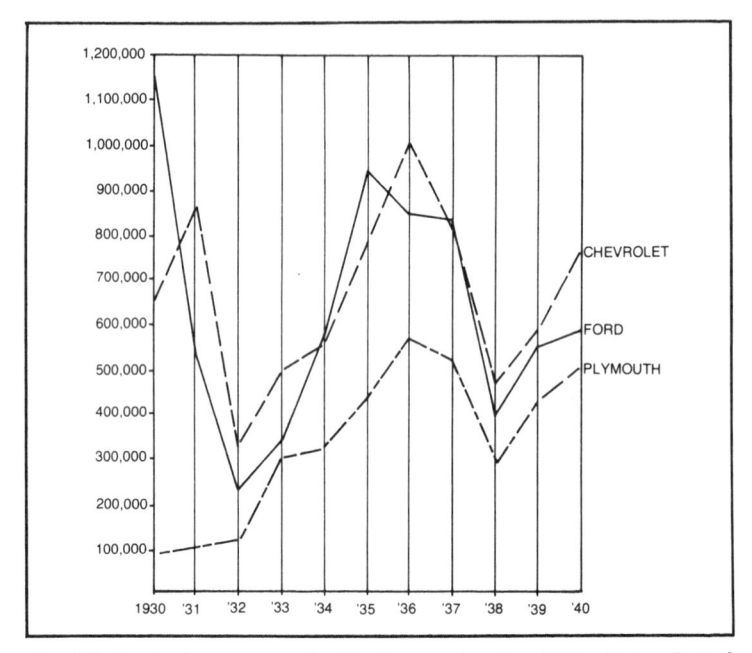

Fig. 5-1. Production rates on the big three during the 1930s. Note effect of depression which struck in early 1930s, then again in 1937-38. As shown here, Plymouth came from nowhere in that decade to become a serious competitor.

of the 1920s had large glass areas with flat vertical glass. In the early years of production cars the glass area was reduced but still mounted in a vertical plane. Windshield pillars were slanted slightly to give a more streamlined appearance, but the windshield glass itself didn't slant until a few years after the production era arrived. The typical 1930s car had a divided windshield, with a chrome centerstrip molding. Some cars had a divided rear window. As the 1930s went by, the slant on the windshield became more acute.

World War II interrupted the series of changes that had made the slab-sided antique cars into the lower, more streamlined production car. Just before the war the first cars with concealed running boards and gas filler tubes appeared. The running board had been shrinking in width all during the 1930s, and after the war it disappeared altogether. Two-tone paint schemes and fender skirts became popular. And the car body, which had ended just behind the back axle on antique cars, grew more overhang which enclosed still larger trunks. The fenders by this time had been blended into the body so that the car had a one-piece look.

Production cars were greatly influenced by the appearance of the first post-war design, the Studebaker styled by Raymond Loewy. Loewy greatly increased glass area, particularly in the rear, making use of more curved glass. The longer rear overhang with a flatter trunk top caused people to make jokes about whether the car was coming or going. But its general shape was remembered by stylists of other companies when they finally produced their post-war models. One notable example of a car that showed the Studebaker influence is the 1949 Ford.

Bumpers on cars have undergone tremendous changes as they evolved from the days of the antiques to those of production cars. The early antiques usually had no bumper. Instead, the front springs extended beyond the fenders and radiator area, two points to impale any pedestrian or stalled vehicle. By the late 1920s, bumpers were offered as standard equipment on some cars. These were usually made from two spaced flat ribbons of steel. Production car bumpers grew vertical guards during the 1930s, then became heavier after the war. Finally, during the early 1950s, the wrap-around bumper appeared.

The production car class includes a wide variety of automobiles. This is one reason that production cars appeal to so many collectors. You can find one to match almost any taste.

## PLYMOUTH

The Plymouth appeared in 1928 as a 4-cylinder version of the larger Chrysler car. The Chrysler company was headed by Walter P. Chrysler, who took over and revived the ailing Maxwell company several years earlier. The first Plymouths sold for more money than a Ford or Chevrolet as Chrysler emphasized value per dollar in their advertising, claiming that the Plymouth was a car of higher quality than either of the two more popular makes. Careful shoppers noted some tempting features in the new 1928 Plymouth: more horsepower, 4-wheel hydraulic brakes, aluminum alloy pistons, silchrome steel exhaust valves, crankcase ventilation and an air cleaner. The car's heavier weight and compensated suspension system gave a better ride than the competition. Even those partial to Fords or Chevys spoke well of the early Plymouth's ride and handling qualities.

Plymouth was the 15th best selling car in 1928 although it was in production for only about half the year. The next year it climbed to 10th place, then in 1930 to 5th place behind Ford, Chevrolet, Buick and Pontiac. Then, in 1931, Plymouth introduced the new 1932 model with a sales pitch that emphasized a new development: floating power. By installing the engine transmission on two rubber mounts, Chrysler claimed that the 4-cylinder Plymouth was as smooth as a conventionally-mounted 8-cylinder engine. This feature helped propel Plymouth into 3rd place during the year of 1932, right behind Chevrolet and Ford. Following that, the Chrysler advertising campaign which suggested that the buyer "Look at All Three" helped impress the public that there was an important new competitor for the two best-selling cars. During the 1932 calendar year Plymouth was the only make to sell more cars than it had sold in 1931.

In 1933 Plymouth introduced its L-head 6-cylinder engine to meet the competition of the Chevy 6 and Ford V-8. Unlike many other makes, the 1930s brought a decade of success to Plymouth. Most other Chrysler products (Fig. 5-2) did well during those Depression years with the top-of-the-line Chryslers finishing the decade with good sales. The sole exception to this success story was the Chrysler Airflow. Those models, although of better aerodynamic design than most other cars of the times, were just too different for the tastes of the 1930s.

If you want to avoid the mass-produced cars of those years, you can find makes that sold in far lower numbers and yet don't fetch a premium price today. Such models as the Willys, mentioned

Fig. 5-2. A 1939 Plymouth pickup. Plymouth pickups are relatively rare, but Plymouth convertible coupes are too, and more valuable.

earlier, the Hudson Terraplane, or the Nash Lafayette are more unusual than a Ford, Chevrolet or Plymouth and yet can be found. If you restore one of those, or another make with similar production figures, the chief difference will be the greater challenge you must meet to find parts. But if you take a Terraplane to an old car meet, you should expect it to attract more interest from collectors than the same model Ford just because it is more rare. And, who knows, someday the Terraplane just might be better recognized as a relatively rare car. But the general public doesn't recognize such cars. If the typical parade goer sees one go by, he will ask, "What model Ford is that?"

## THE PRODUCTION FORDS

People who are old enough to remember the controversy produced by the introduction of a V-8 engine on the early production Fords sometimes mention that there was considerable prejudice against the engine. The fine cars of the 1920s usually had straight 8 engines, so there was some skepticism about a V-8, particularly in a low-priced car. Chevy fans often claimed that all Fords were oil burners. Ford partisans asked in reply, if the V-8 was a bad design, why did Cadillac use it?

By definition, production cars are generally considered to start with the 1930 models, but in the case of Ford that year saw the continuation of the Model A. The big change for Ford came when the first flathead V-8 was introduced in 1932. Early Ford V-8s are rare now and are getting to be expensive. Many of them, particularly the 1932 models, were chopped up and hopped up by hot rodders of a generation ago. Ford issued some unusual body syles that year, especially the Roadster Pickup. The company also produced a Tudor Phaeton and a Convertible Sedan in 1932. These bodies were not offered in later years. The 1932 V-8 Ford is easily recognizable; it is the only V-8 with an almost vertical grille and a body like the Model B, which wasn't significantly different in lines from the last Model A's.

The first Ford V-8s had a bore of 3-1/16", a stroke of 3-3/4", a compression ratio of 5.5:1, and a horsepower rating of 65. In 1933 Ford increased the compression ratio slightly, to 6.3:1, raising the horsepower to 75. In 1934 the single barrel carburetor was replaced with a Stromberg 2-barrel, increasing the horsepower again to 85. Although the engine underwent further design changes, its horespower rating remained at 85 until 1942, when it was increased to 90 horsepower.

One significant difference between Ford engines and many of its contemporaries was the bearing design. Ford used floating rod bearings which turned on the crankshaft. Ford claimed that this feature distributed the rod thrust instead of permitting it to occur always at one place.

Recently, while searching a salvage yard for parts, we were shown a small flathead V-8 engine and asked if we had ever seen one like it. The engine had the familiar look of a Ford product and we remembered the Ford 60 engine, introduced in 1937. Further inspection showed an unfamiliar inscription, definitely *not* your Ford script. Then we remembered that after Ford dropped the 60, so named for its horsepower rating, it reappeared on some French Simca models in the 1950s. Simca increased the compression ratio to 7.5:1 and upped the horsepower rating to 84. (The average compression ratios for any era in automobile history give a good indication of fuel quality of the time. Early gasoline required very low ratios).

After 1932, Ford began to alter the styling in yearly changes that showed a gradual evolution from the upright cars of the late 1920s to the more streamlined models of the '30s. The 4-cylinder engine was dropped after 1933, and engineering effort was concentrated on improving the V-8. Ford made a big styling change in 1933 and again in 1935. The 1935 and 1936 models are particularly popular ones for restoration, partly because Ford sales were good in those years and parts are easy to find. But the highest prized body models of almost any year are the Phaetons, which were discontinued after 1938.

Although many people considered Ford backward in the styling department, a reputation earned by its dalliance with the Model T, production Fords show more advanced styling in some ways than the competition cars. In 1935 Ford abandoned "suicide doors" in front, doors that opened at the front edge, which had made for easy entry but were considered dangerous. Other cars, including some Chevy models, had retained that feature in 1935. In 1937 Ford dropped the traditional discrete headlight, sinking the lamps into the sheet metal between the fender and grille. Most General Motors cars didn't get to that point in headlight placement until the 1940 models.

In 1939 Ford dropped its long-time aversion to hydraulic brakes and joined the crowd. Up until about 1940 the Ford styling showed continuity, less so after that time (Fig. 5-3). The 1942 model, a short production year, had a grille more like those of post-war cars and the first Ford 6-cylinder engine since Henry abandoned his Model K in the early years of the century. The first post-war Fords looked much like the last pre-war models as the factories tried to meet the pent-up demand produced by years with no production.

In 1949 Ford made its first big styling change after the war. This model came out with a new body, lower and wider looking, and with a new suspension that replaced the transverse spring system used on every Ford from the days of the earliest V-8s. Another milestone was passed in 1954 when Ford went to an overhead valve engine.

## MERCURY

The concept and styling design of the Mercury is credited to Edsel Ford, along with the Lincoln Continental. The company introduced the Mercury in 1939 to fill a marketing gap in the Ford line between the low-priced Fords and the upper-middle-priced Lincoln-Zephyr. Unlike another Ford attempt to broaden the market coverage almost twenty years later, the Mercury was obviously successful. It bore a strong family resemblance to the Fords of that year but was slightly bigger and plushier. It had a 95-horsepower engine to suggest better performance than the Ford, but the Mercury was heavier too.

One characteristic of the flathead engines manufactured for the Ford and Mercury cars that inspired affection from the owners was quick starting. A flathead V-8 in good tune would leap into action at a mere jab to the starter button. One man who remembers servicing cars in the 1930s says that was the way he checked tuning. If he had to hold the button down in good weather, the engine needed attention.

## CHEVROLET PRODUCTION CARS

Chevrolet entered the production era with one advantage over the Fords and Plymouths of 1930: it had a 6-cylinder engine. It had overhead valves which in those days was called a "valve in head" engine. The connecting rods were babbit-filled, a feature that Chevy retained until after World War II. Cups on the rod caps supplied oil to the crakshaft journals and the lower cylinder walls, although the engine also had an oil pump. Oil drained back into the pan and collected in the sump at the rear of the engine. Because the front of the oil pan was shallow, these engines did not tolerate low oil levels very well. The first two connecting rods often were oil starved and burned out, especially in cars that were driven at speeds in excess of 55 to 60 miles per hour.

The I-head engine gave Chervolet a theoretical advantage in efficiency but contributed a special sound to motoring, the tap, tap, tap of the tappets. During the 1930s, while Ford and Chevrolet fought a see-saw battle for number one position, engine size of the two big sellers was similar, a little over 200 cubic inches. Each had a horsepower rating of 85 during the mid-'30s. Chevrolet was more

Fig. 5-3. Parts should be no problem for this production Ford.

innovative on suspensions, introducing knee action in its Master Deluxe line in 1934. It also was the first with an all steel top in 1935, a couple of years before Ford, and well ahead with hydraulic brakes, although Plymouth had been the first low-priced car with this feature. Because of its overhead valve engine, some customers associated Chevy with Buick at a time when other GM cars, such as Pontiac, had flat-head engines. Some people who bought the Chevys in the '30s boasted that they chose it because it was a little Buick.

## OTHER PRODUCTION CARS

There was a fairly strong family resemblance in GM cars of the 30s, although that resemblance grew stronger much later when Buick, Olds, and Pontiac cars began to share the same basic body shapes. The line featured "no draft ventilation" early in the decade by adding a wing window in each front door glass. The evolution of body design showed in such details as the placement and shape of the headlights. In 1937 Buick came out with semi-enclosed lights; by 1940 they were fully enclosed in the sheet metal of the fenders or hood.

Dodge bore a strong resemblance to Plymouth in those years, but had added features and a higher price. Many Dodge and Plymouth parts for cars made after the early 1930s are interchangeable.

There were many casualties of the production era, partly because of the Great Depression. The REO car, built by the company founded by R. E. Olds after he sold his Oldsmobile company to General Motors, was one notable example. The REO car was held in high regard because it was conservatively engineered and yet offered many innovations. In the 1920s REO Speed Wagons were well accepted by the trucking industry, and the truck production lasted until after World War II when it became affiliated with White. But 1936 was the last year for the well-made cars such as the REO Flying Cloud. The REO Royal was considered a classic.

Studebaker was well known during the late 1930s for their President Eight. But they also produced a car a bit more in keeping with European politics of the times—would you believe a Dictator Six? Nash cars had some unusual features during the 1930s. The Nash straight eight engine had sixteen spark plugs, two for each cylinder. The top Nash model was called the Ambassador, a name revived by Nash's successor, American Motors, in recent years. Another unusual feature introduced by pre-war Nash was a bed that could be made by folding down the seats, a feature retained by the post-war Nash cars.

If you called a cab during the late 1930s or during World War II, there was a good chance that the vehicle would be a DeSoto. Old movies on the late TV shows often have shots of DeSoto cabs. Many DeSoto owners considered their car to have a much smoother ride than the smaller low-priced models. For many years, DeSoto filled a place in the Chrysler, DeSoto, Dodge and Plymouth line-up that offered competition to General Motors' medium-priced cars. DeSoto was discontinued in 1961.

Graham-Paige cars were noteworthy because of their use of superchargers. On an ordinary car engine the mixture of fuel and air is pushed into the cylinders by atmospheric pressure. A supercharger blows a greater weight of mixture into the cylinders by increasing the pressure on it. This enables the engine to develop greater torque. The Grahams were relatively low production cars, selling about 20,000 cars a year. The make was discontinued in 1940.

During the 1930s, Hudson was the largest producer of cars after General Motors, Ford, and Chrysler. Their low-priced car, the Terraplane, was priced just above the Ford and Chevrolet. The Hudson products of those years had flathead engines with higher compression ratios than the average engine. Terraplane coupes offered special load carrying capacity with a bed that extended from the trunk. During the late production years, Hudson became a high contender on stock car tracks with its Hornet Six. The engine of that car displaced 308 cubic inches and gave a maximum torque greater than any other six, 264 pound feet. It boasted 160 horsepower, a rating that could be increased to 170 by adding an optional power pack. Hudson cars were typically wide-bodied, with more front seat room some years than a Cadillac. In the mid-1950s Hudson joined with Nash to form American Motors.

## LATE PRODUCTION CARS

We of the 1980s would call the cars of the mid-1950s late production cars. By that era the horsepower race was in full swing, affecting almost every car made. In 1951 the average horsepower of all American car models was 118. By 1955 it had reached 181, a gain of over 50% in just four years. All but two makes offered a V-8 engine as an option. And by then the V-8s had overhead valves for better breathing. Some of them, such as the Chrysler and DeSoto models, were famous for their hemispheric combustion chambers. Those engines were prized for their performance on the track.

Along with the swing to V-8 engines, all engines had higher compression ratios, about 8.5 on V-8s, 7.5 on sixes. In 1955 Ford advertised a new I block six, an engine with an overhead valves. Chevys had had overhead valves for decades, but Ford claimed that their new six was the industry's most modern with its short stroke, low friction design.

Veteran engine mechanics were more impressed with another trend of the late production cars—the clutter of gadgets under the hood. These included power options and air conditioners. When they saw the profusion of belts and hoses, they wondered how many owners could afford service on such cars when they got old. These mechanics had lived through the Great Depression and expected another one in their lifetime. Customers ignored such concerns and took to the new accessories.

The gear shift lever, which had appeared on the floor of antique cars, was moved to the steering column during the mid-production car period. This change was greeted as a gain in front seat passenger space, but the coupling was more complicated. Then the automatic transmission did away with the clutch pedal on the vast majority of cars. Only when several small foreign cars became popular did the clutch and floor lever again become desired items which were supposed to return forgotten fun to driving. Those quick shifting foreign cars influenced some of the early compacts, which also sported floor shift levers for a few years.

Suspensions on late production cars had evolved to the point that all American cars had gone to independent front suspension. Antique and earlier production cars had a solid front axle that connected the wheels. This axle ensured that when one wheel hit a hole or bump, the other wheel was also affected. Most late production cars had coil springs on the front, leaf springs at the rear. During the last years of Packard cars that manufacturer introduced torsion bars which had been a part of European car engineering for many years. Chrysler followed this path later.

By the 1950s it was apparent that the auto stylist had become as important to the car manufacturer as the engineer. Some people thought the car stylists had gone mad when their two-tone paint jobs, once rare, became the norm. Then *three*-tone schemes became common, with pastel colors predominant as the first cars in history arrived at the dealers with shades of pink on the sheet metal! The bodies were longer; some 1955 models gained a full 10″ over the same 1954 model. But with hooded headlights and an

Fig. 5-4. This restored 1957 Studebaker Golden Hawk is a desirable collector's item because of its styling and scarcity.

extended fender line to the rear, they looked even longer than they measured. Door posts were eliminated to produce the four door hardtop. And, as glass makers learned how to bend safety glass into sharper curves, the wrap-around windshield appeared.

As the decade of the 1950s ended, stylists went to even greater extremes to attract attention. Cars were bigger, with exaggerated tail fins and heavy chrome grilles that caused some critics to call them rolling juke boxes. Chrome moldings on the sides were curved into wild shapes meant to suggest motion even while the car was standing still (Fig. 5-4). This caused some people to ask, "What will they do for an encore?" The end of that trend was inevitable, with a return to more conservative styling.

One of the trends of the 1950s which affects the price you will have to pay for a car from that period was the number of models offered by each manufacturer. Each company offered an increased number of lines, and some of those were limited edition cars. This practice made for low production figures on some models. The law of supply and demand works with old cars, so you will find some low volume specials selling at above average prices. As a rule of thumb, the sportier the model, the more desirable it is to collectors. Hardtops are probably next to convertibles in demand for restoration. And the more an individual car is loaded with options, the more valuable it is likely to be as a collector's item. There are two reasons for this. Expensive models are always in greater demand, and such cars usually get better care.

Production cars offer you a chance to get into car collecting with a car that you can use every day. Considering the tremendous number and kinds of production cars available, you can surely find one to meet your automotive tastes.

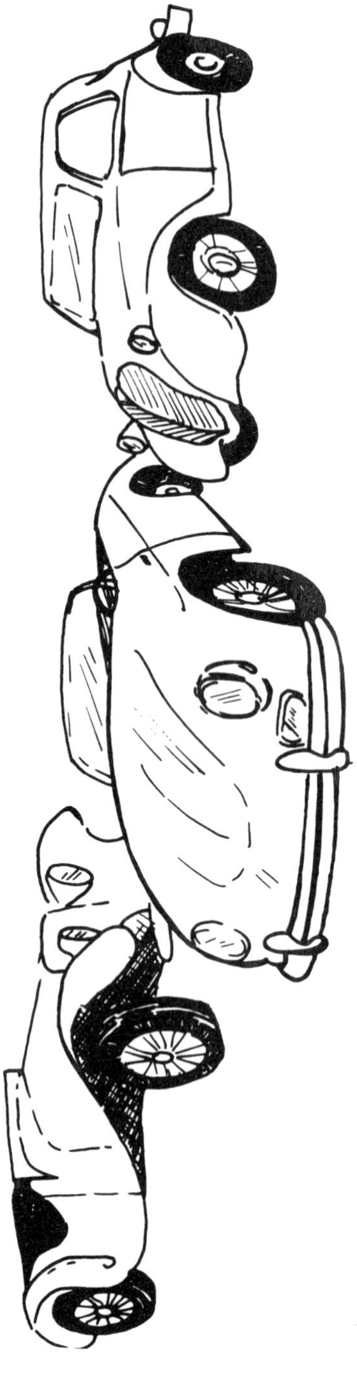

# Chapter 6
# Foreign Cars

The great classic foreign cars, such as Rolls, Mercedes, Bugatti and the like, have *always* been collectors' items. But these cars sell for prices that are far beyond the means of an average collector. Until recently, you could order a used car from England via car magazine ads. England has traditionally been a good source of used cars of interesting design and low production runs. Some Americans have made a good business of traveling to England each year and buying cars for resale in this country. One buyer gave us a sad report of his last trip, made in 1979. Hotel and restaurant costs would have been exorbitant, he says, except for old friends who put him up. And he found few cars at reasonable prices. England, once a candy store for car collectors, has been invaded by oil-rich Arabs. These new car bidders seek out rare and fine specimens because they appreciate such items and also because they are looking for an inflation-proof haven for their dollars. If you have always dreamed of owning an A.C., an Alvis, a Lea Francis, or even a Jaguar—too bad, old chum.

One way to go the foreign car route to car collecting is to find abandoned models of cars that were inexpensive when new. But be careful about parts availability. Preferably the car should have been popular in this country for you to find wrecked specimens in salvage yards or extra parts cars in back yards. We will start with what was once the most popular foreign car.

## VOLKSWAGEN

If there had been a *Family Feud* TV program in the early 1960s with the topic foreign cars, the name at the top of the list would have surely been Volkswagen. In the years around 1960, customers had to put their name on a waiting list to get the car. In 1959 the average price for used current model VW's at auto auctions was actually *higher* than the price for new cars. Year-old models sold for over 90% and two-year-old models for more than 80% of the new price. And these were *wholesale* prices. For a comparison of how another popular foreign car of the times was doing on depreciation, a two-year-old Renault Dauphine averaged about 50% new price at wholesale auctions. A few years later Dauphines sold even lower.

Considering the once high demand for the VW Beetles, it seems a good bet that some of the young people who wanted a VW then will someday want another one in their old age. Early models are the best collectors' items, but rare.

It is hard for people today to imagine how formidable were the odds that VW faced after World War II. After a bitter war and stories of Nazi atrocities fresh in the memory, Americans were hardly ready to buy German chocolate, much less a car made in Germany. And, to most people, the car was ugly, underpowered, and far too small. But VW prevailed. It went on to sell more cars of the same model than any other since the Model T. Although it was often compared to the T, VW showed a steady progression of gradual changes as the car evolved. Ford's flivver had few important changes in the chassis during its life.

To make the VW even less desirable to Americans, it was generally agreed that it was the brainchild of Adolf Hitler. This was true in the sense that Hitler wanted a no-nonsense people's car, a car for the German workers who couldn't afford the big cars of the 1920s. It was because of his concept of a car for the average man that Hitler gave approval for the original VW and encouraged its production.

The designer of the VW, Ferdinand Porsche, had designed an electric car before 1900 that would travel 59 miles without recharging. That car won fame and prizes for Porsche. He later went to work as director of the Austrian division of the Daimler Motor Company. Another branch of this company developed in England, set up to sell Daimler patents in that country. The English company went on later to build cars of the highest quality and price, cars which were the favored choice of English monarchs from the early 1900s until Elizabeth II became Queen and switched to Rolls Royces.

Porsche later worked for the German Daimler company, then, in 1931, set up a consulting office for himself in Stuttgart. Through the years he dreamed of designing a *Kleinauto*, a small car for the masses. During this time he patented a new kind of suspension system, the first torsion bar. He was critical of existing small cars, saying that they showed no original attention to the special problems of small car design but were scaled down copies of big cars. The power system, for example, should be over the drive wheels to provide adequate traction. And special suspensions were needed to compensate for the inherently stiff ride of small cars. His answer: independent suspension for each of the four wheels which reduced the unsprung weight (the parts that move up and down).

Porsche experimented with a radial air-cooled engine, similar to aircraft engines. He later dropped that idea because he thought it would be difficult for the average auto repairman to service.

When Hitler came into power, one of his obsessions was to sponsor a *Volksauto*, a people's car, for the common man. His interest in cars led him to build the autobahns, which could also be used for troop movements, and to prod German car makers to design a low-cost car for the working people. Porsche took his design to Hitler and got his backing. The VW factory was built near Wolfsburg in the late 1930s, just in time to be bombed during World War II, although the plant did turn out military vehicles for use in such varied climates as the North African desert and the snow-covered plains of Russia.

After the war, the badly damaged plant needed repair and complete reorganization. A British officer took control of the plant and got production started. The British military government tried to interest Ford of America and Rootes of England in the plant and its ugly duckling product, but to no avail. Then Heinz Nordhoff, a German engineer, took over management. For the first few years after the war, production was limited to a few thousand cars. By 1949 production was up to about 50,000 cars a year, by 1954 to about 200,000 Beetles plus 40,000 transporters. By 1955 1,000,000 cars had rolled off the line.

One secret of VW's outstanding success in exporting cars to the U. S. was Nordhoff's analysis of why other European manufacturers had failed to reap success in this country. He decided that VW should build up a dealer network with a good parts supply before making an all-out effort to sell the car. A few cars were brought back by soldiers stationed in Germany in the late 1940s, but they were universally judged to be too weird to gain wide acceptance. One man, remembering his first ride in a tiny Beetle in the early 1950s, recalls his impression. He got into the car at

Sunset and Laurel Canyon in Hollywood. Unfortunately, his destination, and that of the young woman who was driving the car, was on Lookout Mountain Road, a mile or two up the canyon. He hunched down into the seat, cowed by the sound of the screaming engine as they went up the canyon road, then stared unbelievingly as the driver appeared to be whipping the car with her right arm to make each curve or increase in grade. Then he realized that she was using the gearbox to maintain their movement toward Lookout Mountain. As he watched bigger cars whizzing past them on each straightaway, he wondered why anyone would buy a car that looked like somebody's doodled design and appeared to have all the power of a sick parakeet. Six years later that same man went into a VW dealer to compare prices. His conversion from scoffer to customer is typical of the change of attitude of many Americans in the decade from about 1955 to 1965.

For a time, the army of VW owners took on the appearance of a cult. Even those people who hated small cars, and especially *foreign* small cars, began to wonder if they were missing something. VW partisans admitted that the car had a few idiosyncrasies, but, they said, these were easy to forgive.

One woman who had long wished for a Beetle bought a bargain car from a man who had put it together from a pile of parts, using a repair manual to guide him. She excitedly showed it off to the women in her car pool, only a bit uneasy when a door handle came off. The next day it was a window crank. She gradually learned to repair the failing parts herself, bridging across the switch with a hair pin when the car wouldn't start.

It was a love-hate relationship, anger when the car wouldn't perform right, then love again when she figured out how to put it right. The affair reached a crisis the day she was driving a couple of women home from work and noticed that the car was losing speed. She gave it more gas. Although the road was level, the car seemed to be slogging down. Gradually her foot went down harder on the gas pedal until it reached the floorboard. The speedometer needle dropped from 20 to 15, then to 10. No one spoke as the car ground down to a halt. The riders got out, leaving the driver speechlessly gripping the steering wheel. Then she got out and walked around the car, kicking it as she went. That was when she found that the wheels were hot. The brakes had locked.

She got the old repair manual out of the glove compartment. It had 20 pages missing from the center of the book.

"That's it," she said, in sudden forgiveness. "Those pages must have covered the parts that have been causing all the trouble."

Although the post-war VW Beetle was based on Ferdinand Porsche's original design, by 1954 the car had been so thoroughly debugged that even the screws no longer were made to the same specifications as in Porsche's first cars. After the mid-1950s the evolution continued. Engine power was increased several times, by increasing the displacement and by raising the compression ratio. In 1954 it went from 30 to 36; in 1961, to 40; in 1966, to 50; in 1967, to 53; in 1969, to 57, and later in the Super Beetle it was increased to 60. Some mechanics consider the early, understressed VW engines to be more durable than the later ones. The changes in 1966 are sometimes particularly criticized in that the displacement was upped from 1300 cc to 1500 cc. The larger engine, critics say, needed more cooling than was available.

Those VW's made before 1960 are somewhat more primitive, but are in greater demand as collectors' cars. After all, in the late 1960s VW sales in the U.S. had grown to over 500,000 a year, equal to that of Plymouth in the 1930s. But even one of these might be a good investment for the long term, if you are still young enough to plan to keep it and show it in the next century.

## RENAULT

VW's were often called by a straight translation of their German name, the people's car. Renault more often went by the title "Fun Car." Some owners said that was just as well because it wasn't good enough for serious motoring. Renaults are cheap now; we were recently offered a running car with a bit of transmission trouble and no top for $60. Such a car *might* be a long shot that the old rule, "Once a dog, always a dog" doesn't necessarily apply to foreign cars that can become rare through a flawed reputation. Actually, Renault was a better car than many owners thought. It *couldn't* have been worse, but the early service was often incredibly bad.

If you find low prices appealing, you can consider the Renault Dauphine (Fig. 6-1) or 4CV of the 1950s or early '60s. But a better way to play the Renault would be to find an abandoned Caravelle, a Dauphine in sports clothing. Such a car, restored, should be fun to drive and would be much more valuable than a Dauphine because of its styling and comparative rarity.

Renault is an old company, having started building cars before 1900. In fact Louis Renault, then 22 years old, launched his company in 1899. He was credited with several innovations, such as the world's first enclosed car, the removable spark plug, the hydraulic shock absorber, and others. He entered his cars in many races and won a large percentage of them, which vindicated his opinion that power to weight ratio was more important than brute power alone. One of the most distinctive aspects of his cars was the sloping front hood that Stanley admired enough to copy in some of its steamers.

In the years before World War I, France was the world's largest producer of automobiles and Renault was the largest French manufacturer. Renault produced many 2-cylinder taxicabs which were instrumental in Marshall Joffre's defense of Paris in the Battle of the Marne. Joffre was in desperate need of reserves who were available in Paris, so taxis were requisitioned to deliver a fresh division to a point 30 miles from Paris. Several hundred cabs, most of them 6 years old, made the round trip twice with but 3 or 4 breakdowns. The rapid troop movement gave Joffre the opportunity to surprise Von Kluck, the German commander, with a flank attack that stymied the German advance.

After World War I, Louis Renault decided to challenge Daimler and Rolls Royce, so he built a huge car, his Model 45. The car weighed up to about 3 tons, and the engine had a displacement

Fig. 6-1. Old Renaults, such as this 1958 Dauphine, are now out of favor and therefore cheap.

of over 550 cubic inches. A sports version of this tremendous car was the first car to average 100 mph for 24 hours. Renault produced the car for about 10 years, before it was dropped from the line in 1929.

During the 1930s Renault cars were modernized, and several small cars were produced, one having independent front suspension that suggested the Dauphine design to come. During World War II the factory at Billancourt was heavily bombed, just as the VW plant at Wofsburg had been. In 1944, when France was liberated, the new French government took over the Renault factory because the company was considered to have collaborated with the Germans.

During the war Renault engineers had worked on a post-war design, the little 4CV. The car was considered a joke by the people who first saw it, a reaction similar to American response to the VW. But the 4CV was even smaller than the VW and had poor weight distribution, which Ferdinand Porsche criticized when he first saw the design just after the war. Even so, a million of the little cars were made and sold between 1944 and 1961.

In 1956 Renault introduced the Dauphine, a car with much more style than the 4CV. This car received international attention when it won the Monte Carlo rally in 1958. Starting about that time it was exported to the United States in considerable numbers for several years, but the inadequate service offered by some of the Renault dealers gave it a bad name with many owners. Renault replaced the car with the Renault 8 in 1964.

The Dauphine engine is a water-cooled 4-cylinder job with wet steel cylinder sleeves. Some mechanics consider the traditional cast iron block engines to have more durability, but the sleeve engine can be easily renewed by installing new cylinder liners and pistons. The engine has pushrod overhead valves. The engine is located behind the rear axle and coupled to the transmission which is located just ahead of that axle. The transmission and final drive gears are encased in a single unit.

One of the delightful surprises in this cheap car is the handling. Its rack and pinion steering gives it a sports car feel. Some owners of early Dauphines found that they could install heavy duty shock absorbers on the car and improve handling even more—with one disadvantage, a stiffer ride.

Restoration work on a Dauphine will offer some tasks that are much easier than the typical antique; for example, engines. The engine is relatively light, so you won't need such heavy beams in the ceiling of your shop for anchoring a pulley. We know one man who overhauled a Dauphine engine on the kitchen table. His wife told us about it.

## MG

The MG sports car was the first noticeable import after World War II. It all started on the West Coast with little MG TCs darting around big American sedans on the winding canyon roads near L.A. The car was distinctive in its old-fashioned styling that looked more like earliest MGs of the 1920s than like the post-war big cars that it competed against. Critics looked it over and said, "Not much car for $2500." But those who drove an MG soon forgot the price per passenger for the little two seater.

The initials, MG, were first used for the MG Super Sports in 1924. Those letters were chosen from the name Morris Garages, because William Morris was a major investor in the company. He had made a car called the Bullnose Morris that competed in England against Ford's Model T. Morris later absorbed the little MG company.

The first MGs had a 4-cylinder 1.8-liter side valve engine with a bore of 75 mm and a stroke of 102 mm, 27" wheels, and a 3-speed transmission. The latest MG engines have an almost identical displacement to that of the early engines, although the bore and stroke have been changed radically to 80.3 × 88.9 mm. A later MG, introduced in 1929, had a 847 cc engine and was called the MG Midget, like its namesake of the early 1960s. There were many variations of these basic sports cars before World War II, and some were extremely successful in racing and record breaking speed runs.

The 1947 MG TC was very similar to the 1936 TA and the later pre-war model, the TB. The TC had 19" wire wheels which made it stand out in any traffic pattern. Americans had to get used to right hand drive on these early imports, but such features only helped to boost demand among drivers who wanted something different. The next model, the TD, came out in 1950. It was a disappointment to some purists who loved the higher wheels and less compromising styling of the old TC. The TD was Americanized to a much greater extent because by then the post-war sports car boom had hit the U S., and MG could afford to make a special car, with left-hand drive, for the American market. The TD was followed in 1953 by the TF, further evolved from the TC.

By 1955 MG retired the T series to introduce the MGA with its streamlined body and sloping grille that replaced the vertical radiator of the older models. You can sometimes find an MGA at a very good price. We were recently offered one with a good body but a missing engine head for $300. When we told a friend about it, he went out and bought it.

If length of manufacturing run or total sales mean anything, the MGB (Fig. 6-2) is the world's most popular sports car. It was introduced in 1962 and was produced without interruption until an announcement in late 1979 that the factory would be closed in 1980. On the announcement MG club members protested strongly and suggested various ways for the company to maintain production in spite of their financial losses. Early in 1980, British Leyland Ltd. announced that Aston Martin Lagonda Ltd. would buy the MG plant and continue production. (Aston Martin was itself saved from a financial crisis by a group of investors headed by Peter Sprague, an American. Sprague has a good record of reviving financially troubled American electronics companies).

During the two decades of the '60s and the '70s MG averaged about 20,000 to 30,000 cars per year, not your Ford or Chevy figures but a sizable number for a special model such as these little sports cars. At the present time, the early models are more desirable for collectors, but as the years pass *any* MGB will become a more interesting car to own.

The original MGB had a 3-bearing crankshaft, but that was replaced with a 5 main bearing shaft in 1965. A GT model appeared in 1967, and the MGB GTs should be excellent choices for restoration. Late models have more smog gear and heavier bumpers which cut performance.

If you like sports cars, the MG would be hard to beat for the value you get for your collector's dollar. Buy one now for restoration later, and you can get it at little more than its normal used car price. Sports cars do depreciate more slowly than sedans, so don't expect to find one in excellent condition for a fraction of its new price. For a *really* low-cost car, you will have to do some restoration work.

## OTHER FOREIGN CARS

Among the many makes and models of foreign cars that have been imported in the past, some appear to be surefire collectors' items. Here are just a few that you can consider.

The Austin Healey Bug Eye Sprite should be a natural. It's hard to believe that about twenty years ago you could buy a new sports car for less than $2000. The car got the name Bug Eye from the shape of the headlights that bulged out of the top of the fenders. It was powered by the same engine used by BMC, the company that then made MG, in the Morris Minor car. Morris Minors are also worthy collectors' cars, giving something of a sports car feel in a small sedan (Fig. 6-3). But the Morris engine, having smaller valves than the Sprite in the years around 1960, had a tendency to burn the exhaust valve of the third cylinder.

The Sprite had a one-piece hood and fender assembly which gave good access to the engine and front end. The car was a true midget with an 80" wheel base.

Another possibility: the larger Austin Healey sports cars. This car, with its 6-cylinder engine, gave considerably hotter performance than the MG. The engine had a displacement of about 178 cubic inches in the 1960 Austin Healey 3000, slightly less in earlier models. This compared to a 97-cubic-inch 4-cylinder engine in the contemporary MGA.

The Triumph sports cars, first imported in 1954, are another likely choice for collectors. The early TR-2 or TR-3 or the later TR-4, TR-6, or Spitfire models would all be desirable. Triumphs sell for considerably lower prices now than MG cars, so they offer a budget-conscious collector a chance to get into sports car collecting.

Fig. 6-2. 1963 MGB. The MGB, with the longest run of any sports car, probably offers your best chance of getting a sports car at a reasonable price.

Fig. 6-3. The Morris Minor's stodgy styling adds to its value as a collector car.

No list of British cars would be complete without the Jaguar. Unfortunately, any good Jaguar will be expensive. Another expensive car, a natural for James Bond fans, is the Aston Martin. But back to cars that most of us can afford.

If you are partial to German cars, the price range is limited. Owners of good Mercedes and Porsches rarely want to part with them, and if they do, they have a full appreciation of what their car is worth. You can sometimes find a rare German car for a reasonable price. For example, an old DKW might sell at a bargain price. This car was an oddball to most people because of its 2-cycle, 3-cylinder engine driving the front wheels. Such cars once aggravated the typical service station attendant's hostility to foreign cars. One California station worker probably still remembers the time he put the oil in the gas tank *after* the gas. The car owner saw him just as he drained the oil can and made him put the car on a lift and drain the gas tank. Instructions for mixing oil with fuel on those cars specified that the oil be put into the tank first to achieve good mixing.

The early imported models of the Swedish Saab were quite similar mechanically to the DKW. The Saab had a fastback styling that limited its trunk space. The car was designed for great body strength, and some owners claimed that it was the safest car on

American highways. If this car with unusual engineering appeals to you, consider the Saab GT model, with a hotter 50-horsepower engine compared to the 38 hp standard model.

Another Swedish car, the Volvo PV-444, was noted for its styling which made it look like a miniature 1940 Ford. This small sedan's 4-cylinder engine gave a sports car performance. Unfortunately its eagerness to go encouraged some owners to over-rev the engine in the lower gears, so you should expect to rebuild the engine of any old Volvo you find. To be realistic you should expect to find well-worn engines in any cheap old foreign car.

If you admire Italian styling, look for an old Fiat. But not all Fiats were considered the epitome of good visual design. The Fiat 1100, for example, was a no-nonsense foreign sedan, but the slab sides didn't appeal to many people. The fiat 1200 Gran Luce, which was developed from the Fiat 1100, was a handsome small car with a beautifully finished interior. But the car's dimensions made it uncomfortable for large or tall people.

What about Japanese imports? Because Japan began exporting cars long after other industrial nations, such cars as Datsun and Toyota offer less interest to collectors who are conscious of the early history of European companies. One collector said, "There is no tradition here." But this situation will change with time. Look for special models, such as the Datsun 240-Z, if you want to gamble on owning a future collector's prize in a Japanese car.

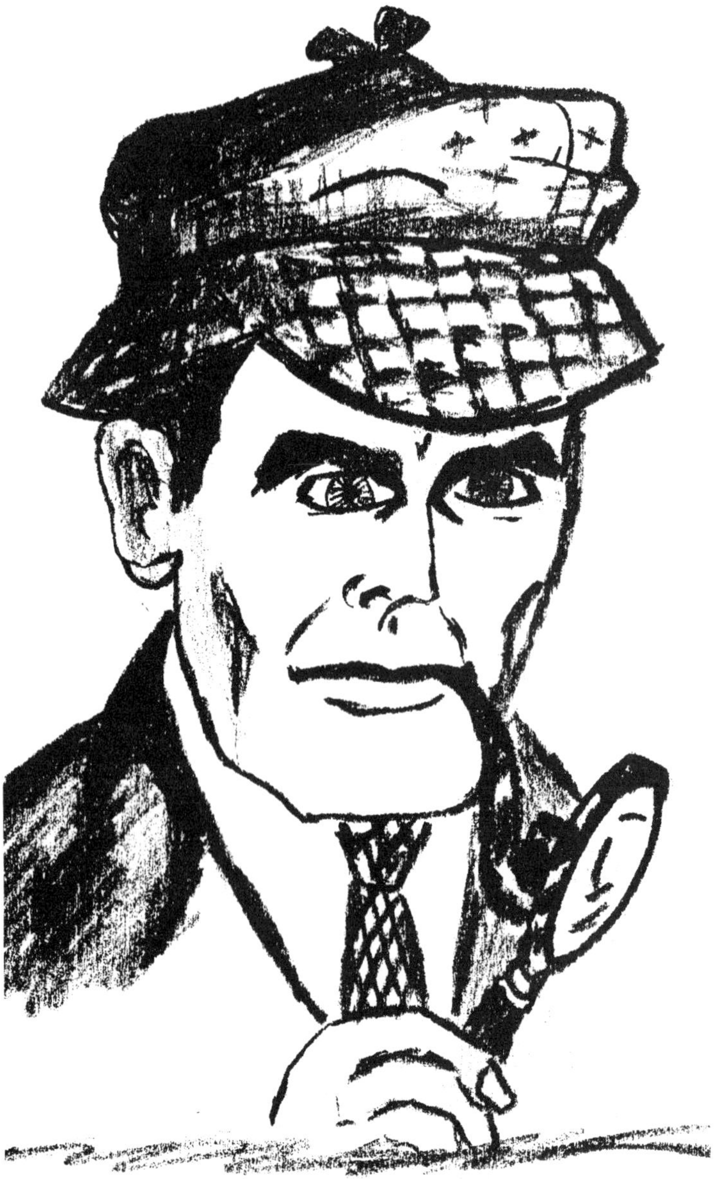

# Chapter 7
# Getting a Car

The best kind of car to get is the hardest to find: one that has been stored in a shed with a good roof. Such cars are out there, but you won't see them on a Sunday drive. To locate one, you must assume the role of a detective, and, just as important, you must exercise a lot of patience. When you find it, such a car will cost more than one of the same model that has been abandoned to the weather. It may *well* be worth the difference. A good rule of thumb is to buy the best car you can afford, even if it means going to a later model or one with higher production numbers. Any car that has been exposed to the weather for a considerable time will have some degree of hidden damage, recesses where water has collected and produced rust. If you have to leave your car outdoors for any length of time before starting to work on it, move it periodically or at least open and close the doors occasionally to dislodge the water. Unused cars rust out much more quickly than cars in daily use.

Even if the car you find has been stored in a shed since it was new, it may have deteriorated in some ways. One man we know found a 1917 Dort about 15 years ago. The car had been stored in a shed since it was new and hadn't been used more than a year or two. The old shed had a hole in the roof, and below that hole the hood of the Dort was rusted out with a hole in it about 1 foot in diameter. The leather upholstery was cracked too, but in other ways the car was in good condition.

Ideally, the car you buy should be in use or have been driven recently. If you are interested in antique cars, you will surely have to accept an abandoned vehicle. But regardless of its condition, how do you find the car you want?

## HOW TO FIND A CAR

First, enlist the aid of your family and friends, including children. *Especially* children. While they won't know makes or models on really old cars, children often know where an old car is parked behind a shed or in a garage.

Be aware that most people's knowledge of exact years or models is hazy or even erroneous. Be prepared to follow some false leads. We recently mentioned that we would like to find a 1935 Plymouth in restorable condition. A middle-aged man immediately said that he knew where a car was parked in a pasture. He said it was a Plymouth, probably a 1930s model. Knowing that this man had long been interested in cars, we went with him to the hillside pasture, a drive of about 30 miles. When we arrived, we found that the car was a 1951 sedan. If possible, have a picture of the model you want to show to people. That can prevent many a wild goose chase.

If your town has alleys that separate back-to-back neighbors, drive through them and look for cars parked in backyards. As the cost of gasoline goes up, you may want to use a bicycle for this game. Your chances of finding a car at a low price by this method is excellent because many owners retain an old car more in procrastination than by design. (And the best part of town to look in is *not* the best part of town).

Next, try the countryside around your town (Fig. 7-1). Again, with energy prices up, you may not want to make endless drives to look for a car, but you can often combine the search with out-of-town trips. Take a different route each time you drive to a neighboring city, preferably one that takes you on back roads. You will almost certainly see a few unofficial car graveyards, ravines or hillsides dotted with a half dozen or more old cars (Fig. 7-2). Many of these will belong to farmers who like to tinker with machines. Such people rarely sell. But occasionally you will find a new land owner or a widow who is glad to find a buyer for any or all of the relics.

Even if the cars you find are not for sale, the owner may be able to suggest the name of a neighbor or friend who has a similar car stored away. But be prepared for all kinds of responses, from friendly to abrupt dismissal. If the cars are located on private property, try to find the owner before you inspect them. To save time, carry a pair of binoculars so you can eliminate distant possiblities without crossing fences, streams, or bull pastures.

If you have friends who travel consistently, ask them to watch for old cars. Again, show the watcher a picture of the model you want. But add that you are interested in *any similar* car; if you restrict yourself to a single year of a particular make, you may end up with nothing. By exploring all cars of similar vintage, you may find a substitute car at a bargain price. Or, in following a lead, you may uncover a second car of the model you wanted all the time.

Old cars are a good conversation topic for many people, so your traveler friends will probably spread the word at their favorite coffee stops. Truck drivers make good contacts for car searches. One driver we know found a car about 100 miles from home because he mentioned what he wanted on CB, and another driver overheard his request. Even if you don't know any truckers personally, you can visit local truck stops and drop the word.

## CAR CLUBS AGAIN

As we have mentioned before, there are many advantages to joining a local antique car club. A club is a good place to hear about where a certain kind of car can be found or more general information about auctions or other car sources. If you don't have a local car club in your city, you can join a national club and reap

Fig. 7-1. Abandoned farms and ranches are good sources of antique cars and trucks.

Fig. 7-2. This salvage yard specimen would be suitable for a parts car.

considerable advantage. You will find the names and addresses of several in the back of this book.

No matter what make of car you favor, there is probably a special club dedicated to preservation of that car. If possible, contact the nearest club that specializes in your make. You will likely find that some of the members have cars for sale. Some of the cars offered will be either unrestored or only partially restored. And of course you can realize many other advantages from a car club, such as advice and help on getting parts and in doing restoration work that is peculiar to your make of car.

## PUBLIC SALES

Your community undoubtedly has numerous estate sales or other public auctions every year. It may even have an occasional antique car auction. You can visit these to observe selling prices, but the cars will likely be restored cream puffs worth a high figure. The kind of auction you should aim for is the general sale of someone's estate.

To find an auction, look in the classified ad pages of your local newspapers. Or look up the telephone numbers of local auctioneers and call them for information on coming sales. Some auctioneers will mail you advance information on sales. In small towns and rural areas the sale bills are often posted at gas stations, stores, or public bulletin boards.

When you receive a sale bill, which describes the property, or attend the sale and hear the auctioneer tout it, allow for a certain amount of exaggeration. A first rule to observe at auctions is to bid *only* on items that you have had an opportunity to *carefully* examine before the auction. After doing that, write down on paper the price you think the item is worth. Then set your top bid at 60% of that price. Finally, under no circumstances should you exceed that figure with your bid.

For example, you find a 1960s car in good condition. You shop around and figure the car is worth about $500. You would write that figure in your notes and calculate that you should bid no more than $300.

The act of writing the price and your top bid is important. It is too easy to get caught up in an auction fever and go far beyond reason. Remember that you are looking for a bargain, *not* a chance to show the crowd your power. Try to be just one of the crowd. Wear clothing that will blend into the mass; avoid any distinguishing feature that makes you stand out. *Don't* arrive at the auction in a limousine or, at the other extreme, dressed like a bum.

Cars for sale at auctions can rarely be tested. You may be able to start the engine in some cases. If the auctioneer says the head has never been off the engine, that the car was driven conservatively, and so on, check it out before the auction. Look for stickers on the door that will identify the service station or garage that serviced the car. Then go and ask if anyone there remembers the owner and the car. One 1956 Plymouth flathead 6 2-door sedan was described as a cream puff that had never had any engine work, but the sticker on the door helped us to locate a service station worker who said the engine had a bad case of burnt valves the last time he saw it.

When you arrive at an auction, you must register and get a bid number. If you win a bid, you show the number to the clerk who records it. You must pay for the item before you remove it. Some auctions accept your personal check if you have proper identification, but if you are unknown in the community, you should have a book of traveler's checks that total the amount you want to pay for a car. This is another way of limiting your bid to a reasonable figure. Take along just the amount of money you think you should pay.

In addition to estate sales, another source of antique items, including cars, is a public administrator's sale (Fig. 7-3). These are held by the county or state public administrator to settle estates that have been acquired by the state. To get on the mailing list for such sales, go to the nearest public administrator's office and leave your name and address.

Some estate sales are held by the attorney who is settling the estate. These often require a sealed bid, so you must examine the items, then submit your bid for them in a sealed envelope. A car, for example, will typically be stored at a local garage for bidders to inspect. Bidding at such sales is often limited to dealers or people who make a practice of buying at sales. Watch the pages of your local newspaper for announcements of such sales, or leave your name with the offices of local attorneys.

When buying at any kind of sale that requires a bid, remember that auctions are unpredictable. The excitement of an auction often sends prices soaring to unreasonable levels. But on other days you can get a bargain. Remember, it takes only one other interested buyer to drive up the price. Be careful.

## PUBLICATIONS

Many national car clubs publish magazines or newspapers which go to all members. Some of these are good sources of cars and parts. While the cars may be located many miles from your home, you can often find a rare car listed in these publications.

Don't overlook the possibility of running an ad yourself to tell the kind of car you want. Start with your local newspaper. Probably the best kind of paper is the give-away kind that you pick up from a stack at your local stores. These publications consist purely of ads, so people who take them do read the ads. Describe what you want in the fewest possible number of words, but be specific. Then add your name, address, and phone number. You may want to accept collect calls if the paper covers an extended area. But make sure the members of your family know to expect the calls and can get the information for you. We have sometimes been disgusted to find that the person who answers the phone when we have called knew nothing about the ad.

**DEALERS**

While you may think an antique car dealer (Fig. 7-4) is the *last* person to contact for a car, don't overlook any in your area. You can sometimes find exactly what you want from one, and at a surprisingly reasonable price. Obviously, the dealer must make a

Fig. 7-3. You can sometimes find parts or manuals like this at public sales.

profit, so you can expect to pay him more than to a private owner. But there are several advantages to buying a car from a dealer. First, you can eliminate what could be a long search time, and with further inflation, prices could advance enough that you would have to pay as much later to a private owner as the dealer would ask now. Also, a dealer will probably have several cars that fit your tastes and pocketbook. These cars will probably be in various states of repair, so you can choose one that fits your skills. If you have a car or any automotive equipment that you don't need, you may be able to use it for a trade-in. And if you have no way to transport the car to your workshop, you can probably arrange to have the dealer deliver it. Even if the dealer has no cars that you like, he can often find an unusual car through his contacts with other dealers. And a visit to a dealer can give you information on prices.

Old salvage yards are another possibility. The cars you find at these places may be too badly damaged, unless they are rare, for restoration. But they will have many usable parts. Remember that you are buying a parts car on these, so the price must be low.

## THE REO IN THE SHED

Here is how one man found a car. Carl, a friend of ours, told his friends that he would like to find a restorable antique or production

Fig. 7-4. The easiest place to find a car is at an antique car lot.

car. One evening Carl's children, hearing him mention what he wanted, told him that they had been peeking into a closed shed on the way home from school and had seen an old, old car inside. Carl followed them to the place and located the owner of the shed. It turned out that the car, a 1933 REO Flying Cloud, was owned by a young man who had rented the shed space. Carl found the young man and asked him if he wanted to sell the car. The fellow said he'd started to restore it, but the job had gone wrong and he was he was disgusted with his investment. He said he'd spent $350 on having it painted. After some discussion, he offered to sell it for $350. Carl was delighted with the car and the price. He had to rework the car's interior and rebuild the engine, but when he finished, the car was a thing of beauty. At that time he was offered $5000 for it. Pictures of the REO appear in this book.

Another friend was looking for a small foreign car that he could restore and use for a work car. One day in July he was hauling cement and some cold drinks to a work party when he saw a roadside watermelon stand. He stopped to buy a melon and noticed a gray 1961 Morris Minor in the barn yard. Was it for sale? Yes, the farmwife said: it belonged to her son who was in the service. This was the third Morris the man had found within a few weeks, but the first two had not been for sale although they seemed to have been abandoned. Persistence pays.

## A SECOND LOOK

When you find a car, be prepared to make an extensive examination of its condition before you even consider a purchase. Take along a flashlight, to inspect cars in unlit sheds or the underside of a car, and a small screwdriver. You can use the screwdriver to probe for rust on the frame. You will also want to examine the body for semi-concealed rust, but do that by eye. No car owner will appreciate your probing the body with any kind of tool.

Another useful item to take with you is a check list, such as the one shown in Figure 7-5. Unless the car is an obvious bargain, check every category on the list. Write in the parts that are damaged or missing. Don't buy the car until you have had time to explore the cost of each part you need and can add up the total. The list offers two advantages over just looking. It forces you to arrive at a total cost and compare that to the price of a better car. And it will show you how much restoration work is necessary. Make sure the car you buy doesn't need more time than your patience and interest will permit.

You will notice that the first item on the list is the car frame. Some old cars have a ladder-type frame, composed of side rails plus several cross members. Others have the side rails connected by beams shaped into an X. Such frames collect dirt at the points where the X pieces attach to the side rails. Probe this area on these frames to see if dirt has collected there and if the frame has rusted out in those areas. Mike found one 1940 Ford that had the center section of the side rails completely rusted through. Only the upper and lower lips held the frame together.

## IS THE PRICE RIGHT?

In one way, buying a car is like buying a stock that is listed on a stock exchange. Investment counselors often say that the more active the trading in a stock, the better idea you can get of its real value. A stock that sells in some volume each day sells for a price that represents the appraisal of many buyers and sellers. The bid and asked price for such a stock will have close spreads. For an issue with a thin float, that is few shares outstanding, and low trading volume, there is likely to be a wide spread between bid and asked prices. The price of a widely traded issue will normally be much more stable than that of a low volume stock.

The same situation exists with cars. If you buy a car that is frequently offered for sale, you can get a good indication of the going price. But if you seek a rare model, who knows how much you should pay? Like an inactive stock, the price may jump up or down with each sale. The only sure rule for such cars is that the price will be whatever a seller and buyer can agree on.

You can find market reports on many American and a few foreign car makes in the *Old Cars Price Guide*, published by Krause Publications, Iola, Wisconsin. This magazine is available at most newsstands, or you can subscribe to it. It gives the going price, as monitored by the publisher, of cars in various grades of condition. Such prices should be regarded as an *average*, not a set figure. Local supply and demand for old cars in general or for a particular model may skew the prices in your neighborhood up or down. But we recommend this source as a rough guide.

## LEGAL CONSIDERATIONS

When you find a car at the right price, you have one *more* item to consider before you pay your hard-earned money: the title. If the car is complete, the title is more important than if it is a basket case. You wouldn't want to spend a considerable sum for parts and a

| PARTS TO CHECK | PARTS TO BE REPLACED | EST. COST |
|---|---|---|
| BODY<br>   *EXTERIOR*: FRAME, TOP, WOOD BOWS, RUNNING BOARDS, DOORS, HINGES, FENDERS, WELTING, COWL, TRUNK OR TOOL BOX, GLASS, WINDSHIELD FRAME, RUBBER MOLDING.<br>   *INTERIOR*: FLOOR, DOOR HANDLES, DASH, INSTRUMENTS, STEERING WHEEL, RUBBER PEDAL PADS, SEATS, UPHOLSTERY, HEAD LINER, FLOOR MATS.<br>ENGINE<br>   BLOCK, PISTONS, RODS, CRANKSHAFT, VALVE TRAIN, HEAD(S), MANIFOLDS, EXHAUST SYSTEM, GASKETS, CARBURETOR, FUEL PUMP, LINES, TANK, DISTRIBUTOR, COIL OR COIL BOX, REPAIR MANUAL.<br>ELECTRICAL SYSTEM<br>   BATTERY & CASE, GENERATOR, STARTER, WIRING, LIGHTS, GAUGES, WIPER MOTOR.<br>COOLING SYSTEM<br>   RADIATOR, FAN, PULLEYS, BELTS, WATER PUMP.<br>POWER TRAIN<br>   TRANSMISSION, CLUTCH, PRESSURE PLATE, TRANSMISSION, DRIVE SHAFT, UNIVERSAL JOINTS, DIFFERENTIAL.<br>STEERING, SUSPENSION, & BRAKES<br>   STEERING COLUMN, STEERING GEAR BOX, STEERING LINKAGE, FRONT AXLE, KING PINS, BUSHINGS, SPRINGS, SHOCK ABSORBERS, WHEELS (LIST KIND), SPARE.<br>ACCESSORIES<br>   OWNER'S MANUAL, RADIO, HORNS, HEATER, TOOL KIT, JACK, VACUUM MOTOR ON WIPERS, SPECIAL LIGHTS, HUB CAPS. | | |

Fig. 7-5. Car condition checklist. Use this to systematically evaluate the parts you will need to restore a car.

year or more of your spare time, only to have somone claim that the car was stolen from him—or his grandfather.

Title laws vary from state to state, so you should learn the facts about your state. When did it pass a title law? Some antique cars were probably made before your state had a law requiring registration of vehicles. If the car was in use after the law was passed, it probably was registered. For cars without a title, the problem can sometimes be eliminated by having a check made on the car's serial number. If the computer kicks it out as a stolen vehicle, that's it. The way to get this information is to apply for a title through your local office of the department of motor vehicles in your state. Better yet, have the owner of the car apply. Buy the car *only* on condition that the seller can provide you with a valid title. Don't pay for it until you can get a title. If you write a check, make a note on it, "Title attached." The check can't be cashed then without the title.

You won't need a title for a parts car. Suppose you find two or more old cars of the same model, all of them basket cases, but you find enough parts from the lot to make a good car? Here again, a title is less important. But be sure to take pictures of each car in its original condition, showing that it would pass for junk except for its desirability as a parts car. If challenged later, you can produce the pictures as proof that you built a car from parts. When the car is completed, you can apply to your state motor vehicle department for a new title.

Suppose you find a desirable car and there is no title? You will be taking some risk if you buy it. Because laws in various states will be different, you should get legal advice if a considerable sum is involved.

For any car you buy, get a notarized bill of sale from the owner. Or pay for it by check so you have a receipt. Get as much of the car's history as the owner can provide, the names and addresses of previous owners and the length of time each one owned the car. In some states length of ownership is a factor in title applications. If the seller is a minor, as defined by the laws of your state, make sure you get the signatures of the parents on the bill of sale or a statement from them approving the sale.

Before making a payment for any car or parts, get a statement on what you are buying. Then examine the car or the parts to make sure nothing is missing. After you become the owner any loss of parts by theft will probably be *your* loss, so make plans to move the car to your work area as soon as possible. Eliminate problems by making sure the deal is right *before* you buy. It's much easier than to try to get deficiencies corrected later.

## MOVING YOUR CAR

If you buy a car at a car or swap meet, you can usually find someone there who has a trailer to move your car for you. Such people have money already invested in the equipment, and they will have proper insurance for the job (Fig. 7-6). A hauling fee helps them to defray some of the expense of buying a trailer and keeping it licensed and insured.

Before trying to move a car yourself, check your insurance with your agent to see if you have liability coverage while moving a car. It is safer to drive the car than to tow it, but many states will not permit an unlicensed car to be driven on their highways. The first step in preparing to move a car is to go to the nearest office of the highway patrol and ask for information on your state laws regarding car towing. If you travel through more than one state, you will have to learn the laws of each state. Some states require a sign, such as "Car In Tow." Others require a redundant tow system to back up the primary system. A tow bar would have to be backed up by a chain, and so on.

Choose an appropriate vehicle for the tow car. It should be heavier than the car you are towing because, if you use a tow bar, you will have only 4 wheel brakes for both cars. Add weight to the rear of the tow car so that it will track straight on sudden stops.

Get a set of trailer lights and install them temporarily on your antique car. Clamp them to the rear bumper or license plate bracket and run the wires under the car to your tow car. Avoid placing the wires so they will mar the paint on your old car if the paint is in reasonably good condition.

We strongly recommend that you do not attempt to tow a car very far, not more than, say, about 50 miles. To go farther requires a number of precautions. For example, you will have to take some measures to prevent damage to the transmission. The specific steps will depend on the individual car. If the car has an open driveshaft, you can simply remove it, and the transmission will not be driven by the rear wheels. Or you can stop at intervals and drive the old car some distance in each gear, if it is in running condition, to lubricate the transmission. All cars should have the wheel bearings packed before starting on a trip. To avoid any problems with car damage by towing, get a trailer or hire someone with a trailer to haul your car home.

Fig. 7-6. Salvage yards and old car dealers will have equipment to help you move a car.

Regardless of how you move the car, avoid the main thoroughfares, large cities, and rush hour traffic. Check maps to find secondary roads that parallel the main routes.

While tow bars are considered satisfactory by some car owners, they have serious disadvantages over tow ropes or chains. They often don't fit the car's bumpers. Ideally, the tow bar should be made to fit the car it will be used with; universal tow bars can be dangerous. And it is difficult to fit a tow bar to a modern car and an old car. If you use a tow bar, you should stop after a few miles to check it, then again after 10 or 15 miles to inspect for loose nuts. If there is a driver in the rear car, he can use brakes, but he should *not* touch the steering.

The November, 1971 issue of *Spoke Wheels*, a newspaper dedicated to old cars, described how one car was destroyed during towing. Bill Coleman, of Houston, Texas, bought a fine 1940 Buick Limited Convertible Sedan, a very rare car, at the Hershey, Pennsylvania swap meet. The car was moved by a pickup truck with a tow bar. Near Baton Rouge, Louisiana the pickup blew a rear tire while driving at a moderate speed. The problem of a blow-out was compounded by the heavier Buick which caused the vehicles to jackknife and the Buick to roll over about three times. The Buick, which had just been purchased for $5000, was totaled.

This accident shows why valuable antiques should be carried on a trailer. A tow bar is dangerous because, as shown here, the bar gives the towed vehicle leverage to force the pulling car in any direction. These effects are especially dangerous if the towed car is as heavy or heavier than the pulling car.

When using a rope to pull a car, get a nylon rope. Ordinary hemp rope quickly wears out when wrapped around car parts. Keep the rope or chain *tight*. To maintain communication between the driver of the tow car and the towed car, use hand signals or a CB. Make sure you arrange for signals before you start. Use signals well before stopping so the rear driver can brake and keep the chain tight. If there are no brakes on the rear car, you can put the pull chain through a pipe and hook the chain so that the rear vehicle is as close as possible to the pipe.

The main rule with this kind of towing is to anticipate each change of direction or stop and signal it to the rear driver well in advance of the event. The lead driver must avoid sudden stops. And the rider in the towed car should be ready to apply the brakes on a downhill run. The tow car can reduce speed on uphill slopes, but the driver must permit the rear car to control the speed going downhill so the chain will stay tight.

## TRAILERS

Car collectors who use trailers often make their own (Fig. 7-7). Some make single axle trailers, others use a double axle. Double axle trailers, having four wheels, can haul a heavier car without problems (Fig. 7-8). Some trailers have brakes, some have none. Trailers without brakes are not as safe as fifth wheel trailers

Fig. 7-7. A homemade 2-wheel trailer for hauling cars.

with electric brakes. A trailer could be a sensible investment after you have restored an antique car that you won't want to drive to meets or parades. You can rent a trailer for temporary use, such as moving the car you buy to your home. If you rent a trailer with springs, you must boom the car down, that is, chain it down tightly, to prevent a rhythmic action that could wreck you. It is better to have no springs on the car trailer.

When pulling a trailer, you must hold your speed down; speed limits for cars pulling trailers are always below that for general traffic. The same rules apply to pulling a trailer as in towing. Choose routes carefully and anticipate problems.

If you buy a trailer, look for one with a wheel bolt pattern that matches that of the car or truck that will pull it. This will permit you to use the same spare for either. Some car collectors use radial tires on the trailer, but a stiff-walled tire is better, preferably a 6-ply. This kind of tire reduces sway.

When stopping for the night, choose out-of-the-way spots. Plan to stop at a small town rather than a major city, and off the main drag. Old cars generate interest, perhaps more than you'd like. To prevent any problems, choose a motel where a limited number of people will see the car.

## TRUCKS FOR CAR HAULING

To use a truck for car hauling, the bed must be longer than that of a typical factory-made truck. A one-ton truck, for example, would be too short. Most welders lengthen a truck frame by various kinds of bridge work. These patchwork methods may make a messy job.

Here is how to do the job right. Support the frame just behind the cab before you do any cutting. If you have enough jacks, it's a good idea to support the frame with jacks so you can make slight adjustments in the height.

Remove the drive shaft. (For procedure on this, see Chapter 15). You will have to either lengthen the drive shaft or find a longer drive shaft and lengthen your truck frame to match the length of the longer drive shaft.

Cut the frame, leaving about 2 feet of frame to extend behind the cab so you can get around this section with a welder. Find some frame steel of the same size. You can use pieces of frame, but they must be exactly as long as the length you are adding to the frame. Align the truck frame and the extra pieces. You can use extra pieces of steel and clamps to hold the extension pieces in place while you tack weld the four junctions. Then weld the frame as securely as

Fig. 7-8. A homemade double axle 4-wheel trailer which can haul heavier cars without problems.

possible. In doing this you must make some judgments on the best way to weld according to the design of the frame. Fish-plating may be used.

The next step most welders use is to put bridgework under the frame. Instead, get two pieces of 1" bar stock to reinforce the frame (Fig. 7-9). Bar stock comes in 20 foot lengths, probably longer than you need for each piece. Cut the bar stock so it reaches to a point about 12" from the end of the springs or at least 16" past the splice. Then jack the bar stock up under the frame until it is tight against the frame. If you apply enough pressure to just slightly raise the truck on one side, you will know that the weight of the truck is holding the bar stock against the frame. Go to one side of the bar stock and weld about 4" on that side. Then go to the other side of the bar stock and weld the next 4" to that side of the frame. Continue this step by step welding to the end of the bar stock. You should now have welded the bar stock to the frame at 4" intervals in each side—a 4" weld on one side of the bar stock opposite a gap in the welding on the other side. The welding will slightly shrink the frame, putting a slight arch in it and increasing its strength. This kind of frame reinforcement is often used on boom trucks that are subject to tremendous stress.

## FINDING PARTS

One reason for using the check list shown in this chapter is that it provides an orderly way to estimate how many replacement parts you will need for your car. When buying any car, be careful about getting a car with missing parts. If a part is bad, it must be replaced; but if it is missing, you must not only find the part, but you must find the right part without an old one for comparison.

One of the most economical ways to get parts is to buy a parts car of the same model as your restoration car. The chances are that you will find more parts cars than good cars, so it's a good idea to get a price on each one you see and keep a record of the car's condition and price. Old salvage yards often have useful parts cars, but the price there will usually be greater than you would expect to pay a private owner.

Mike once needed a grille for a 1956 GMC pick-up and went to a salvage yard for it. The salvage yard price was $40 for a fender and grille, but the fender had a rusty area in it. Mike declined the parts and started home, but on the way he saw an old pick-up of the same model. The door on the driver's side was missing, but the truck was otherwise fairly complete except that it had no engine. It had obviously been abandoned, so Mike looked up the owner. The man said he'd take $15 for the old truck. So in addition to paying less money, Mike got better parts and many more of them. People will sometimes almost give away parts of old cars just to have them hauled away.

Almost every weekend swap meet or flea market will have some vendors of old car parts. Unless you can easily identify the parts you need, take a sample with you. Never rely on the vendor's claim that a certain part will fit your car. Most of them won't know exactly what parts they have, and many care less. Also you should have an idea of the going prices for a part, by shopping several sources before you buy (unless the part is *extremely* rare).

One man we know needed a grille for a 1938 Nash Lafayette. He found the grille at a flea market. Instead of immediately asking the price, he asked the vendor what kind of car it came from. The vendor said he didn't know and no one had ever wanted it so he would take $10 for it. Then he added, "Unless you'd rather give $7.50." By letting the vendor commit himself first, the buyer got a much more reasonable price than he had expected.

The best sources for parts are usually the same as those for cars: swap meets, small town garages, and public sales. But at auctions the parts often go to volume buyers. Sometimes you can buy a single part from a buyer at an auction for less money than he would charge you after transporting the part and storing it at his place of business.

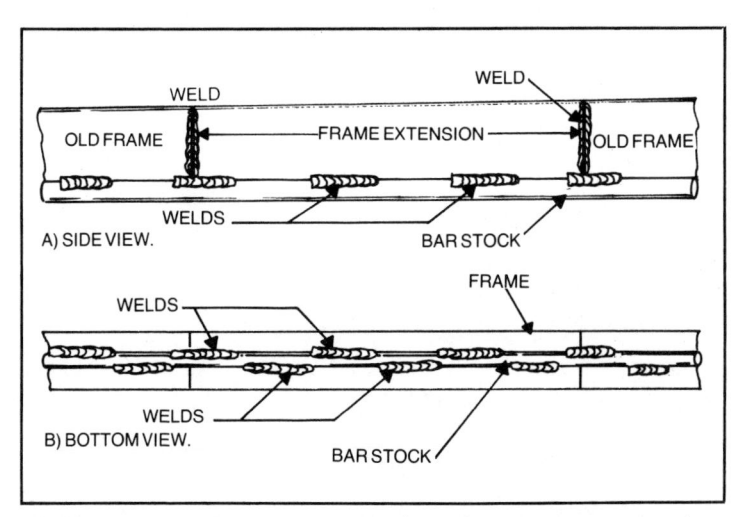

Fig. 7-9. How to use bar stock to reinforce a truck frame extension to make a car-hauling truck.

Dealers in antique cars often have NOS (new old stock) parts. These are parts the dealer has bought from old garages or parts houses when they went out of business. The prices on these parts are usually high because NOS parts are often rare.

Specialty manufacturers make new parts that meet the specifications of old parts exactly. In some cases the new parts are better than the original part. For example, one man who restored a 1924 car found that the outboard oil pump on the car had deteriorated because of poor metal. He found a company that manufactured an identical pump and bought one for his car. When he examined the new pump, he decided that the steel used in it was far superior to the "pot metal" in the old pump. To locate a parts manufacturer, check with a club that is dedicated to the restoration of your make of car.

Occasionally there may be legal obstacles to using authentic parts. For example, in the 1940s, blue dot tail light lenses were popular. Later many states passed laws making such lights illegal. You could install these on a car if you intended to use it only during daylight hours.

If the tires on your car are old and weather cracked, use care when you try to inflate them. One safe method is to remove the wheel from the car and attach the air hose while working from around the corner of a building or behind some obstacle. Such tires may blow out, sending pieces of rubber into your face or eyes.

If the tires inflate without blowing, drive carefully for the first few miles. They may go at the first bump. Tires that are old enough to have cotton fabric in the casing instead of nylon or other modern fabric are especially susceptible to blowing.

In fitting new tires, make sure you have the right size wheel for the car if you want to do an authentic restoration. Cars that went through World War II may have had a wheel change or the wheels altered to a different size rim. Tires were extremely hard to get during that time, and many old cars were adapted for more popular sizes. Some people even traded cars for no other reason than to get a set of good tires with the car they were buying.

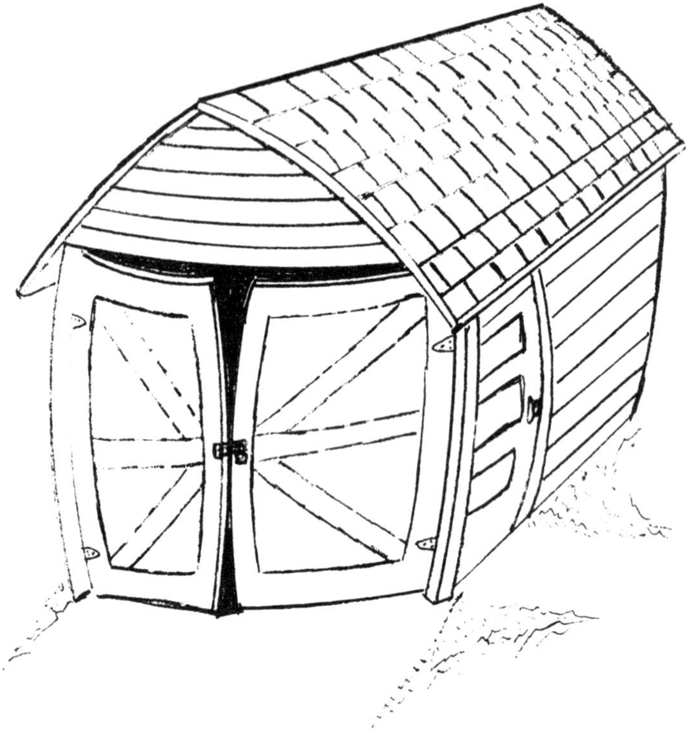

# Chapter 8
# Workshop and Tools

The number of tools that you need to restore one old car is highly elastic. You may get by with very few, but there are many tools that would be desirable to own. Choose the size of your tool kit with regard to whether you intend to rework just one car or whether you expect this to be a continuing hobby.

The first rule in the selection of tools is to buy the general purpose tools first. Some tools will be needed very seldom and should only be purchased when there is a direct need for them. A few special purpose tools, while nice to have, can be rented or borrowed. Or jobs that require special tools can be sent to a local machine shop.

There are a couple of factors which argue for tool purchase, especially for tools with a variety of uses. First, most of the tools you will buy for restoration can be used in the routine maintenance of any car. If you have paid out for any car repair work lately, you don't have to be told how much do-it-yourself car care can reduce your transportation budget. And one fact of life suggests that you should start collecting your tools now, even if you aren't ready to go to work on an old car: *inflation*. The longer you wait to build up a tool kit, the more you can expect to pay for it. Study the list of tools described in this chapter and give extra priority to those that can help in routine maintenance jobs on your present cars. If you have done no car work, choose the less expensive items first. Then, if you find the job distasteful, you can shove them under the workbench without too much concern over the lost investment.

Later in this chapter we will list the tools we think you might need for the most complete restoration job, but the first item to consider isn't a tool in the usual sense. It's a place to work.

## WORKSHOP

If you live in southern California, or in a place with a similar warm, dry climate, you can start without an enclosed work space. But even there you will probably want some kind of shelter for your car when you paint it and thereafter. In the long run the outlay for a small shed can be considered part of your investment in your vintage car, a part that protects the money that goes into the car.

If you own a house, you probably have a carport or a garage than can be converted to a satisfactory shop. Renters are somewhat more restricted, but even those who rent a place without a garage can probably find a vacant shed within a practical distance from home. Old residential areas are good bets to have empty buildings. To get the use of one you may have to use considerable diplomacy and give character references. Sometimes you can get reduced rental charges by providing some service that will save the owner substantial labor costs. For example, you can make repairs on the building if they are needed or maintain parts of the property, such as doing the gardening and lawn care. Be flexible and you may be able to strike a bargain that benefits both you and the owner.

Except for the cost of heating the building in winter, the best rule for choosing the right size of building is *the bigger the better*. Whatever size you choose will prove to be about a stall and a half too small after you have had it for a few years. To plan a minimum work area, measure the size of the car you intend to restore, or just measure a typical car, and allow at least 3' to 4' for work space on all four sides. Then allow about half this much space for storage room for fenders, doors, and other parts that you will remove. Better yet, leave as much space for storage as you design into the building for work area. Then add enough space for a work bench, a large tool box, a wash vat, and for any special equipment you plan to own such as welders or an air compressor.

## LIGHTING

In addition to enough work area one of the most important requirements for a workshop is to have good lighting. When you are painting a car, you must be able to see the work without shadows that can hide the details. If you own the building, you have a better chance of getting good light. Daylight is the ideal light, but not always practical. Big doors let in light but, if you live in a cold climate, lose heat around the door.

One way to make the most of any lighting system is to paint the interior of the building white. A white interior not only aids vision but gives the work area a more cheerful atmosphere.

Shop lights get dirty at regular intervals. Install your ceiling light fixtures with a receptacle and plug so that they are removable. You can then take out the fixture to clean the lamps.

While wiring your shop, put some outlets near the door so you can use power tools outside the shop if necessary. Tools to be used outside should be grounded or in insulated housings. Use heavy Romex cable for extension cords, particularly for tools that draw heavy current, such as electric welders.

A good trouble light is a necessity. You can get lights with oridinary incandescent bulbs or with fluorescent bulbs. The fluorescent type has the advantage that it produces little heat and so is more comfortable in close quarters in hot weather. An incandescent bulb can cause minor burns under such conditions.

Either kind should be protected from damage. If you use the ordinary incandescent kind, ask for a "rough service" bulb instead of the kind of lamp bulbs sold in discount and department stores. There is another kind of incandescent bulb with a plastic skin that prevents danger from broken glass if water or other cold liquid falls on the bulb while it is hot.

## SHOP FIXTURES

There are several ways to improve the usefulness of any shelter which you will want to add, particularly if you own the building. One of these involves the structure of the building itself. Other additions can be movable.

The structural change involves beefing up the ceiling joists to permit you to use them as an anchor for an engine hoist. Estimate the approximate position of the engine of the car when it is parked in position for rebuilding. Then choose the ceiling joist that is directly overhead and reinforce it. Most sheds will have ceiling joists made from 2" × 4" or, at most, 2" × 6" material. You can increase the dimensions of the overhead beam by nailing an extra joist to the one already there. The extra beam should be heavier, but the ideal dimensions will depend on the length of span it must cover. If it is convenient to add extra vertical supports for the beam, you can economize on its thickness and width. In some buildings the joists may run parallel to the car position and there is no joist directly over the one possible location for the engine. Such a situation is unlikely, but if you face this problem you can run a girder across the joists, using the girder as an anchor for the hoist. It will also add extra strength to the building by tying the joists together. A couple of 2" × 6"s or 2" × 8"s nailed together and set on edge should be adequate.

The first additional fixture to your workshop should be a workbench. You can build this, but it is often cheaper to buy one from someone who is moving or no longer has use for it. It should be strong enough to support heavy parts, which means that if the top is made of wood, it should be 2" thick. You will need a vise on the bench, but *don't* use the vise as an anvil. To prevent the temptation of doing that, find a piece of railroad iron or other heavy piece of steel and place it on the workbench near the vise. You will want to add other workbench items later, such as a grinder and buffing wheel.

Another useful feature for your shop is to add plenty of shelving. Shelves provide space for oil, grease, parts, and any other small items that can add clutter to a shop with no shelving. Again, you can build shelves, and this is probably the most satisfactory way to get them because you can plan them to fit your needs and your space. But be open to any bargain shelving that will do the job.

## SHOP TOOLS FOR GENERAL USE

In buying hand tools, you may be tempted to choose the brand name strictly by reputation. This is sometimes a mistake. The best quality tool is no good if replacement parts aren't available from a local supplier. Another reason to avoid highly touted brands is price. You can buy a whole set of sockets of some brands of satisfactory quality for the price of a few sockets of other brands.

One brand that can be purchased in every part of this country is the well known Craftsman brand available from your local Sears store. Or you can shop your neighborhood discount store; these marts often carry Thorsen tools which seem to offer good value for their low price and are more convenient to use than some high priced tools.

The first item is one you may be tempted to omit: a fire extinguisher. Don't (Fig. 8-1). Mike has operated a shop at his present location for 7 years and has needed a fire extinguisher twice. Each time he would have lost the shop without an extinguisher. There are many flammable materials in a shop, and with a fire the first few minutes are *critical*. You can get disposable extinguishers.

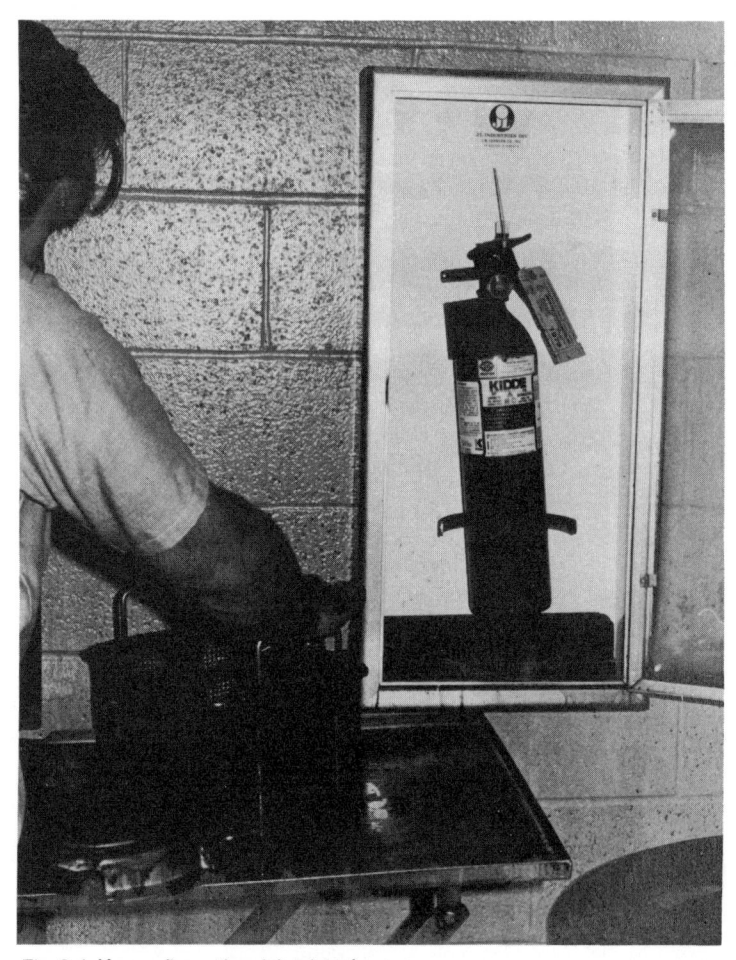

Fig. 8-1. Keep a fire extinguisher handy.

Another item that you may not consider a tool, but which is helpful, is a tool catalog. This is useful if you get stuck on a difficult task. A tool catalog may show a special tool that will help you do the job. Sometimes you can make a substitute tool, based on a picture or description of the tool you need.

*Screwdrivers:* Choose these to fit every common use. You should have several standard screwdrivers of various sizes plus a couple of Phillips-head drivers. Get one standard and one Phillips-head driver in short, and stubby lengths that can be used in close spaces. Since standard screwdrivers should not be used as pry bars or with pliers or locking pliers to give extra torque, you should have at least one heavy duty screwdriver that is strong enough to take punishment. One screwdriver should be long enough to reach inaccessible spots, preferably about 2' long.

In some cases you will need special screwdrivers, such as a clutch-head screwdriver if you are working on certain General Motors cars, or an Allen-head screwdriver to adjust points on some GM cars. Screw-holding screwdrivers are often handy but usually not essential. These work by holding the screw in a clip or by having a magnetic head. An offset screwdriver will cost you very little and can be absolutely essential to remove screws from some tight places. A combination screwdriver with quick change heads, including both Phillips and standard heads, is useful to carry to salvage yards, where you can buy parts at lower prices by removing them yourself.

*Hammers:* Your first hammer should be a light ball peen hammer, one with a head that weighs about 2 ounces. These are useful to lightly tap parts to loosen them and also in gasket making. When you cannot find a gasket for an old car, you can make the gasket from gasket material. Then place the gasket into position and strike the position of the bolt holes under the gasket to make holes in the gasket at the right points.

Your next hammer should be a much larger ball peen, about 20 ounces, for heavy general use. Following that you should have a rubber hammer to use on metal parts that are subject to damage. A typical use would be to knock on hub caps. A plastic hammer is also useful for hitting easily-marred materials.

If you do any body work, you will need some special body hammers, to be described later.

Probably the last hammer you will buy is a heavy sledge hammer, one with a head of, say, 8 pounds.

*Wrenches:* If you had just one wrench, it should probably be a 10" adjustable wrench. Such a wrench will be too bulky to use in tight places, but it is versatile. You can add one or two smaller adjustable wrenches, such as a 4" or a 6" size, for smaller parts.

A set of end wrenches are especially useful, covering the range of nut sizes from ⅜" to 1". If possible, you should have two end wrenches of the ½", 9/16", and ⅝" sizes so you can use one on the nut and the other to hold the bolt. Such wrenches should not be used as striking wrenches unless they are old ones that you consider expendable.

Box-end wrenches are useful in some places that are too tight for the open-end wrench to work, but they will work only on nuts where the end of the bolt or other part on which the nut is located is free. You will probably use these less often than your end wrenches, so they should have lower priority.

Some mechanics consider combination wrenches, with a box end at one end and open end at the other, to be more convenient than plain end wrenches or box ends. One trick sometimes used with these on hard-to-crack nuts is select the proper box-end wrench to fit the nut, then slip another box-end over that wrench so it holds the open end. This gives extra leverage. But don't hold the joint; the wrenches can slip and either badly pinch or drive the end wrench into your hand.

Unless you can borrow a torque wrench, add one to your collection of tools. When you replace a cylinder head, for example, it is important to know exactly how much torque you are applying to the bolts or nuts. If you apply too much force to a bolt or nut, you may distort the part you are installing. Or, if the part is extremely rigid, you may strip the threads on the nut or bolt. On the other hand, if you don't apply *enough* torque, the nut or bolt will loosen with vibration. Practice using a torque wrench on a junked part before using it on your car.

If you keep working on cars, you will sooner or later want to invest in at least one socket set. Your first choice should be a ⅜" drive set with sockets that vary in size from ⅜" to ⅞". The typical socket set has only shallow sockets, but you can add a set of deep sockets. And if you are working on an old car, you will find a screwdriver socket handy for working on drag links and tie rod ends.

A small ¼" drive set of sockets are convenient for working on parts under the dash. And, if you do much work on the chassis or other areas where you need to apply more force, you will find a larger ½" drive set worthwhile. Still larger sockets, such as ¾" drive sets are very expensive. If you need one or two of these, you can buy only the sockets you need and use them with an adaptor in ½" drive tools.

Along with your sockets, you will have a choice of driver tools unless you buy an exceptionally complete set. Get a suitable ratchet with each set. Ratchets that have the drive shift directly behind the drive mechanism are less convenient to use than those that have it on the side or extending down from the drive area. The disadvantage of the shift directly behind the driver mechanism becomes obvious if you ever back a nut or bolt off in a restricted space and get the shift button jammed against an obstruction. When this happens, the tool is stuck, and you can't reach the shift to reverse it.

You may find that you need special socket tools. For example, you can buy a special socket to fit the spark plugs on your car. A flex socket is best if the space around the plug is restricted. Also if you plan to work on any foreign cars, you will need a set of metric sockets. Or to restore an old English car you will need some Whitworth tools. Whitworth wrenches are different from ordinary U.S. wrenches in two ways: the sizes available and the way the wrench is labeled. Instead of the usual 9/16" and other common nut sizes, older British nuts were measured in 32nds of an inch. And a wrench that is labeled 5/16" does not fit a 5/16" nut. Instead it fits the nut that would have been used on a 5/16" bolt in Britain several years ago. One couple we know who drove from California to mid-continent in a 1950s British car broke a crankshaft in Texas. The mechanics who fixed the car had no Whitworth tools, so they had to file each nut they removed to make it fit their American wrenches. When our friends got the labor bill, they were shocked.

A speed handle does what it says, makes nut or bolt removal much quicker. It is especially useful where you have many pieces to take off, such as the bolts around the edge of the oil pan. A few extensions help to put your sockets into tight places. About three of these will do, a 5", 12", and a 23" or 24" will handle most situations. Adaptors that will let you use sockets of one set with the drive tools of another set will save the cost of extra tools and make your sets more versatile. And, finally, a couple of flex sockets, ½" and 9/16", will be useful for some tight spots.

There are a variety of wrenches for special purposes that would be convenient to have if you plan to work on several cars. For example, if you plan to do much engine work, you should consider investing in a flywheel wrench. This fits into the teeth of a flywheel and permits you to turn the engine over with ease and without the risk of scraped knuckles. For work on metal lines, such as brake lines or fuel lines, line wrenches are much more effective than end wrenches. End wrenches tend to round off the fittings. Some line wrench sets have a line wrench fitting at one end of the wrench with an end wrench fitting on the other end. To save money you can get a set with line wrenches at each end. Finally there are the powered impact wrenches. These can be considered almost a luxury because, while they save effort, the same work can be done with other tools. But a hand operated impact wrench is a good tool to have for installation of door striker plates. This tool can be purchased with two heads, standard screwdriver and Phillips-head blade. After tightening the screws to maximum torque by the usual method, you can hit the impact tool with a hammer to cinch the screw.

*Pliers:* Get an assortment of pliers, such as standard pliers, lockjaw pliers, diagonals, water pump pliers, and needle nose pliers. The latter are especially useful for electrical work. Brake spring pliers are useful on old cars with early hydraulic brakes. *Don't* use pliers on nuts or on hardened steel parts that can damage the jaws of the pliers.

*C-Clamps:* These are useful in many shop procedures, for example, in disassembling or rebuilding leaf springs. The larger ones will work in many applications, so look for at least a couple of 8" to 10" clamps. Smaller clamps are inexpensive and can be added for use on more delicate parts.

*Used Bolts and Nuts:* Collect all you can find at garage sales or flea markets. New hardware is expensive. Separate the bolts according to size, especially the more useful sizes such as ⅜" and 5/16". Use coffee cans or add valve covers for bins. You can get many bolts from a junk or parts car. You will probably find more usable bolts than nuts, so you can buy a box of ⅜" and a box of 5/16" nuts to use with your old bolts. You should also save old washers, especailly lock washers, if they are usable.

*Pry Bar:* If you have no pry bars or can find no bargain bars at flea markets, you can make them. Get two rear axles and remove the flange from one end. Weld the two together and put a point at one end so you can insert it into tight places. It's a good idea to save short pieces of steel for the same purpose. Pieces of old pipe can also be used. If the pipe is large enough in diameter, it can be slipped over other tools as a "cheater" to give extra leverage.

*Chains:* Buy any bargain piece of chain that you can get. Save random lengths of broken chain too. You can get repair links and make short pieces of chain into longer chains that have many uses around a shop or even on the road. Short lengths are useful for engine lifts.

*Fender Covers:* These are essential if you have to work on the engine after you have painted the car. They should be used when working on any car with a decent finish to protect the paint from belt buckles or buttons on your clothes. You can buy these, but you can make one that is in some ways superior and it will cost you nothing. Get some remnants of foam-backed carpet from a carpet layer or furniture store and cut out a piece to fit your car.

*Oil Cans:* The squirt cans with a triggered pump are the most convenient to use. They permit you to squirt the oil into the area where you want it even if you have to work against gravity. They have the disadvantage that they leak after considerable use. We suggest you get one of these, but keep an ordinary oil can, the kind without the pump, to use where the can with the pump isn't needed.

*Wash Vat:* You can make one of these from nothing more than a 5-gallon can or other container. For solvent, use either kerosene or diesel fuel. Add a brush and you have a vat for cleaning small parts.

*⅜" Electric Drill:* This tool will be essential. The ⅜" size will handle much heavier work than a typical ¼" drill, but even it isn't rugged enough to serve as a grinder. It can be used with sanding discs and a buffing wheel for light work.

*Don't* buy bargain drill bits. Cheap bits are easily dulled, and almost worthless. Good bits are hard but can be broken if carelessly used. When a bit breaks, save it until you have time to regrind the point. The shorter bit will do many jobs and will be harder to break than a long bit. If you have a friend who works in industry where broken bits are discarded, try to get some of these and resharpen them. Industrial bits are the best you can find.

*Threading Tools:* Your first purchase of this kind should probably be a couple of thread files, sometimes called thread chasers (Fig. 8-2). These can be used to renew the external threads on a bolt, but they can't reach internal threads. The K & D Mfg. Co. makes some of these, such as their #2229 with sections that have 11, 12, 13, 14, 16, 20, and 24 threads per inch and their #2249 with 9, 10, 12, 16, 20, 27, 28, and 32 threads per inch. These are a low-priced alternative to a tap and die set. A tap and die set is, of course, more versatile and can be used to put threads on a non-threaded part.

*Gear Oil Pump:* Very useful. Transmissions and differentials usually have the fill plug located where you can't reach it with an ordinary pour out container of oil. You can buy small squeeze tubes

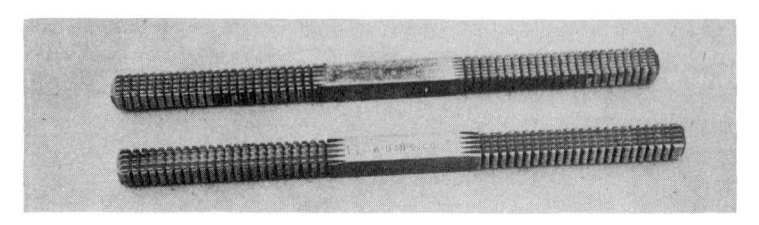

Fig. 8-2. These thread files offer a low-cost method of renewing external threads.

for occasional use, but if you intend to maintain your cars, this tool can save you money because you can buy gear oil at a significantly lower price in the bulk.

*Air Compressor:* Again very useful. You can use the air to clean parts and choked lines, and to inflate tires.

*Feeler Gauge:* Inexpensive and necessary. Get two of these, one for careful work and an extra to use to set valves while the engine is running. The valve setting gauge will soon be hammered out of shape.

*Handy Retriever:* You can make this from an old hand choke pull cable. Remove the inner wire and put a ¼" bend in the end of it. This is good for reaching into holes and retrieving small objects. Short lengths are useful for removing ignition switches.

*Tire Gauge:* Cheap and useful.

*Line Cutter and Flaring Tool:* Useful for installing metal lines. Buy this when you need it.

*Funnels:* Get a small one for steering gears and similar use. A large one with a flexible nozzle is useful for transferring liquids. You can make your own out of plastic bottles.

*Hydraulic Jack:* You should have a small 1½-ton hydraulic jack. Buy this tool new unless you find a used heavy duty jack at a good price. Most hydraulic jacks must be used in an upright position. Some German and English jacks can be used in any position. These are useful for jacking out damaged car bodies.

*Wood Blocks:* Save random lengths of 2" × 4"s, 2" × 6"s, and other 2" or 4" blocks for use under the hydraulic jack to extend its usable height. These blocks should be used with great care to see that you have a solid foundation under the jack.

*Jack Stands:* Small jack stands are useful under A frames and other similar jobs. These have an adjustment range of from about 13" to about 21". Heavy duty models go from about 16" to about 25".

*Ramps:* We don't recommend these. One man we know bought a set of new ramps and drove his 1976 Dodge Pickup on them to change oil. That went just fine. Then he drove his 1969 Dodge Dart onto them to do the same job, and the ramps collapsed. He was lucky the collapse occurred with the lighter vehicle. We know of other such cases with ramps of various price and quality range. They also tend to skid on a smooth surface but can't be used on uneven ground. Another disadvantage for restoration work—the car must be in good running condition to get it on a ramp.

*Roll Around Hydraulic Jack:* Sometimes handy in close quarters. But only if you feel affluent.

## ELECTRICAL SYSTEM TOOLS

*Electrical Meters:* To check voltage and resistance a volt-ohm meter is a very useful gadget. But you can get by with simpler equipment. For example you can make a simple test light with just a car lamp bulb and two leads. Put an alligator clip on one lead, an ice pick or sharpened screw driver blade on the other. You can clip one lead to the chassis and use the ice pick to penetrate insulation to check for voltage at that point in the wiring. The voltage rating of the bulb should be the same as that of the car battery.

You can remove an amp-meter from an old car and use in series with the electrical line to check current drain from any component. Or you can buy a current indicator that works by induction. Place it against a wire and it will tell you if current is flowing in that wire.

*Battery Charger:* When working with old cars that won't be driven very often, you will probably have a problem keeping the batteries charged. A battery charger is a great convenience and will pay for itself. You can economize here with a trickle charger, but you must plan ahead because of the time they require. Also, you should have a good jumper cable for times when you forget.

*Battery Hydrometer:* Very useful for monitoring condition of electrolyte in battery.

*Ignition Pliers:* These prevent shock when you remove a spark plug lead to locate a miss or other single cylinder malfunction. You can make a satisfactory pair of ignition pliers by bolting together two pieces of ½" × ½" wood 8" to 10" long. Place a 3/16" bolt about 2" from one end. Shape the jaws with a knife, and with them opened slightly, drill a ¼" hole between them to make a circular grip on each jaw.

## TOOLS FOR ENGINE WORK

*Vacuum Gauge:* A low-cost useful diagnostic tool.

*Homemade Engine Lift:* This is nothing more than a flat piece of steel with a steel loop on top and with holes drilled at the proper points to fit your engine where the carburetor fits on it (Fig. 8-3). Remove the carburetor and bolt on the engine lift tool. This tool will work only on cars with downdraft carburetors.

*Valve Lapping Tool:* This simple hand tool is sometimes used for final valve lapping.

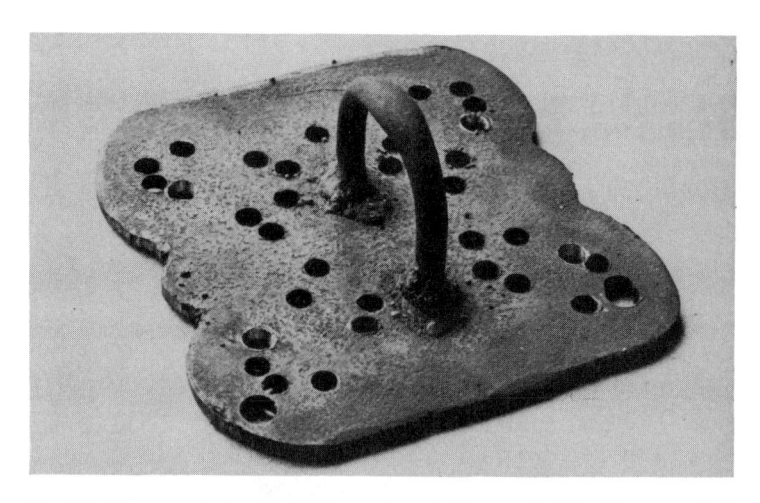

Fig. 8-3. Homemade bracket that mounts on intake manifold to lift engine. Drill holes to match your bolt pattern.

*Cylinder Hone:* A tool needed only if you plan to do several engines. You can have a machine shop rework one or two engines.

*Piston Ring Compressor; Cylinder Ridge Reamer;* and *Piston Ring Groove Scraper:* Same as above. Buy only if you plan to do extensive engine rebuilding.

*Stud Extractor:* These are very convenient for getting broken stud bolts out of old engines. Sometimes you can get a bolt out by filing a groove in it and using a screw driver, but if the bolt is broken below the surface of the block, the job is more difficult. The standard procedure is to drill out the stud, leaving little more than the threads intact, then screwing in an "Ezy Out" tool. Get a tool of the right size for the broken stud. This is something you will want to buy only as you need it.

*Pilot Shaft:* Get the main driver gear from an old transmission and use it as a clutch aligning tool. Very useful for clutch work (Fig. 8-4).

*Compression Gauge and Oil Pressure Gauge:* Good diagnostic tools, but not absolutely essential (Fig. 8-5).

*Timing Light:* If you can borrow this, buy something you need more often.

*Lathe:* Expensive. Good for making parts that you can't easily find. A small combination lathe and drill press will probably be adequate. Or take occasional jobs to a local machine shop. A nice hobby gadget if you can afford it.

## TOOLS FOR BODY WORK

For body work you will need specially designed hammers (Fig. 8-6). Some of these should have flat faces and others should have a convex face. At least one should have a pick at one end. You can start body work with no more than one or two such hammers, but you will also need a dolly to use with the hammers. The dolly is a lump of steel about the size of your fist, or smaller, that is flat on one side and is rounded on the other side.

*Body Filler Tools:* Body filler can be spread with a wide blade putty knife, one with a 3" blade. You can make a smaller tool from a piece of old metal venetian blind. Get a flat board, with an area of about 1 or 2 square feet, for a mixing board. You will also need some body files to grind off excess filler. These will fit into a holder, called a cheese grater, and can have both round and flat faces.

For finish work on body filler, or on old paint, you should have some wood sanding blocks. A 1" board about 2-¾" × 16" is right for holding a single piece of sandpaper of similar size to that used on powered sanders. An orbital or straight vibrator sander is a time saver. But belt sanders are of no use on car work because you can't move the sander fast enough to avoid gouges.

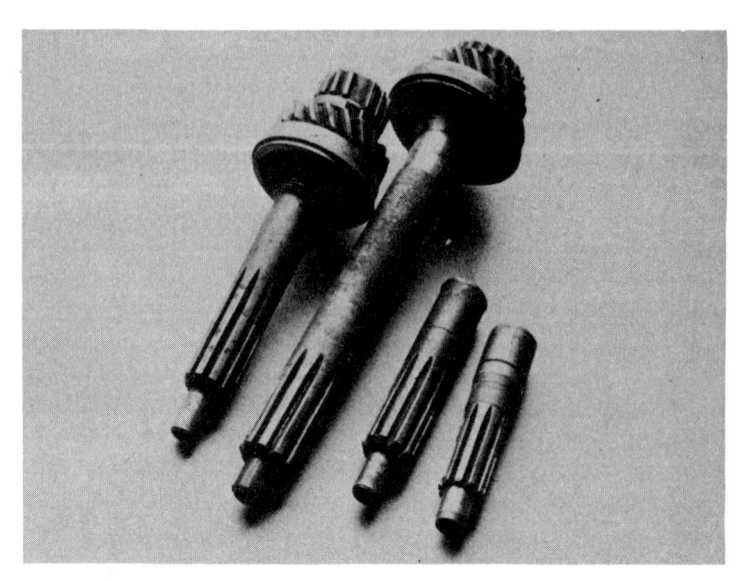

Fig. 8-4. Pilot shafts from old transmissions are handy to align the clutch during replacement.

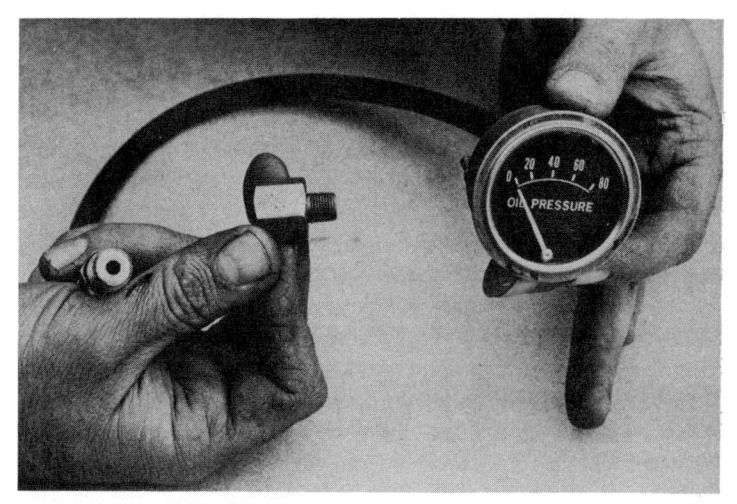

Fig. 8-5. A manual oil pressure gauge to test gauge in dash.

*Disc Grinder:* This tool is essential if you plan to do much body work. You can use it to remove old paint as well as to remove excess filler before finish sanding.

*Small Metal Cutting Tools:* Some small metal cutting tools are almost essential for any kind of car restoration. You can make one tool from an old pair of scissors. Grind off the points of the blades, and you will have a tool for trimming gaskets, shim stock, and other thin metal. A pair of heavy tin snips are good for cutting slightly heavier metal. Add a hack saw with an assortment of blades, and you have a versatile set of cutting tools. Use coarse-toothed hack saw blades to give good chip clearance in thick metal and fine-toothed blades for thinner metal and small tubing.

*Body Sling:* If you use a chain to lift a body from a chassis, or to return it to the chassis, you will almost certainly damage the body. A host of strong friends can do the job, if you can get them together when you want to do the job. A better method is to use a body sling, which protects both the car and you. Instructions for making a body sling from surplus conveyor belting are given in Chapter 9.

*Sand Blaster:* Not a high priority item. Useful if you must remove all the paint from a car or part of a car. Some smaller ones hold only about a quart of sand, good for small jobs. Get one with porcelain nozzles. You can make extra nozzles by removing the electrodes from old spark plugs.

*Sand for Blaster:* Get fine grades only. Coarse sand is no good for use on cars, leaves a surface that is too rough. You can save money by buying builder's sand and screening it. First dry it in the sun, then sift it through a piece of screen wire to remove large particles. If you live in a damp climate, bake it in an oven. Moisture in the sand will cause particles to stick together and clog the gun. Unless air is very dry, a water trap should be used.

*Door Handle Tool:* Good to have if you must rework interiors.

*Carpenter's Square:* Very useful for aligning body parts.

## WELDING EQUIPMENT

Think about how much you will use any welding equipment before you invest in it. If you think you would be happy with, for example, a cheap work car such as the one shown in Chapter 17 then you will need some welding equipment. If not, you can rent equipment or hire your welding done by a shop.

Fig. 8-6. This minimum set of hand tools for body work is all you need to repair minor body damage.

An electric arc welder is probably the best all around piece of welding equipment to own. You can get special rod and use it to cut metal, a job that is usually assigned to a torch. The main limitation of an electric welder is that you cannot weld very thin metal. Also, the weld is often rather crude until you grind it down or fill it. But you can use the electric welder for an almost endless range of repair jobs, from fixing broken wheelbarrows to metal furniture.

One difficulty with electric welders after they have been used for a while is that the spring on the ground clamp weakens and doesn't make good contact. This adds resistance between the ground lead and ground, producing heat there. To cure this ailment, get an old pair of small lockjaw pliers and weld a washer to the handle. You can bolt the ground cable to the washer and use the lockjaw pliers for a ground clamp. If you replace a cable, save the old one. Old welding cable makes excellent jumper cable.

A small propane torch is fine for soldering jobs. You can use one of these to solder radiator joints and any other thin metal soldering.

For cutting sheet metal an oxy-acetylene welder is the best choice. It gives a hotter flame than the previously-mentioned welders, but it also offers a good degree of control over the flame. You can use one of these for brazing work. You will have to lease the gas bottles from a gas supplier who will fill only his own bottles. In typical use you will use 2 bottles of oxygen for each bottle of acetylene. If you plan to do most of your welding with an electric rig, you will want a cutting torch with the gas welder.

If you get an oxy-acetylene rig, make sure it is properly installed. The gas bottles must be firmly fastened to either a movable cart that is stable, or chained to a wall. We have heard some horror stories about rigs that were tipped over, breaking off the nozzles. When this happens, the rapid gas release turns the bottle into a rocket, but a rocket with no guidance system. Such a self-propelled object can do considerable damage to your shop, your car, and even to you.

Another precaution: make sure your oxy-acetylene bottles have a check valve positioned in the line after the gauges. Sometimes fire starts back in the hose. A check valve will permit you to shut off the gas.

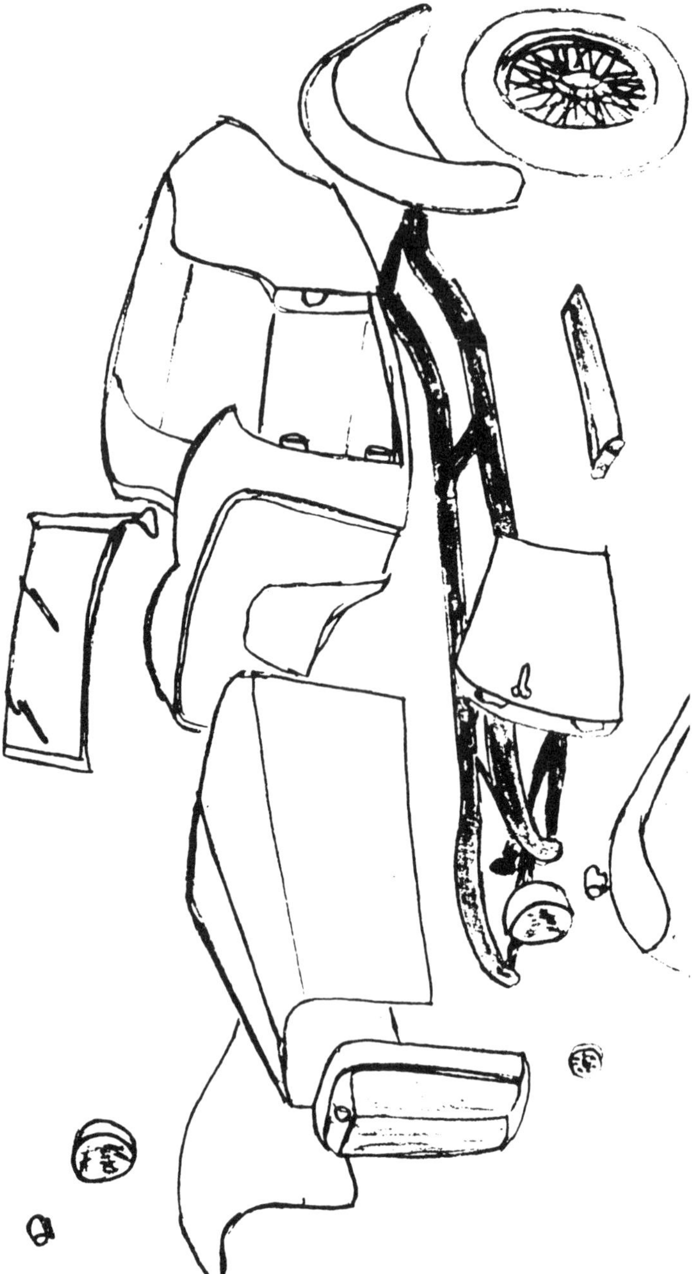

# Chapter 9
# Strip Down

The extent of disassembly for any car should be keyed to the ultimate value of the car. We recently looked at a 1947 Oldsmobile sedan that was basically sound, but the body was in bad condition. At today's prices this car would not be worth enough, even after the best restoration, to justify a total strip down and rebuilding job. If the car were about 20 years older, it would automatically qualify without regard to make or model. Any classic car in the same condition would deserve the best possible restoration.

In some cases you may have other grounds for complete restoration. Mike was once given a 1950 Chevy. This car in no way warranted complete restoration, but because Mike has a high regard for the dear lady who gave it to him, he did it for sentimental reasons.

Some restorers take every car down to the frame and then paint the frame. After rubbing down the frame paint, they may have restored the car to a *higher* quality than it had when new. Some car collectors say that any step beyond the standard factory practice is false restoration. But the best job usually lacks something because most people tire and quit when a little more time would do the job right. One man says that he finally gets a car in good condition the third time he does it.

## PREPARATION FOR DISASSEMBLY

If you are planning a complete strip down, begin by spraying every nut and bolt with penetrating oil or a rust solvent. Give the solvent time to work (a day or so) before you try to break the nuts loose. If the car has an excessive amount of grease on it, take it to an auto cleaning service to be steamed. This will rid it of rust scale and loose paint as well as old grease.

Get a clipboard or, even better, a spiral notebook to keep records of each step. The clipboard makes a handy writing surface, but loose sheets of paper can easily be lost. Get these items before you start to work. If you wait, you will be tempted to trust your memory for such details as the arrangement of adjacent parts. Make frequent sketches to supplement your written descriptions.

Number each wire you remove by sticking a numbered piece of masking tape around it (Fig. 9-1). Record the number in your notebook with information on the purpose and location of the wire. Do this even if you plan to replace the wiring; the old wire can be measured to find the proper length for its replacement.

If you have a camera with a sharp lens and the ability to focus at close distances, a single lens reflex for example, you can put it to good use. Photograph each assembly before you take it apart. The pictures will be insurance against forgetting the order and orientation of each component.

As in any kind of disassembly, prepare some cans with blank labels on them for bolts and nuts. Then write the location of the bolts on each can label as you store the part in the can. Valve covers also make good small parts holders. They are shallow, so you can

Fig. 9-1. These wires and cables behind the dash of a Studebaker pickup show why you should label wiring before you remove it.

look to the bottom of the containers for parts. Deep containers require dumping to find a part, and then you must pick up the mess. Whatever kind of containers you choose, they will save considerable time and prevent mistakes when you reassemble the car.

In addition to the materials above, keep a roll of masking tape handy for labeling parts. Although a part may seem obvious when you take it off, you may later forget how it was installed. A note on the tape can show which end goes forward, or which side goes up. Some parts look alike at first glance but have minor differences. Even if the two are the same, each will have established wear patterns that match those of the part it works on. It's bad enough to get a new part to work well with a used part, but it's asking too much to expect that from two used parts that didn't wear in together.

## STRIP DOWN PROCEDURE

The exact procedure will vary according to whether the engine hoist you use is portable or is installed permanently in one location. If you must move the car to the hoist, the engine should be pulled before the wheels. In some cases you may want to work on the car at a location away from the hoist, so you would remove the engine, then move the car to the work area.

There is no single order of procedure that everyone must follow in removing car parts. Various people can start at different points on the car and all arrive at a successful strip down. Regardless of the order followed, the individual steps will be the same. For example, various wires and tubes connect the engine to the driving compartment and must be removed. On a total strip down, try to determine each wire's destination and disconnect it at each end. Some wires seem to disappear when they go into a harness. If the wiring is to be replaced, separate each wire with a knife so it can be labeled and measured. When you unhook lines, such as an oil gauge line or a water capillary tube from the engine, unhook the other end from the dash at the same time. When you remove linkages to the engine, tape any clipping devices that hold a linkage to it. Don't forget to label each part.

Regardless of the kind of car you have, there are certain questions that must be faced: What parts will be sent out for repair? Will the engine go to a rebuilder? And will the body be sandblasted? Your car may present special questions that are peculiar to it. These questions must be answered with respect to the tools you have available as well as to your confidence in doing each job.

The steps that follow are no more than a general guide; you can improvise to make the work fit your car and your workshop.

Begin by draining the coolant and removing the hoses. On most cars old enough to warrant a full strip down, the fenders will be bolted on and can be easily removed. On many cars the front fenders will come off with the radiator; this assembly is called a front end clip. Remove the bolts that hold the fenders to the body and then see if the fenders are bolted to the radiator support. If the car is very old, this section may have to be disassembled piece by piece. Such a car will also have a hood that is hinged down the center and easily removed. For cars made starting about 1950, with a hood that lifts from the front, be careful to avoid injury by the hood spring that is separate from the hinge (Fig. 9-2). With the front fenders, radiator, and hood removed, the engine is exposed and easy to pull.

After removing the radiator and front fenders, take off the gas tank. This reduces the risk of fire from cutting torches if they are used. Empty the tank first; gas in the tank adds unnecessary weight and can be spilled, increasing the chance of accidents. Most old cars will have a drain plug in the bottom of the tank; if there is none, you can siphon the gas out. Remove the line to the tank and the wire that goes to the gas gauge sending unit. Label the wire so it won't be confused with the tail light wires. The tank may be bolted in by straps or by flanges. Or it may be supported by the frame, the body, or by a combination of these methods. For safety, remove the tank from your working area; if possible get it out of the shop for storage.

**ENGINE**

At this point you can remove either the engine or the body, but our procedure will choose to pull the engine next. Since the transmission linkage must be removed in either case, do that now. Check to see if there is a removable section of floor pan near the transmission. Many cars had these to provide access to the transmission for repairs. Locate the speedometer cable and remove it from the transmission. If the car has the gear shift level on the steering column, disconnect the linkage from it to the transmission. Floor levers must be removed if you intend to take the transmission out with the engine, but can be left on the transmission if it will be removed separately.

Our procedure will separate the transmission from the engine, but in case you want to remove a floor lever, here is how to

Fig. 9-2. Using homemade tool to remove hood spring on 1950 Chevy. Block of wood protects fender.

do it. The lever will probably have a rubber boot over its base, the lever held in place by either a snap ring or a threaded ring. Identify the kind of ring. A snap ring will have a space to insert a screwdriver to pry it out; a threaded ring will be shaped like a large thin nut. Push down on the lever as you remove the ring. When the ring is off, push down on the lever and twist it counterclockwise. It should lift out easily.

Next, the engine. Although the coolant was drained before the radiator was removed, there will be some liquid left in the block.

Look for a draincock or a plug in the block to let it out. Drain the oil also. After draining the oil, replace the drain plug and tighten it with a wrench. Never trust your memory to do this later; good intentions won't save your engine if it falls out.

Remove any easily damaged parts from the engine, such as the carburetor, the fan, and the fuel pump. Keep the bolts with these parts so that when you are ready to install them, you won't have to look for bolts. Also unhook the wiring to the engine, labeling each wire. Unbolt the exhaust pipe form the exhaust manifold.

Make a cradle under the transmission by hooking a chain across the frame rails to support the transmission. Then unbolt the engine from the hogshead (clutch housing). Remove these bolts carefully. The main drive gears and dowel pins will keep the freed part from falling, but if you notice slippage, leave a bolt in until you are ready to pull the engine.

Remove the engine mounting bolts. Don't be afraid to do this; the engine's weight will hold it in place. You can now bolt your engine-pulling bracket onto the intake manifold, or hook your chain to a couple of bolts, one near the front of the block and one near the rear. Put a washer over the chain link to prevent the bolt from pulling through. Or you can wrap the chain around the whole engine, but this method gives less control of the engine.

If your car has open drive shaft, remove it next. Enclosed drive shafts can be removed later. To remove an open shaft, look for four nuts on the pinion flange at the rear end. Remove these, move the drive shaft slightly forward, then drop it and slide it out to the rear. Some drive shafts will have four bolts at the front, connecting it to the transmission. And some old cars will have the emergency brake working on the drive shaft, so it must be disconnected. If the drive shaft has a slip-joint, be careful that it doesn't slip apart. You can take it apart, but if you do that, check the position of the U-joints first. They must be in-plane, or timed. This means that the yokes must be in-line or at 90° to each other. If you fail to observe the proper relationship on these, the drive train can develop serious vibrations.

Next, remove the rear fenders if they are bolted on. On most cars made before World War II you can take out a few bolts to get the fenders off; later cars will have welded fenders. Bolted on fenders often have a cushion between the fender and the body, called the fender welting, which is often chrome-edged or plain black. Save the old welting to use as a pattern in preparing new welting. The odds are against your finding ready-made pieces of welting to fit your car. If the tail lights are mounted on the rear fenders, this is a good time to remove them.

## INTERIOR STRIP DOWN

It's a good idea to remove the steering wheel and steering gear before removing the seats because you can sit in the driver's seat and use your knees to apply pressure under the steering wheel while removing it. If there is a horn button in the center of the steering wheel, remove it first. Unscrew the nut that holds the wheel on the shaft until it is flush with the end of the shaft. Now, sit in the driver's seat and brace your feet against something solid so your knees are against the underside of the steering wheel. Place a large brass punch against the end of the steering shaft and strike it sharply with a hammer while you push upward on the wheel with your knees. One hard blow will knock the wheel loose with less damage to the shaft than several light pecks. The nut will prevent the shaft from mushrooming when you strike it. When the wheel breaks loose, remove the nut and the wheel.

The steering housing will probably be fastened to the dash with a horseshoe clamp and two bolts. The gear will be held to the frame with no less than three bolts. Steering arms are held into the steering linkage by various kinds of joints, depending on the age of the car. Antique cars are likely to have more precision-made joints which come apart by simply unscrewing the members. Modern cars usually have tapered joints, one member fitting inside the end of the other member. To release a part from a tapered joint, remove the cotter pin on the nut, then the nut, and strike the female member with a hammer to break the joint loose. Don't be afraid to hit hard, but be careful not to damage the threads with a misdirected hammer blow. When free, the steering gear can be pulled out from under the car, but you may have to jack the car up to get the steering column out because of the angle of the column.

To remove the windshield from the car body you must examine it to see how it was installed. On modern cars the windshield is removed by pushing it out, on many old cars by pushing it in. But regardless of the age of the car you must remove the trim first. On a typical old car there will be a centerstrip molding to remove also. Remove the molding, the rubber weatherstrip material, then the glass.

To remove the side glass, take off the door panel and the window moldings. To remove the interior door handles, press the trim ring inward and use a nail or other tool to push out the pin that holds the handle. When you have taken off the door panel, remove the screws that hold the lifter mechanism. At this time you can probably tip the window glass inward and lift it out. In this procedure, as in all others, make a complete record of the step-by-step method you followed. When you are ready to replace the glass, you can simply reverse the order of the procedure.

The dash and its instruments also require individual decisions on disassembly procedure. Only a thorough examination can tell you whether to remove the dash and instruments separately or as a single unit. For example, some gauges can be disconnected at the back of the gauge, others have a permanently fixed tube on the back of the gauge. This latter kind must be disconnected at the engine block and the entire tube drawn out with the gauge. After removing the dash, remove any other interior parts that are peculiar to your car.

Go under the car and find the bolts that hold the seats down. Unbolt and remove the seats. Unless the headliner is good, you must remove it. Check around the edges for a beading that can be removed to expose the fasteners that hold it.

## BODY REMOVAL

The brake and clutch system must be disconnected to permit body removal from the frame. Manufacturers have used many different set-ups for these, from pedals installed with the traditional lower pivot to swung pedals. Again, make careful sketches and label the parts of your car's clutch and brake system so you will have no trouble putting it back together.

Now, go under the body and check to see if you have missed any parts, such as ground cables, that must be disconnected before you remove the body. Locate the mounting bolts for the body. There will usually be six or more of these. The bolts will be fairly large, at least 7/16" or larger. These bolts will be insulated by rubber or wooden shims or washers which prevent vibrations in the frame from being transferred to the body. In addition to the rubber parts there will probably be several steel washers which alternate in position with the rubber parts. Some of the washers may be square, some round. Make sure you make a sketch of the order in which these parts are installed before you remove them.

These body bolts are usually difficult to remove because they will not have been loosened since the car left the factory. If you have a torch, you can cut the bolts (Fig. 9-3). Even if you have to cut them, save the pieces of one to get a replacement bolt of the same

Fig. 9-3. Using the "gas wrench" to remove body mounting bolt.

diameter and length. Save every part of the body mounts; parts men don't stock body mounts.

There are various ways to remove a body from a frame, but some of them result in serious body damage. Chains are especially bad. Here are some ways to get the body off the frame without denting it.

A body sling, as described below, is a helpful tool to safe body movement. If you don't have a sling, you can use the method that requires the least preparation; enlist any friends or curious onlookers that you can find to simply lift the body off the chassis. If you intend to use strictly human power, you will want to remove the doors to reduce body weight. But if you have a sling, the doors will help support the body and prevent damage.

To make a body sling, find a factory in your area that uses a conveyer belt production line. Old conveyer belts are usually discarded when new ones are installed, so try to have someone who works at the factory save a section of belting for you. Cut the belting material so it will be 2½ to 3 times as long as the width of your car. It should be long enough to reach through the windows of the car and touch ends when folded back over the top of the car body. The method you use to connect a chain to the belt will depend on what kind of tools you have. The simplest method is to cut holes in each end of the belting and run a chain through the holes. If the belting is wide enough, cut more than one hole in each end and lace the chain through like a shoe string. This would take the pressure off one spot and lessen the possibility of the ends ripping out. It would also spread the lifting surface out to more of the body and reduce the chances of crushing the body. Body crush is why cables and chains can't be used; they apply too much pressure at one point. Another way is to prepare two pieces of steel with hooks or loops attached to them. Drill holes through the pieces of steel and also through the belting and bolt the pieces of steel to the belting. Then hook the chain to the steel loops. Back the bolts up with large washers to prevent their pulling through.

Sometimes a factory will give the belting to you if you take the whole roll. It's heavy, so take a muscular friend with you. Since you may have extra belting, it also makes good floor mats at the work bench to protect your legs and feet from the hard concrete.

To lift the body you will need a set of chain falls which you can either borrow or rent. You will need strong ceiling joists in your shop if the falls are anchored to them. If you are working outdoors, look for a large tree with a heavy limb above the work area. When you put the sling on the body, it's a good idea to protect the body with a heavy sheet of plywood across the top (Fig. 9-4). The plywood should extend a fraction of an inch beyond the body on each side. This precaution is particularly necessary if the car doesn't have an all-steel top.

Still another method of body removal is that used by people who take camper beds off pick-up trucks. You will need two beams, each one about four feet longer than the width of the body. Wood is better than steel for this; it offers more friction and so isn't as likely to slip. Oak is a particularly good choice because of its strength which, weight for weight, is greater than that of steel. If you must use pine and are in doubt about its strength, add another board.

You will also need four supports for the beams. The supports must be long enough to hold the body well above the chassis so the chassis can be rolled out from under the body. If you can find some 55-gallon steel barrels, these make good supports and are usually high enough.

Lift one end of the body, either by hand or with a pry bar or jack. If you have nothing better, a bumper jack will do. Place the beam under that end and support the ends of the beam with your barrels. Then go to the other end and follow the same lifting procedure.

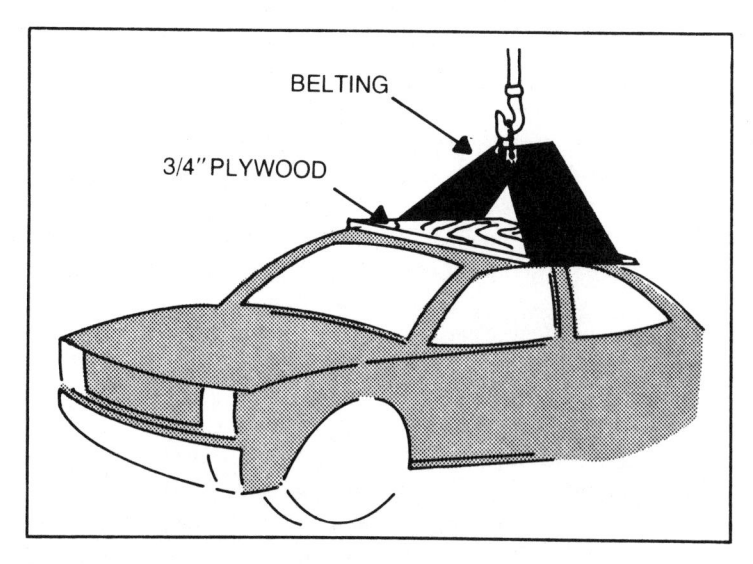

Fig. 9-4. Use a board or a sheet of ¾" plywood to protect the top when using a body sling. If the body is heavy, use two sheets of plywood. Plywood should extend slightly beyond widest part of body.

When you roll the chassis out, you must guide the car by kicking the front wheels or by aiming them with your hands. With the weight off the front end this should be easy to do.

## FINAL STRIP DOWN

Now that the car is in pieces all over your shop (and perhaps, your back yard), you must have prepared yourself to face this point without panic. Many cars change hands in this condition because the rebuilding task looks so monumental that you think you will never finish it. This is a good time to send out any parts that must be reworked by a commercial shop. For example, you can send the chrome to a plating plant, and the seats to an upholsterer. This reduces the tasks before you, improving your morale, and it also makes more room in your shop while getting some items vulnerable to damage in a safe place.

Jack up the chassis and support it at four points, two at the front and two at the rear. Take off the wheels and store them or, if they need special repair or sand blasting, send them off. If the car has a closed drive shaft, now is the time to remove the cradle you made to support it.

Remove the front and rear shackle pins on the springs. Lower the rear axle to the floor and slide it to the rear. If no work is necessary for this unit, clean and repaint it.

The front end is somewhat more complicated than the rear axle, but if there is a straight axle, as in many old cars, the removal procedure is similar. Check the kingpins and tie rod ends carefully for wear. Front springs are more likely to break than rear springs because there is more weight on the front end. Check these carefully. Some breaks are hard to see because other leaves will hold the broken leaf in place. If you disassemble any leaf springs, use a couple of C-clamps to hold the leaves together while you remove the center bolt. Without a clamp the springs can move apart with such force that they will injure you when you unscrew the last threads. Number the spring leaves and mark the end of each that goes to the front. The center hole is usually offset from the center, but the offset is sometimes very slight.

Remove any final items that remain on the frame, such as brake cylinders or rods, battery boxes, and bolted-on brackets. Don't remove riveted items unless they are damaged. If the running board brackets are damaged, for example, you can remove them and bolt them back on. But bolts are no substitute for rivets. They usually loosen and eventually fail.

With the frame stripped of parts it can be sanded and painted. This is the point where many people overrestore the car to a better than new condition with multiple coats of paint on the frame, each one rubbed to mirror finish. While this overrestoring is frowned upon by some car buffs, after so much work you can see why it is done.

It's a good idea to wait to change small items that are to be replaced, such as spring hanger bushings, until after the frame is painted. These items will add contrasts in color, giving the finished job more eye appeal and showing that they are new rather than painted-over, worn-out parts.

Now that the strip down is complete, you can start rebuilding the car. The first step in that job is the engine.

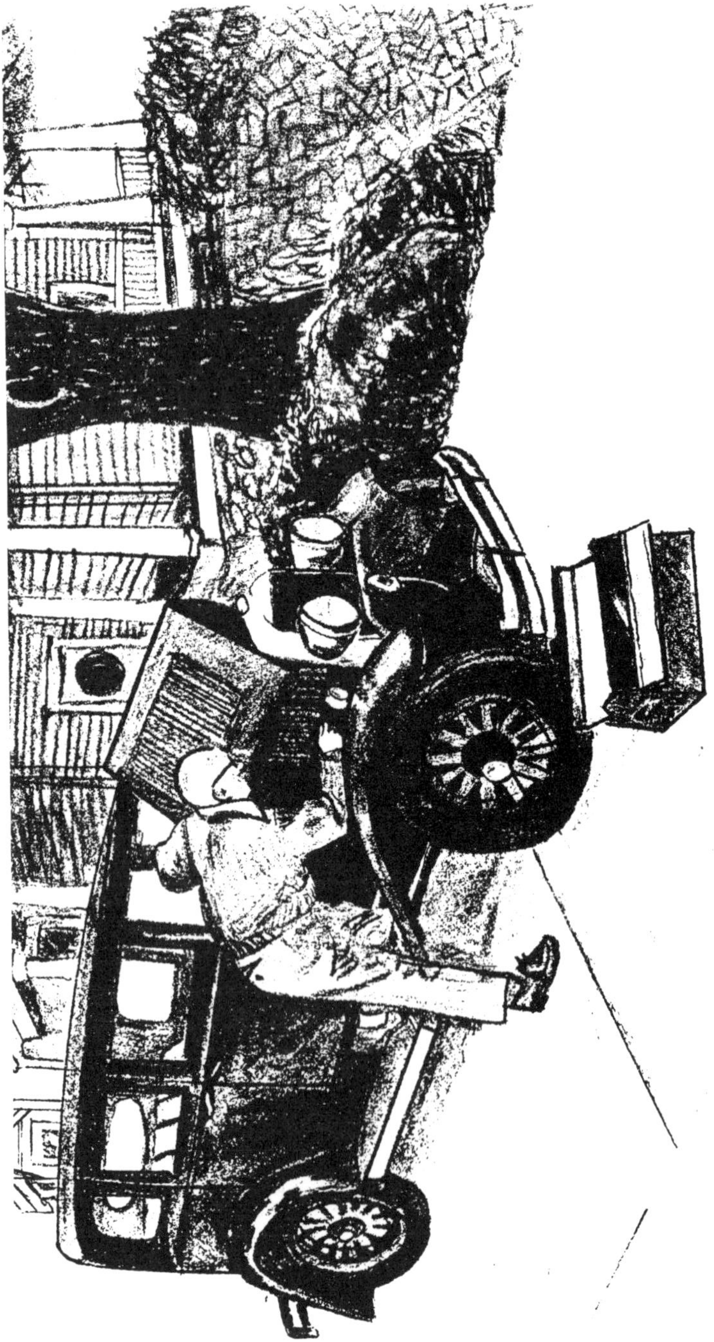

# Chapter 10
# Engine Restoration

Restoring an engine on a car that has been abandoned is quite a different task as compared to the overhaul of a working engine. You can get a repair manual from the library and learn how to work on the engine of the car you drove to work yesterday, but there are problems with abandoned cars that aren't mentioned in the manuals. Before we get to some of those problems, let's take a look at the kinds of engines you may encouter.

## KINDS OF ENGINES

The engine in your vintage car will probably have from four to eight cylinders. Except for a few makes, such as the VW, 4-cylinder car engines will have the cylinders arranged vertically in line, with the cylinder block cast from a single piece of iron. Such engines typically have three main bearings that support the crankshaft. The crankshaft will have all four throws, or cranks, in a single plane, with the two inside cranks offset from the outside cranks.

Except for certain GM cars built after 1960, any 6-cylinder car that you restore is likely to have an in-line engine. Most of these will have four main bearings on the crankshaft; some will have seven mains. The crank journals are arranged in pairs, each pair offset 120° from the adjacent pair.

Many classic cars have straight 8 engines, the 8 cylinders in a line. The crankshaft normally has five or more main bearings. Some 8-cylinder engines have crankshafts that look like two 4-cylinder shafts connected end to end, with one set of four cranks off-set 90° from the other set. Better balanced engines have crankshafts that appear to be made by placing a 4-cylinder crankshaft in the center section, then adding the two front cranks and two rear cranks from another 4-cylinder shaft. The front and rear sections are offset 90° from the center section.

Almost any Cadillac, Lincoln, and post-1932 Ford cars will have V-type engines. The most common is, of course, the V-8 with two banks of four cylinders each, the banks set at 60° to 90° from each other. The crankshaft for a V engine is much shorter than that for a straight engine with the same number of cylinders and has two connecting rods mounted on each crank journal. The crankshaft can have the same shape as that of a 4-cylinder engine, but the crank journals are usually offset at 90° to the adjacent journal. Special models of some classic cars have V-12 or V-16 engines.

The Volkswagen is well known for its pancake engine, a 4-cylinder engine with the cylinders in a single plane but composed of two banks of cylinders. There are 2 cylinders in each bank, and the banks are opposed, that is the pistons move outward at 180° from those of the other bank. The Corvair engine is similar in construction but has three cylinders in each bank or a total of six.

## VALVE ARRANGEMENTS

Modern engines almost invariably have overhead or "I" head valves (Fig. 10-1C). For many years these were called "valve-in-head" engines. Chevrolet and Buick have had such a valve arrangement since the days of the antiques. It requires a more elaborate arrangement of valve parts, such as push rods and rocker arms which work the valves. The I-head engine is taller but narrower than the "L" or flathead engine. The cooling system for the head is more complicated because the coolant must control valve temperature as well as engine head temperature.

Many old cars will have the L-head design, with the valves set beside the cylinder where they open by moving upward (Fig. 10-1B). This engine is easily recognized by the postion of the spark plugs, set vertically in the top of the head. The only other kind of engine you are likely to find with this spark plug arrangement is the T-head but it will have the intake manifold on the opposite side of the engine from the exhaust manifold (Fig. 10-1A). A T-head requires two camshafts, one for the train of valves on each side of the cylinder, but an L-head needs only one camshaft. A flathead engine is easier to overhaul than the I-head models because there are no working parts in the head to interfere with head removal. But the valves on the flathead are more difficult to service.

A few engines have the F-head, with one valve overhead and the other valve in the block (Fig. 10-1D). Then there is the even more rare sleeve valve engine, such as the "Silent Knight." These engines are especially difficult to restore because of the great amount of moving sleeve surface area that can freeze to the adjacent sleeve.

## MATERIALS USED IN ENGINES

Most engines in old cars will have been cast from gray iron, in one piece. In very old antiques the engines may be made up of several pieces, a casting for each cylinder. The exhaust valve seats usually consist of inserts made from special metal rings that can withstand higher temperatures.

Some engine blocks are made from nickel-steel or chromium steel. A few engines may have aluminum blocks. Some notable examples of the latter are the Buick Specials and Olds Cutlass models, introduced in 1961. Those engines, like most other aluminum block engines, had steel cylinder liners. Cylinder liners may be wet liners, cooled directly by the coolant, or dry liners. A few aluminum engines, such as those used on the Chevrolet Vega, have no liners.

Cylinder heads may be made from iron or aluminum. An easy way to identify whether your engine has aluminum parts is to test it with a small magnet. The magnet will be attracted to iron but not to aluminum. VW engines also have magnesium parts. To identify magnesium, try to cut a shaving off with a knife. If the metal yields a shaving, it is aluminum. If it crumbles, it is magnesium.

Magnesium has one characteristic that sometimes causes problems. Mike once came upon a traffic jam on the open highway, with cars backed up for a quarter of a mile. A highway patrolman had stopped the traffic because a Volkswagen's engine was burning. A wheel had come off the VW, and some part of the car had dragged across the pavement with enough friction to produce a spark that ignited the magnesium on the engine. It was burning like a Roman candle, setting off shooting stars of sparks into the night sky. If you have a car with magnesium parts, avoid hot sparks.

Another material that you will find in engine blocks is babbit, a metal made up of lead, tin, antimony, and copper. The upper part of the main bearings are set in the bottom of the block, and the lower halves of these bearings are made into removable caps. On old cars these bearings were made by pouring babbit into the bearing cap or into the proper space on the block. A jig that was identical in shape and size to the journal that would run in the bearing was inserted

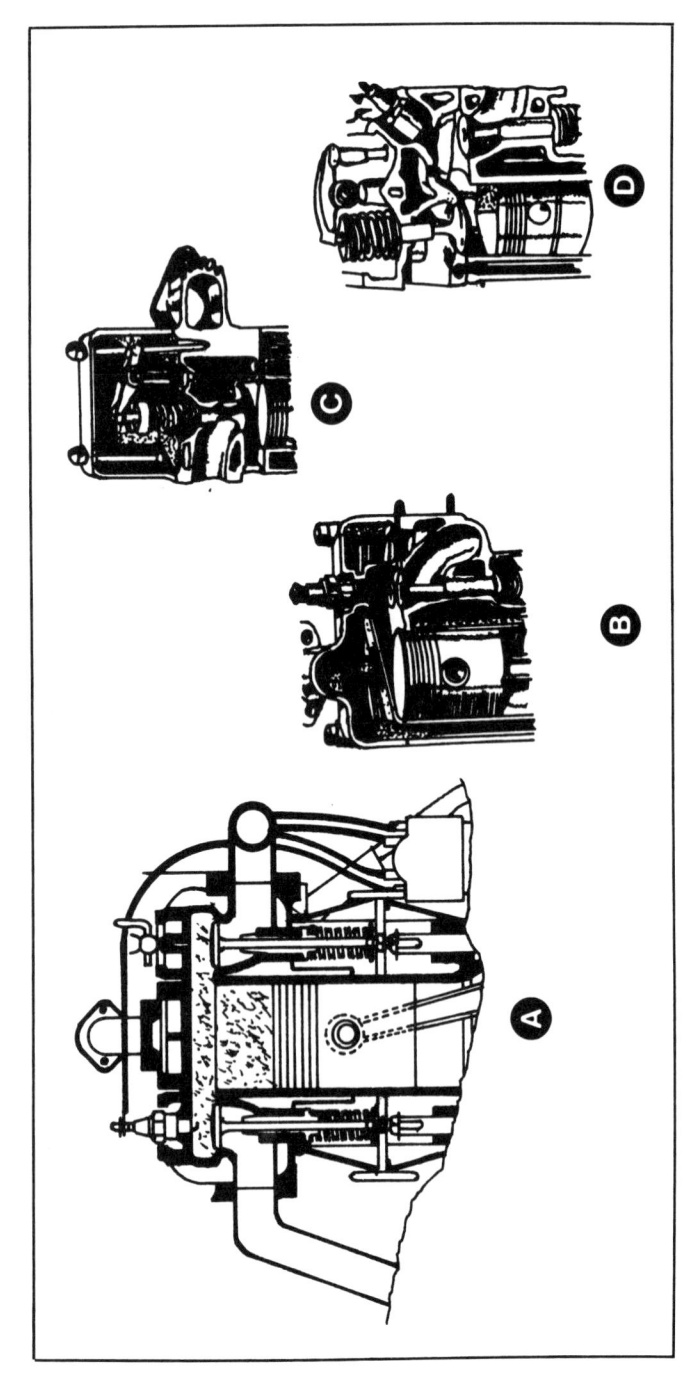

Fig. 10-1. Types of valve arrangements. (A) T-head. (B) L-head, or side valve, valves in block. (C) I-head, or overhead valves, valves in head. (D) F-head, 1 valve in head, other in block.

into the block where the melted babbit was poured. After the babbit hardened, the jig was removed, and the bearing was scraped and machined to precisely fit the journal. On old engines this job can be done in a machine shop. Ford V-8s and most modern engines have bearing inserts that can easily be installed by hand.

Pistons in your vintage engine may be made of cast iron, steel, or aluminum. Aluminum is used in most modern engines because of its low weight. When the engine is operating at high speed, the piston must stop and reverse its direction of movement in as little as a few thousandths of a second. The high inertia of a cast iron piston makes this sudden stopping and accelerating use up too much power. Cast iron does have one advantage over aluminum; it expands less when heated, so the piston can fit the cylinder more closely.

Some pistons have been made from more than one kind of metal. These have steel struts inset into the piston so that they oppose the expansion or shrinkage of the piston with changing temperatures. Many pistons depend on slots that permit expansion of the metal without changing the diameter of the piston significantly or are cam-ground to an oval shape that changes to round when hot. Pistons in an old car probably have a simple cylindrical shape with a flat top. Some may have a dome top or a more complex head shape.

Piston rings can be made from cast iron or various kinds of steel. Most compression rings for old cars are made from cast iron. The compression rings are simply made, usually with straight joints. Some rings of old design have angled or step joints to avoid leakage, but research has proven that such measures are unnecessary. Oil rings are more complicated, and you can get special rings for engines that are badly worn. These have expanders that hold a double ring against the cylinder walls even if the cylinder is tapered.

The camshaft is made from hardened steel that can break like cast iron. It is driven off the crankshaft by a timing chain or gear and rotates at one-half the speed of the crankshaft. It operates the valves, the oil pump, the distributor, and, usually, the fuel pump. On in-line engines it usually works in bearings in the side of the engine block; on V-type engines it is usually located between the cylinder banks. In special models the camshaft can be located above the valves, an overhead camshaft. If an engine is worn badly enough to need overhauling, the camshaft probably should be inspected for excessive wear.

## ENGINE DIAGNOSIS

Since your vintage car may not have been running for a long time, you will want to determine the condition of the engine, if possible, before doing any significant work on it. The first step is to check to see if the engine is free or frozen. Try turning it with the starter or with a crank. If it is free, go on to a compression test.

To test the compression, remove all the spark plugs and insert the compression tester in each spark plug hole, to get a compression reading on each cylinder, while someone operates the starter for you. Make a record of the readings so that you can compare the condition of the rings and the valves in the various cylinders. The readings you get will depend on the condition of these components but also on the compression ratio of the engine. A modern high-compression engine in good condition would be expected to give a reading of about 150 p.s.i. or even higher, while a low-compression engine in a pre-World War II car would produce a reading of perhaps 80 to 90 p.s.i. when new.

If your engine gives some very low readings, pour a little heavy oil into the cylinders that gave the low readings and retest. If the new readings are normal, you can consider that the rings, and possibly the cylinder walls, are in bad condition on those cylinders. If there is no significant change in the readings, the trouble is probably burned valves (Figs. 10-2, 10-3), weak valve springs, or a bad head gasket. Improper valve adjustment is also a possible cause and should be checked. If equally low compression readings occur in two adjacent cylinders, the problem is almost surely a blown head gasket between those two cylinders.

Although a compression test does not always indicate the precise cause of low compression, it can give the basic engine a clean bill of health if all cylinders are up to specifications. If the engine won't start, the next step is to go to the flow chart in Fig. 10-4. The last item on the flow chart, as you will notice, is the timing chain. With a jumped chain, the valves and distributor shaft will be off in timing; with a broken chain, they won't work. You can often verify this problem without tools.

First, push the starter button, or key, and listen to the sound of the engine turning over. Better yet, have someone else operate the starter or do it yourself by shorting across the solenoid or working the starter lever with a bar while you are standing over the engine. Does the engine appear to turn over easily as if there were no compression against it? And do you hear a hum? These are indications that the timing chain or gear is not working. This may

Fig. 10-2. Burned exhaust valve.

mean no other problems, but if the chain jumped while the car was running at a good speed, the momentum of the car and the engine is likely to have continued the piston motion long enough to have hit valve heads and done considerable damage to any overhead valve engine.

To confirm timing problems, crank the engine until the timing mark on the crankshaft pulley at the bottom front of the engine is lined up with the timing index mark on the engine block. Now carefully remove the distributor cap without disturbing the rotor. The rotor should be pointing to the position of the contact in the cap for either cylinder #1 or the contact opposite that one. Engine cylinders are numbered from front to back, so the front cylinder will be #1. Note that any other rotor position is confirmation of timing gear problems, but if the rotor is pointing to #1, that does not necessarily eliminate the possibility. To eliminate that possibility, crank the engine again and watch the rotor to see if it turns.

Another confirmation of a jumped chain can be gotten from the compression test. If the valves are in equal condition, the compression on the cylinders will be low, but uniformly low. If one cylinder has a compression figure of 50 pounds per square inch, all will have a similar test value.

Many old cars with 6-or 8-cylinder in-line engines have timing gears which permit direct meshing of the camshaft gear with the gear on the crankshaft. On V-8 engines the gears are spaced with a chain used to connect them. The old timing gears on the in-line engines were almost universally noisy. They sometimes consisted of 2 steel gears or an aluminum and a steel gear meshing. Later plastics were introduced and are now extensively used for this purpose. Plastic gears are good for perhaps 60,000 to 90,000 miles on the average, but some last much longer than that.

Regardless of how carefully you follow the troubleshooting charts, you can run into a problem that defies simple solutions. One car that we know had a low vacuum reading on the engine. The engine would misfire, with little power to move the car on the highway. The spark plugs were removed, one at a time, for a compression test. It showed good compression. The symptoms didn't make sense until the trouble was identified as valve float. The car had hydraulic valves, which depend on oil pressure. In this car the pressure was maintained at a high level because of a fault at the oil pump. The oil pump check valve wasn't opening to by-pass the oil, so a constant high pressure pumped up the valve lifters and caused valve float.

Your vintage car probably won't have hydraulic valve lifters, but any combination of parts as complex as an automobile engine offers the possibility for unexpected problems. If you run into one of these, don't be discouraged if your first guess is wrong. Just keep on eliminating possible causes, and you will succeed.

If your old car engine is running, but badly, you can make an estimate of its condition by careful listening. Even a distinctive

Fig. 10-3. Burned valve and pitted rod inserts must be replaced.

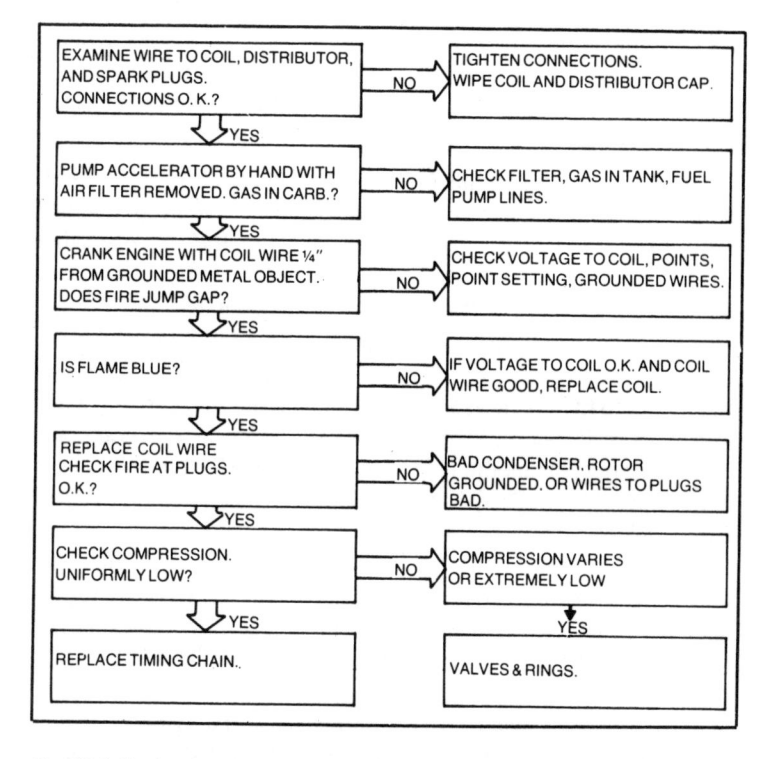

```
┌─────────────────────────────────────────────────────────────────────┐
│  ┌──────────────────────────────┐      ┌──────────────────────────┐ │
│  │ EXAMINE WIRE TO COIL,        │      │ TIGHTEN CONNECTIONS.     │ │
│  │ DISTRIBUTOR, AND SPARK PLUGS.│──NO──▶│ WIPE COIL AND            │ │
│  │ CONNECTIONS O.K.?            │      │ DISTRIBUTOR CAP.         │ │
│  └──────────────┬───────────────┘      └──────────────────────────┘ │
│                ▼YES                                                  │
│  ┌──────────────────────────────┐      ┌──────────────────────────┐ │
│  │ PUMP ACCELERATOR BY HAND     │      │ CHECK FILTER, GAS IN     │ │
│  │ WITH AIR FILTER REMOVED.     │──NO──▶│ TANK, FUEL PUMP LINES.   │ │
│  │ GAS IN CARB.?                │      │                          │ │
│  └──────────────┬───────────────┘      └──────────────────────────┘ │
│                ▼YES                                                  │
│  ┌──────────────────────────────┐      ┌──────────────────────────┐ │
│  │ CRANK ENGINE WITH COIL WIRE  │      │ CHECK VOLTAGE TO COIL,   │ │
│  │ ¼" FROM GROUNDED METAL       │──NO──▶│ POINTS, POINT SETTING,   │ │
│  │ OBJECT. DOES FIRE JUMP GAP?  │      │ GROUNDED WIRES.          │ │
│  └──────────────┬───────────────┘      └──────────────────────────┘ │
│                ▼YES                                                  │
│  ┌──────────────────────────────┐      ┌──────────────────────────┐ │
│  │ IS FLAME BLUE?               │──NO──▶│ IF VOLTAGE TO COIL O.K.  │ │
│  │                              │      │ AND COIL WIRE GOOD,      │ │
│  │                              │      │ REPLACE COIL.            │ │
│  └──────────────┬───────────────┘      └──────────────────────────┘ │
│                ▼YES                                                  │
│  ┌──────────────────────────────┐      ┌──────────────────────────┐ │
│  │ REPLACE COIL WIRE            │      │ BAD CONDENSER. ROTOR     │ │
│  │ CHECK FIRE AT PLUGS.         │──NO──▶│ GROUNDED. OR WIRES TO    │ │
│  │ O.K.?                        │      │ PLUGS BAD.               │ │
│  └──────────────┬───────────────┘      └──────────────────────────┘ │
│                ▼YES                                                  │
│  ┌──────────────────────────────┐      ┌──────────────────────────┐ │
│  │ CHECK COMPRESSION.           │──NO──▶│ COMPRESSION VARIES       │ │
│  │ UNIFORMLY LOW?               │      │ OR EXTREMELY LOW         │ │
│  └──────────────┬───────────────┘      └──────────────┬───────────┘ │
│                ▼YES                                   ▼YES           │
│  ┌──────────────────────────────┐      ┌──────────────────────────┐ │
│  │ REPLACE TIMING CHAIN.        │      │ VALVES & RINGS.          │ │
│  └──────────────────────────────┘      └──────────────────────────┘ │
└─────────────────────────────────────────────────────────────────────┘
```

Fig. 10-4. Engine troubleshooting chart.

noise can be hard to identify at first hearing. The first step is to find which area of the engine is producing the noise. You can make an instant listening tool from any long piece of iron, an old gas hose, or even a broomstick. The principle is similar to that of the stethoscope. Place the iron bar, or other listening tool, to various points on the surface of the engine. The sound that travels up through the bar to your ear will be much louder than it was without the bar. By moving the bar over the engine, you will be able to focus on the site of the sound. Use care to keep the listening tool away from moving parts, such as the fan or belts. With a little practice you can quickly locate the source of the sound. Once you have tracked down its location, you can make a good guess as to what is causing the problem.

Sometimes the noise will be inconsequential. Fuel pumps are notorious for producing noise that can be mistaken for anything from a faulty lifter to a connecting rod. The noise is usually produced by the lobe on the timing gear which activates the lever arm in the pump. If your listening device shows the loudest response when it is held against the fuel pump, you can relax. Vacuum leaks are another source of often unrecognized sounds.

## CLEANING ENGINES

Even if your old engine is in running condition when you get it, it will almost certainly need internal cleaning. The proper way to clean an engine is to strip it down and do the job manually. Restorers often use other methods to save time. We will mention some of these even though they are not recommended.

One quick and dirty way to clean a gummy old engine is to dilute a quart of oil with 3 or 4 quarts of diesel fuel. Pour the mixture into the crankcase and start the engine. Let it run at a low idle until it is warm, then shut it off and drain the crankcase immediately. This method is not recommended for two reasons: it doesn't provide good lubrication for a hot engine, and there is some danger of fire.

You can also get certain commercial cleaners that are designed to be added to the oil. You put them in, drive the car for from 20 to 500 miles, depending on the specific additive that you use, then drain after a run long enough to get the engine up to temperature.

All of these cleaners are somewhat risky to use. If the cleaner works, it knocks loose sludge that must go through the screen in the oil pick-up, through the oil pump, and only then to the filter. Some old engines don't have filters, and most of those that do have filters have a by-pass system instead of a full flow filter. This means you will have all of the gunk that was in the crankcase floating around in the oil, going through the bearings. In some cases the "cleaned" engine will start to use more oil.

A better way to clean the engine, although there is still some risk, is to change the oil, putting in a detergent oil. Most old engines will have been run on non-detergent oil, so the detergent oil may kick loose some particles. Don't leave the oil in the engine for the full period. Instructions with modern oils may suggest an oil change every 6,000 miles. When you are putting a detergent oil into an old car, you should change the oil at 500 miles the first change, and at 1,000 miles the second. Drain the oil while it is hot, so you will remove as much of the suspended material as possible.

Some engines have a gray metallic-looking sludge in the bottom of the pan. If you remove the pan and notice this kind of sludge, don't be alarmed. It was caused by lead compounds blowing by the rings. It has no great significance except that it may mean that your engine needs overhauling. If you suspect this kind of sludge in the pan, you can remove it by draining the oil while it is hot.

Almost all used engines will have some degree of carbon build-up. This applies to those which seem to be in the best of condition. One elderly man that we know took his immaculate 1963 Chevy to a shop for a tune-up. He had babied the car since it was new, always carefully driving it in short, slow errands around his home town. He also kept it serviced, changing the oil and having it lubricated at regular intervals. On this tune-up the mechanic servicing the car checked the spark plugs and found them carboned, so he removed all the plugs and installed new ones. When he completed the tune-up, he tried to start the engine. Instead of the purr of a well-tuned engine he listened in surprise as the engine turned over, then seized.

What had happened? When he remembered the carbon on the plugs, the cause of the engine lock was clear. The engine had become heavily carboned by the old man's relentlessly slow driving habits. Carbon had bridged over from the interior head surface to the base of the spark plugs, and when the plugs were removed, and new plugs screwed in, this bridge had cracked loose. Then as the mechanic tried to start the engine, more carbon had come loose, enough to freeze the engine. He then had to remove the head and clean the engine. If you remove spark plugs and find heavy carbon, you should plan to remove the carbon, though head removal may not be necessary.

Some mechanics use a quickie method of removing carbon that is frowned upon by other mechanics. We'll mention it only as a possiblity but *don't* recommend it for a valuable engine. Remove the air cleaner and set the throttle to run the engine at a fast idle. Get a cup of water and pour it into the air intake of the carburetor. *Pour the water very slowly*. Many people have used this shortcut to carbon removal with success, but again we must warn you that it *isn't* a recommended procedure.

Then there is the laxative method of carbon removal. Pour a quart of oil very slowly into the throat of the carburetor with the engine running at a fast idle to keep it going. After about a half quart, pour faster and drop the engine speed until the engine stops. Let the car stand for at least 24 hours, longer if possible. Restart it and drive it until the trail of blue smoke fades. The oil softens the carbon so it can pass out the exhaust without damage to the engine.

## FROZEN ENGINES

As mentioned earlier, restoring an old engine requires different techniques to that of overhauling a running engine. One of the most difficult steps is the first one you face, tearing it down. If the car has been abandoned for any period of time, left standing in the weather without any attention, there is a good chance that the engine is "frozen." Engines that haven't run for years will almost surely seize so that you can't crank them. Getting them unstuck requires careful work and great patience. Sometimes even that isn't enough. Probably the best way to suggest how to go about freeing an engine is to describe the problems one engine presented to Mike.

About ten years ago a man offered a 1941 Dodge for sale. He had gotten the car from his father who had been driving it regularly. But the man had left it standing, unused, for two years. Mike bought the car, knowing that two years is not a long time for old cars, so he expected no unusual problems with the engine. But when he got the car, he found that the engine was locked. He towed it home, removed the spark plugs, and filled each cylinder with penetrating oil. After a week the engine was stuck as solid as ever.

Considering that time and solvent alone weren't doing the job, Mike removed the head. He mopped out the excess oil and found that two cylinders were much worse than the others. He cleaned the excess rust out with sandpaper and removed the scale. Then he applied more penetrating oil and let the engine set for another week. No luck. He removed the pan, the rod caps, then pulled out the rods and pistons that were free. Because of the car's history of regular use until it was parked two years earlier, Mike had thought that he could simply free the engine and drive the car. Now he could see that it should be overhauled. He got an oak board and tried to knock the stuck pistons loose. Two pistons refused to move. Next he tried a piece of brass. Finally, in desperation, he grabbed a piece of steel and broke the pistons out of the engine. Even then, pieces of pistons clung to the walls near the position occupied by the rings. Rust had gone deep into the cylinder walls at those points. All this in *two years*.

Mike had to reassess the situation. This occurred while he was working as a mechanic but before he had his own shop. He lived in a city of over 100,000 population, renting a house with no garage. He began the work in the autumn, hoping to get the car fixed up mechanically before winter set in, but here it was

November and no shop to protect him or the car from the weather. So he bagan to improvise.

He put the car up on blocks, then crawled under it and unbolted everything in sight that would be in the way for engine removal. He unbolted the hogshead. Then he placed some heavy boards across the front fenders with a beam running parallel with the engine on top of those boards. He borrowed a manually operated fence stretcher, the kind that works like a miniature block and tackle, from a farmer. He put a chain around the engine and attached it to the fence stretcher which was attached to the beam above the engine. With that in place he could remove the final engine supports and then carefully lower the engine to the ground. Using the fence stretcher again, he dragged the engine from under the car and up an inclined plane made with the boards to the bed of his pick-up truck. Then he took the engine to a machine shop.

As restorations often do, the job had become much more expensive than Mike had estimated when he bought the car. He was just married and his budget was tight, so he asked the machine shop for an estimate on reboring the block, turning the crankshaft, and running the main bearings. When he heard the estimate, he told the shop foreman that he couldn't pay for the entire job now, so some of it would have to be postponed. The foreman made a suggestion that proved helpful to both Mike and the shop. He said they could keep the engine in the shop and work on it only when they lacked other work to do. The rate would be lower, but he couldn't guarantee a delivery date for the engine. Mike was delighted with that arrangement, so he left the engine.

Four months later, in the early spring, Mike got a call that his engine was ready. The shop had bored it out at 0.060″ oversize, far larger than the usual reboring job, to rid the cylinder walls of corrosion. Even so, there were discoloration marks in some spots, but the shop workers considered the discoloration to be insignificant at that point. The shop had put in new oversize pistons.

Mike took the engine back home and slid it along some boards into position under the body that was still up on blocks in his back yard. Then he moved an old, *sturdily* made swing set over the body. This time he borrowed an engine hoist and hung it from the pipe at the top of the swing set. With that he pulled the engine up into position and bolted it to the frame.

Mike's experience suggests that you should be prepared to overhaul and possibly have some machine work done on any engine that has been idle for more than a year or two.

## DISASSEMBLY PROCEDURE

Before you start to tear down an engine, get a set of clean cans for bolts. Glue a blank label to each and keep a fiber tip marker handy so you can write the location and purpose of the nuts and bolts or other parts you save in the cans. This is especially important for parts that are hard to replace.

Before you tear the engine down, make sure that disassembly is necessary. See if you can get the car running without major surgery. If the engine is frozen, or if you have found internal problems, you have no choice. More disassembly than necessary will probably add much more time to your restoration job than you'd expect because many old parts that would work unmolested can be damaged by trying to remove them. Old bolts can twist off, for example.

When you remove a nut that holds more than one part under it, or a combination of parts and washers, make a quick drawing to show the order of the parts. It is all too easy to go on to the next operation and later wonder which lock washer went where. For easy assembly you can sometimes replace bolts in the parts they held, using tape to hold them there until you are ready for them. Look first, then look *again* before you remove a part.

Begin disassembly by draining the cooling system, if there is any water or anti-freeze left in it. Remove the hoses, including the heater hoses. Disconnect the fuel lines, the accelerator rod, and the vacuum line at the carburetor. Remove the spark plugs (Fig. 10-5) and wires, making sure you know where each one goes. Take out the temperature sending unit, if the system is electrical. Remove the choke cable or the heat pick-up pipe if the car has an automatic choke. If it has overhead valves, remove the valve cover, then the rocker arm assembly and the push rods. You can handle this easier if you remove the carburetor. Unbolt the exhaust pipe from the exhaust manifold.

Now you can remove the head. Take it easy on the old nuts and bolts. If a nut is locked, use some penetrating oil and give it time to work. If you use brute force, you may break a bolt.

On old flathead engines the studs usually are set in the block, running up through the head with nuts holding the head down. Trying to lift one of these can be a difficult problem, particularly if the head is stuck. To solve this problem, get two old spark plugs and weld handles or hooks to the base of the plugs. Screw the plugs into two of the spark plug holes and you have a handhold near each end to help you pull the head.

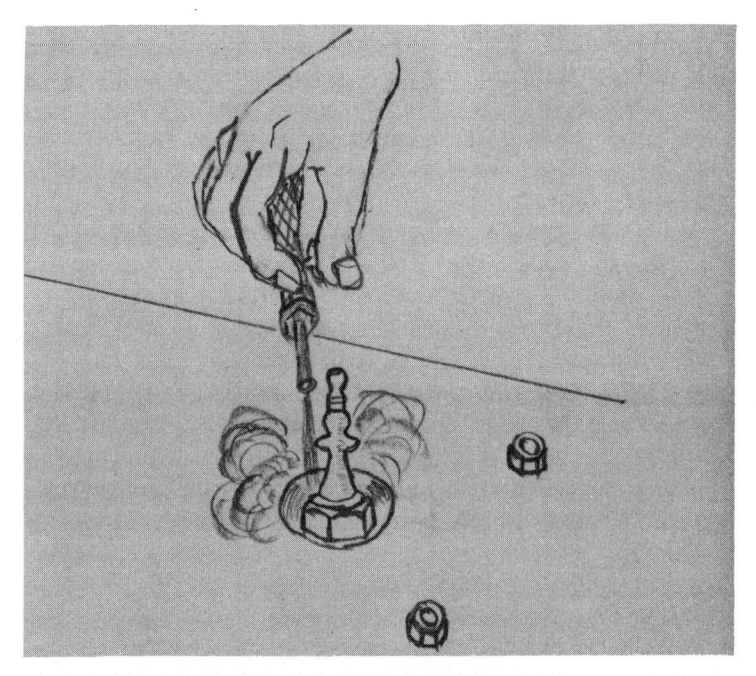

Fig. 10-5. Blow dirt out of depression around spark plugs before removing them. A piece of gravel could fall into cylinder and break a piston.

With the head removed you can get a much better estimate of how much rebuilding you will have to do. Be careful in scraping parts to check their condition; you may score some of them, espcecially aluminum piston tops. But this is a good time to clean the top surface of the block with a flat blade, removing all the old gasket or any other material. If the cylinders have a significant ridge around their tops, it should be cut off while the pistons are in the block so they will catch the cuttings.

Clean the scrapings and cuttings away and examine the parts you can see. The next step in disassembly is to remove the pan. Pan bolts rarely cause much trouble because oil seepage prevents them from corroding to the extent of head bolts. If the car has an internal oil pump, remove that next. The oil pump should be cleaned and the cover removed so you can inspect the gears. If they are smooth, you can continue to use the pump, but if they are badly marked, you should get a new one. An oil pump that breaks down in any way can ruin an engine.

Next, remove the valves. On an L-head engine you must take off the valve chamber covers to get to the springs. If you are

167

removing valves on an L-head engine with the pan on the engine, stuff pieces of cloth in any open spaces to prevent the valve retainers from falling into the crankcase. To get the valves out, compress the valve springs to raise them on the valves that are closed so that you can remove the locks. Then turn the engine over until the valves that were open are closed and remove them. Hang the valves in a numbered board so they can go back into the same position they occupied originally.

Pay special attention to the timing set-up. Make a complete sketch of the electrical hook-up, particularly the high tension wiring from the distributor cap to the spark plugs. When you remove the cover for the timing chain or gears, make a careful study of the position of the camshaft gear compared to the crankshaft gear. There may be notches or other timing marks on these gears; if there aren't, you must mark them so you can put them back in proper relation to each other. These parts should be taken down only if you have to do a complete engine rebuilding job.

After removing the valves, check the springs for proper tension. You may not be able to get specifications on this, but you can use a simple spring scale to measure the amount of tension needed to compress the springs. If you can't get the specifications for your engine, compare the readings with those required for a similar engine.

On many engines the rods will be numbered; on most in-line engines the numbers face the camshaft side of the engine. When you remove the rod, put your two thumbs on the opposite rod bolts and push the rod upward. Do this very carefully so you won't push the rod off to one side and rake the threaded portion of the rod bolt across the journal of the crankshaft. In fact, you should not touch the crankshaft journal with the rod if you can avoid it. If you doubt your ability to remove the rods without nicking the crankshaft, you can get plastic guards to cover the rod bolts.

Normally you will remove the piston and rod assembly from the top of the engine block after you push it upward in the cylinder from below. But on some engines the big end of the rod is too large, so you must remove the assembly from the bottom. This would require engine removal so you could take the crankshaft out.

When you get the pistons and rods out on your work bench, put the rod caps back on the rods. Examine the rod-piston pin attachment to see if new bushings are needed there. There are several ways that rods can be connected to the pin. The pin may be clamped to the rod, clamped to the piston, or it can be free-floating.

Except for the first type, the rod will have a bushing in it that can be replaced if badly worn. When replacing a bushing, the bushing must be reamed for proper fit. When the fit is right, the pin will not drop through the bushing of its own weight but it can move freely in the bushing if pushed. Don't forget to align any oil holes in the rod and the bushing so these parts can be lubricated.

Remove the old rings and clean the pistons, including the grooves for the rings. If you don't have a ring groove tool, you can use a broken piston ring for this job. The edges of old piston rings can be jagged, so be careful with them not to gouge the top or bottom of the ring lands on your pistons.

Ideally these jobs should be done while holding the piston in a piston vise that works something like a C-clamp with curved jaws, or you can do the job easily by clamping the connecting rod in an ordinary vise. But don't try to hold the bare piston in a vise. You will probably distort the piston or at least mar its surface.

Check the oil return holes behind the oil ring. Some pistons have slots and aren't bad about stopping up; others have drilled holes. If you find that the holes are closed, probe them with drill bits of various sizes until you find the size that fits the hole. Put the bit in your drill and redrill the holes. If you don't have the right size bit, use a smaller one. *Don't* use a larger bit. Removing extra metal from the piston is undesirable because of the possibility of weakening the piston and also because careless removal of metal can unbalance your engine.

After you have cleaned the ring grooves of all pistons, buff off the piston above the skirt with a wire brush wheel on a grinder. Don't buff the skirt.

Rinse the pistons with solvent, then dry with a clean cloth or with compressed air. Set the pistons on a clean area of your work bench. Set the first piston in your vise so that the vise clamps the shank of the rod.

## CYLINDER DAMAGE

If you find any badly damaged cylinders, your engine must be rebored. This means all new oversize pistons, of course. Any potentially valuable car will be worth the expense, but if you feel that you can't afford the whole job, there are alternatives. Suppose you tear down the engine and find just one bad cylinder. One solution would be to have the cylinder bored out and a sleeve, made to original specifications, inserted. This assumes that you can find a sleeve of the right dimensions. If you can't find a sleeve, there is one other possibility. You can have the one cylinder rebored and put a single oversized piston in it. This isn't the kind of thing your repair manual would recommend, but it has worked successfully as an emergency repair in vehicles put to far more use than your antique car will be.

Here is one example. A hauling service had an engine failure on their largest truck, one that they used daily. They had ordered a new truck, and so they didn't want to invest in a new engine or even a completely rebored engine for the old truck. The instructions to the mechanics were to get it fixed within two days. When the mechanics tore down the engine, they found that a piston pin had broken and badly scored the cylinder wall. But only one cylinder was affected. They honed the cylinder walls (Fig. 10-6), trying to remove the damage. Even after they had enlarged the cylinder diameter by 0.030", they hadn't erased all the scoring. They fitted a 0.030" oversize piston to that one cylinder, but it made a loose fit, so they knurled the piston. Knowing that there would be a certain amount of blow-by at the damaged area on the cylinder walls, the mechanics hoped that the engine would serve until the new truck arrived.

The truck went back into service and ran satisfactorily. Delay followed delay on the new truck, forcing the hauling service to use the old truck far longer than they had planned. Finally the new truck arrived, and the old truck was retired, but only after 30,000 miles had been logged by the damaged engine. This experience indicates that you can rebore a single cylinder and put in an oversize piston and have no fear of driving your vintage car in parades and to car meets. It wouldn't be a recommended procedure for a heavy-use vehicle.

## RING INSTALLATION

When you get out the package of new rings, read every word of the printed information on the package. It will tell you which ring goes in the top position. Leave each ring in its envelope until you are ready to install it so that you won't mix them. Install the oil ring first, then the ring that goes just above the oil ring, and so on up to the top ring.

To test the new piston rings for size, insert a ring into each cylinder and use a piston to push it down about one or two inches (Fig. 10-7). Use a feeler gauge to measure the gap at the joint of the ring. As a rule of thumb this gap should be about .003" to .005" per inch of cylinder diameter. If the gap is too small, the ring can break.

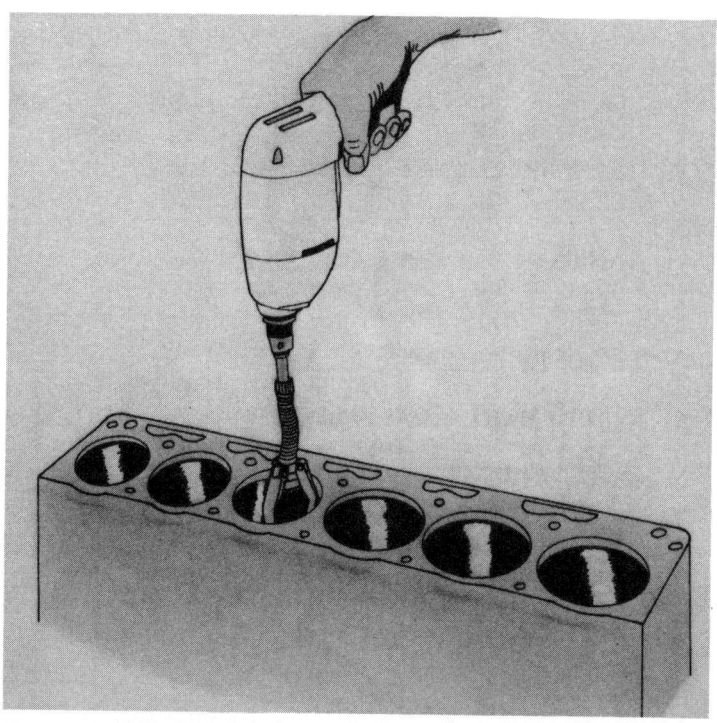

Fig. 10-6. Honing a cylinder.

When you install a ring on a piston (Fig. 10-8), twist the ring around in the grooves to see if it moves freely. If it doesn't, the groove is not clean. Remove the ring and clean the groove once more.

Remove the piston from the vise and pour some oil over the rings. It's a good idea to smear some oil over the cylinder walls, too. Put the piston back in the vise and arrange the compression ring gaps so they are 180° away from the gap on the adjacent ring and so all are 90° away from the ends of the wrist pins. Place the ring compressor over the rings, being careful not to rotate the rings, and tighten it down. Remove the piston from the vise and set it on the bench upside down. Remove the rod cap and wipe it clean of oil or other material.

When you handle the bearings, don't touch the bearing surface. And use extreme care so you don't scar the bearing surface. Carefully remove the bearings from the package and insert them in the rod and cap. Make sure each tang on the bearing goes into the notch designed for it in the rod and cap. Select a small amount of good, clean grease, such as white lithium grease, and smear a layer of it over the bearing surface. The grease should cover the inside surface of the bearing, but it should not extend onto the cap or rod parts which fit together.

Take the piston assembly to its proper cylinder. Rotate the crankshaft until the crank journal for that cylinder is at its bottom position.

Watch the position of the notch in the piston, it usually goes to the front of the cylinder. Place the piston into its cylinder. Use a hammer with a wood handle to bump the piston down, holding the hammer upright so the end of the wood handle thumps against the top of the piston (Fig. 10-9). Drive the piston down until its top is flush with the top of the block and the ring compressor is free.

At this point the work will go easier if you have a helper. One person should be under the car to guide the bolts past the crankshaft journal so they won't touch the journal and possibly nick it. When the bearing surface is firmly against the crankshaft journal, place the cap on the rod. Make sure the tangs go together; that is, the numbers should be on the same side of each. For 6-cylinder engines the numbers usually face the camshaft. Tighten the nuts snugly, but postpone the torquing until all are installed.

Fig. 10-7. Wear in old rings is shown by gap width with ring in cylinder. New ring, below, should have a gap of .003" to .005" for each inch of cylinder diameter.

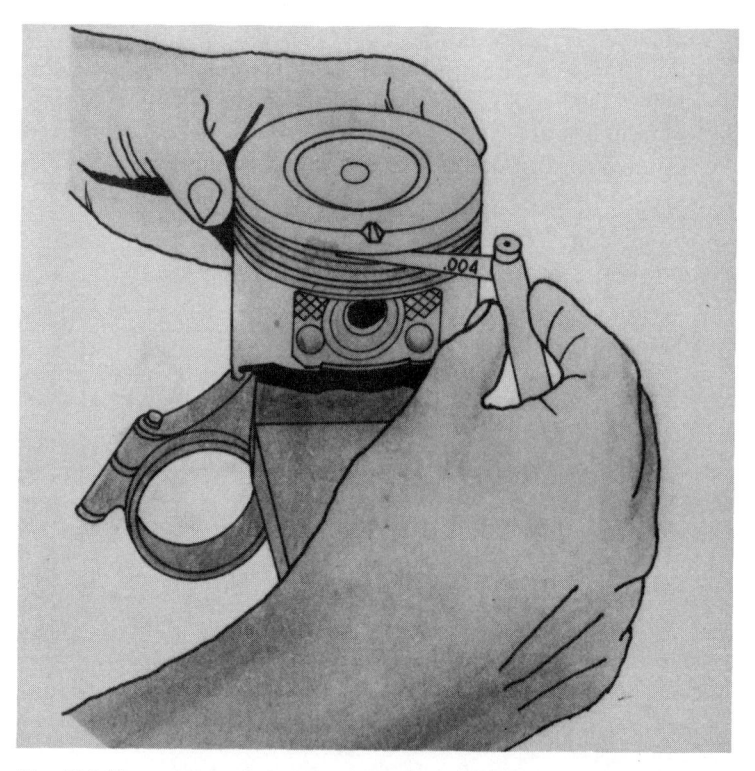

Fig. 10-8. Measuring gap between side of rings and ring lands to check ring land wear.

When you have all of the pistons in the cylinders with the rods installed on the crankshaft, look up the proper torque figure in a repair manual for your car. After the rods, replace the oil pump, making sure the distributor shaft is in place.

## BEARINGS IN OLD ENGINES

The previous procedure for installing connecting rods bearings assumes that your engine will have inserts. But if you are working on a car with poured babbit bearings, the procedure will obviously be different.

Some authorities on old car engines recommend that you resist any impulse to have the crankshaft journals machined unless it is absolutely necessary. Broken crankshafts are more of a problem with old engines than with modern ones, particularly with some old 4-cylinder engines. If you have the old crankshaft ground off, it will not be as strong as when it was new. Also the hardened surface of the journal may be impaired by grinding, making the shaft

173

wear faster. To prevent causing more problems than you solve, you should check the journal for any rough places and smooth these without removing any more metal than you have to.

If the bearing surfaces are rough, you will have to have new bearings poured. For most cars made after the late 1930s this

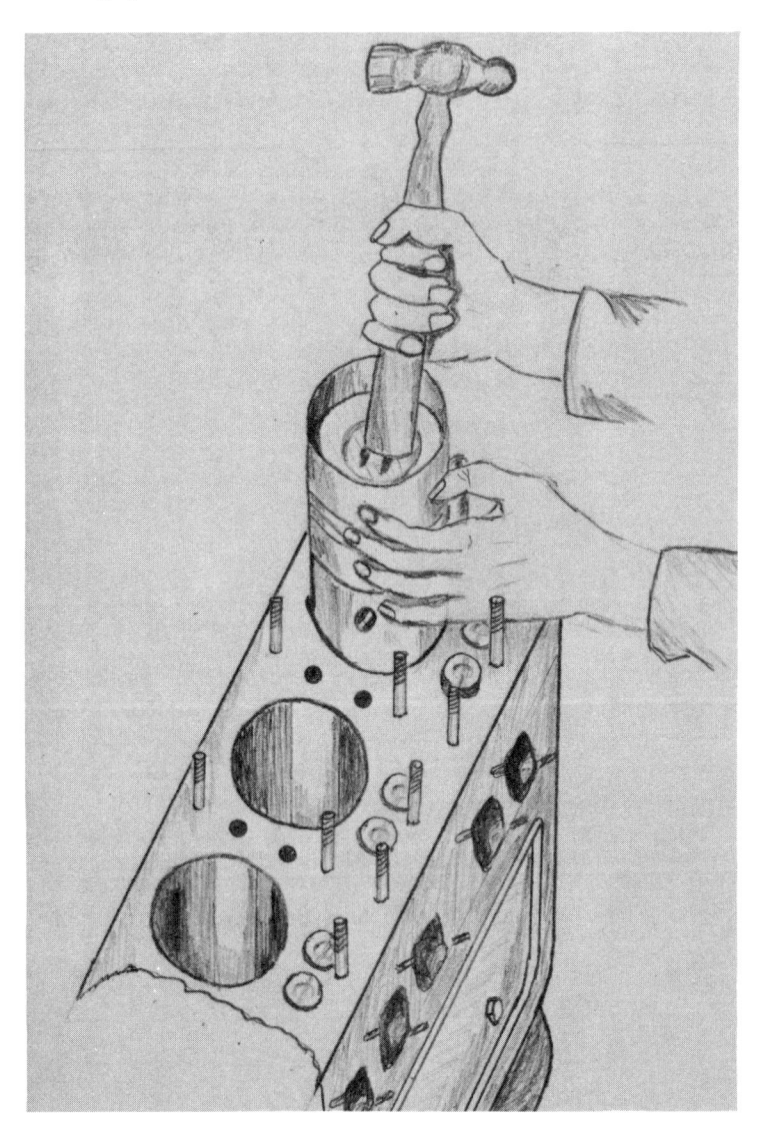

Fig. 10-9. Use wooden hammer handle to bump pistons into cylinder. Don't use steel tool for this.

means nothing more than installing inserts, but for many Chevrolets made up to the 1950s and for older cars the babbit must be poured. These old cars have babbitted connecting rods as well as main bearings. When the engine was new, the rod cap was often separated from the rod by several thin shims. As the bearings and the crankshaft became worn, the slack could be eliminated by removing one or more shims from the rod cap. After all the shims were removed, the mechanic removed the rod cap and filed it and the end of the rod until the proper fit was obtained. If you rework an old engine, you may be able to renew the bearing tolerances this way without investing in expensive new rods or having a babbit bearing poured in an old rod. Altering a connecting rod by filing is not approved for rods with inserts, but it has been used by some restorers in emergencies.

Early day mechanics who filed rod caps would install the filed cap, then tap it with a hammer and listen to the sound. Theirs was a skill that had to be learned by experience alone. Now there is an easier way to judge the right fit. You can buy a package of "PlastiGauge" and use it according to directions. To check the tolerance between the rod bearing and the crankshaft you can place a small strip of the plastic gauge material between the bearing and the crankshaft journal, then tighten the rod bolts. Remove the cap and check the width of the plastic strip against the gauge shown on the package. The width of the strip will show the clearance between the bearing surface and crankshaft.

If you are working on an engine with rod inserts, you can use pieces of shim stock to get a better fit. If the bearings are too loose, you can remove the inserts and place strips of shim stock behind the inserts. If the bearings are tight, you can use pieces of shim stock between the rod caps and the rods. The same procedure can be used for main bearings.

The easy way to fix any engine with bad bearings is to take it to a local machine shop. But if you don't want to invest that much in the engine, there are other ways to do the job, particularly if you are adventurous and can use your imagination. Here are a couple of case histories of improvisations that worked. Although these involved engines that are smaller than car engines, the principle is the same.

A man brought a tiller to Mike for repair. The engine had thrown a rod, breaking a small piece out of the block. It also had chipped a piece out of the piston skirt and chewed up the crankshaft. When he learned the cost of fixing it right, the owner vetoed the idea. So Mike began to improvise. He got a new rod, but decided to use the old piston, which he ground off until it was smooth. He bolted the new rod onto the crankshaft to test the fit. It showed considerable slack. He removed the cap and filed both the rod and the cap until the rod fit the crankshaft journal with a tight fit. Next, Mike smoothed the worst ridges off the crankshaft with emery paper. Then he put valve grinding compound on the shaft and installed the cap, and, with the crankshaft in a vise, he rotated the rod around it until he could tell by the reduced drag that the clearance between the rod bearing and the crankshaft had been increased. He removed the rod cap and filed it and the rod again. Then once again he put valve grinding compound on the bearing and the shaft and installed the cap. He rotated the rod again until the clearance was increased. After several grindings the rod and cap were seated to the crankshaft. Then he used a piece of Plasti-Gauge to set the proper clearance. The engine has been used during each summer for five years since that repair. It is still running.

Someone may point out that this was an engine with aluminum rods, and a small engine at that. But this was the kind of repair often done by small garage mechanics in the early days of the automotive era. It can easily be applied to any old car with babbit bearings in any case where repair parts are hard to find or it isn't convenient to take the engine to a machine shop.

In the days of the Model T some Ford owners repaired worn bearings with such unlikely substitute materials as bacon rinds or pieces of an old leather belt. This kind of makeshift repair is going too far for expediency, but there are other ways to substitute bearings that will work satisfactorily.

Here is how another mechanic that we know used an almost unrelated part to fix an engine. The engine was a small power plant for an old Cushman pickup, a vehicle not much larger than a moped with a small carrier on the back. The engine had a bad rod bearing, and no parts could be found. The mechanic who fixed it carefully miked the inside of the rod, with the cap bolted to the rod, then went to a storage room where he kept extra parts. He checked each bearing, no matter what its purpose, until he found a cam bearing that was just a shade wider than the required size. He put the cam bearing into the rod, then put the rod in a vise. While a helper held the bearing firmly in place, he sawed off the excess width with a hack saw, using a fine-toothed blade. Then he removed the cam bearing, which is a full circle bearing, and sawed it into two pieces so it would fit around the crankshaft. Rod bearings have tangs to keep them from turning on the shaft, so he put a tang at the proper point with a sharp chisel. Then he filed the edges of the bearing he had made to smooth it.

He carefully miked the crankshaft and then the rod bearing, finding that the bearing would be too tight for the shaft. He then got a commercial brake cylinder hone and honed the new bearing until it was about .002″ greater in diameter than the shaft. While honing he quickly went through the babbit on the bearing into the brass sub-surface. Even so the engine, after the rod was installed, ran for years doing light duty trash pick up for a college campus. Considering that an antique car will be driven very little, this same method can be used to replace a hard-to-get bearing, and the repair should be quite satisfactory.

One method of fitting bearings is to put a thin layer of Prussian Blue on the bearing surface, replace the rod on the crankshaft, and rotate the shaft. When you remove the rod, you can see any high places on the bearing where the Prussian Blue will be rubbed off. This tells you where to make significant changes in the level of babbit, either by scraping or with emery paper. You can do the final fitting with valve grinding compound.

If the crankshaft was removed from your engine, we assume that you sent it to a machine shop for reworking. In some engines you may want to replace the oil seal. The rear seals sometimes leak, causing excessive oil consumption and making a mess wherever the car is parked. Loosening the crankshaft will help in the removal and replacement of this seal. The new seal should be tapped into the upper and lower grooves behind the rear main bearing. Use a smooth rounded tool to do this. Then cut off the end of the seal with a razor blade. It is almost impossible to do this without nicking the crankshaft. If that occurs, rotate the shaft away from the cut and work the nick out of it with emery paper to prevent rapid seal wear. Clean out the dust. Braided seals seem to wear the crankshaft more than the newer neoprene but hold better on a worn engine with blow-by. If a braided seal doesn't hold the oil, run a small stiff wire behind the seal so the seal will be held against the crankshaft with more pressure.

## VALVES

Any foreign material, such as gum or carbon, on the valve stems, in the guides, or on the seats will impair valve performance. Worn valve guides, weak springs, and improperly set tappet clearances will also cause problems. In adjusting the tappets, too much clearance can cause noise, compression loss, and undue oil consumption. Tappets that are too tight will hold the valves open, causing them to burn.

In the engine disassembly, the valves will have been removed so that all the parts can be cleaned with a wire wheel brush and solvent. For difficult jobs, carburetor cleaner is effective. Inspect the seats for cracks, pits, or improper angles. If you are installing new rings and rod bearings, you should probably have the valve seats refaced regardless of how they look. This is a job you will probably want to send to a shop. If guides are needed, replace them before doing the seats. To check the fit of the valves in the seat, spread a film of Prussian Blue on the face of the valve and install it in the seat. Rotate the valve ¼ turn, then remove it and check the appearance of the Prussian Blue left on the seat. Any unevenness indicates inaccurate valve/seat surfaces. Typical seat widths are 1/16" to 3/32" for intakes and 3/64" to 1/16" for exhaust valves. Narrow seats seal better than wide ones, but unfortunately the narrow seats don't last as long. Racing engines usually have narrow seats, but racing engine mechanics expect to tear down the engine several times each season. For practical engines the seats should be at least of average width.

In some cases you will need only to remove all the old residue from the valve stems and guides to make them work properly. Test the valve stems and guides for wear by trying to shake the valve. If there is much wobble to them, replace the valves and valve guides. Bad guides can cause the valves to burn out quickly, often within a thousand miles of driving.

When removing valve guides, if you don't have the special tools that are sometimes required to correctly position the guides, you can measure that part of the guide that extends from the cylinder head on overhead valve engines and install the new guides to the same position.

Some engines do not have removable valve guides. For example, some Pontiac overhead valve engines have the valve guides cast in the head, and to repair sloppy fitted valves you must install valves with oversize stems. Reamers are available to match the hole size to the stems. This job is best done by steps. For example if you have valves with .005" oversize stems, you would ream with a .003" reamer first, then a .005" reamer. After reaming the valve guide, you must reface the valve seat and the valve.

If you check repair manuals and talk to various mechanics, you can get conflicting advice on how to set valves. Some people set their valves as the minimum clearance because they want a quiet running engine. Sometimes this not only causes burned valves, but doesn't even produce a quiet engine. While the burned valves should have been expected, tappet noises with close-set valves often bewilder the mechanic. An engine that sounds noisy because of tappets is likely to have non-uniform clearances in the valves. If the specifications call for the valves to be set at .012" and most of the valves are set perfectly but one or two are set looser, say at .015", the engine will probably make more noise than if all of the valves were set at .020". It's the out-of-beat noise that grinds on your nerves.

Experienced mechanics agree that some repair manual specifications just don't seem to work for the average repairman. For example, the old Chevrolet 6 valve specifications called for .006" on the intake valves and .012" on the exhaust valves. If you rework one of the old Chevys, set your valves at .010" and .020", and you'll have far less trouble. But make sure the settings are uniform for each type.

### Flathead Valve Adjustment

Books usually recommend that you set the valves with the engine running. You can always recognize mechanics who follow these instructions on flathead engines by the burn scars on their arms and hands. Our method on flathead engines is to measure the clearance with the engine warm but not running. Turn the engine over until the lifter for the valve you want to set is at the lowest position. If you are in doubt on this, watch the valves as you crank the engine until you can predict their sequence. When setting the exhaust valve, for example, you would turn the engine until the intake valve for that cylinder opens and closes. Most tappet adjusting screws have a lock nut that must be loosened before you can make the adjustment. The screw itself is set with a wrench, so you need two wrenches. Other adjusting screws are self locking. Turn the adjusting screw until the feeler gauge can be moved under the valve stem with a slight drag. If a range of values is given for the proper setting, always use the widest tolerance.

Old flathead Ford engines had no provision for adjustment of valves. On these engines the valve clearances must be set by grinding off the valve stem to increase the gap or by grinding down the valve seat to reduce it.

### Overhead Valve Adjustment

Overhead valves can also be set with the engine warm but not running, but, because it is much easier to reach overhead valves, these can be set while the engine is running. Instead of using two wrenches, you must use a wrench and a screwdriver to set the clearances on overhead valves. The procedure is similar to that of the L-head engines except that you use the wrench to loosen the lock-nut and the screw driver to turn the adjusting screw in the rocker arm until you feel the proper drag on the feeler gauge.

## HYDRAULIC VALVE LIFTERS

Most problems with hydraulic valve lifters are due to two causes: inadequate oil supply or dirt. If you are reworking an engine in bad condition that has hydraulic valve lifters, a complete disassembly and cleaning of the valve system is probably a good idea. To remove the lifters, first take off the rocker arms and push rods, then lift them out. If they are stuck because of carbon or varnish, tape the jaws of some adjustable pliers and use the pliers to pull them. Clean the lifters with solvent.

If several lifters quit working at once, the problem is likely to be air bubbles in the oil supply. Such bubbles are caused by an air leak at the intake side of the oil pump or by overfilling the crankcase with oil.

To adjust valves with hydraulic lifters, start the engine and get it warm. Back off the adjustment of each valve until it rattles, then turn it down until it is just quiet. Go through each valve until each one is adjusted to that point. Then shut off the engine and close the adjustment to the specifications for your engine. Specifications for cars with hydraulic valve lifters should be easy to find, but if you can't find them for your car, close the adjustment by ¾ turn.

## GASKETS

If you are working on an old car with hard-to-get parts, you should save the gaskets in case you have to re-use them. Old cork gaskets are often brittle and must be handled carefully to avoid damage to them. The passage of time causes these gaskets to dry out and to shrink. If you can remove one in a single piece, you can probably renew it well enough to use it again. Put the gasket in boiling water and watch it carefully so that you can remove it from the water as soon as it has enlarged to normal size.

Another way of solving the cork gasket problem is to buy sheets of cork of the proper thickness and cut out a new gasket. Or you can buy new cork gaskets that are similar in shape and adapt them to fit your car. Avoid butt joints on these. Instead, when joining two pieces of cork, lay one on top of the other and make an angled cut that will leave a sharp angle at the leading edge of each gasket. Then use a sealer to seal the cut edges.

The older the engine, the greater the chances that you will have trouble finding a new gasket. Mike once helped a friend, John, rework an old 1933 International truck. The engine was frozen, so Mike and John had to remove the head to bump the pistons loose with a piece of oak. They sanded the cylinder walls lightly and lubricated them with oil. When it was time to replace the head, they tried to find a new gasket, but apparently 1933 International trucks were a low volume item. After finding no new gaskets from local sources, they inspected the old gasket and found it intact. Considering that the 1933 International truck had a low compression engine, they decided that the old gasket might hold. So, after carefully cleaning the block, they used various sealers to help the gasket. Around the cylinders they used a metallic sealer; back near the water passages they used a sealer designed to seal against moisture. Then they sprayed both sides of the old gasket with a sealer and installed it. The gasket worked just fine.

## GASKET INSTALLATION

When installing pan gaskets, make sure you get all the oil off the matching surfaces. Use a sticky gasket sealer, such as 3-M Weatherstrip Adhesive on the block. The sealer holds the gasket while you work, avoiding the nuisance of having it fall into your face. When you have the gasket in place, put a fingerfull of a heavier sealer, such as #1 Permatex, at each seam between the gasket sections, if the gasket is made of more than one piece. Before you try to install the pan, place it so that the edge with the bolt holes rests on a solid surface, such as a vise or an anvil, and strike the area around each hole lightly with a flat-faced hammer. This will remove the distortion caused by previous bolting. If you fail to do this, the holes will contact the gasket before the rest of the area, possibly rupturing the gasket. Neoprene gaskets are especially subject to damage, so care must be taken with them to avoid overtightening the bolts. The older cork gaskets often shrink but, as mentioned, can be soaked in hot water for 5 or 10 minutes to bring back to proper size. When you have replaced the pan, don't forget to check the drain plug to see if it is tight. Forgetting this one step can waste all the hard work and money that you have invested in the engine.

Next step is the head. If you are rebuilding a relatively modern engine, the chances are that the head will be installed with bolts that screw into holes in the block. Engines in older cars often have permanent stud bolts in the block that protrude through the bolt holes in the head. If your engine has removable bolts, you must have some method of aligning the head with the block to avoid damaging the head gasket. Look at the block to see if there are any dowel pins that fit into short holes on the underside of the head to guide you. If there are none, you can make some guides from a couple of bolts that have the same thread as the holes in the block. Choose bolts that are at least 2 inches longer than necessary to reach through the head. Cut the heads off these bolts and screw one into the block at the rear and the other at the front. Make sure there is enough bolt sticking up to permit you to unscrew each one with lockjaw pliers after the head is down.

Check over the gasket to see if the directions on it say "use no sealer." If you don't find those words, you can assume that a sealer should be used. The sealer has two purposes: to act as a lubricant under the extreme pressure produced by torqueing the head and seal the sections between the water and oil passages. Early day mechanics often used wheel bearing grease for this job. You can check with your jobber for a useful sealer.

Apply a coating of sealer to both sides of the gasket. Install the head, then the head bolts. Before using a torque wrench to tighten the bolts, you should check a diagram for your engine that gives the bolt tightening sequence. The sequence typically starts at the bolt nearest the center, then goes to the bolts near it, alternating from one side of the center to the opposite side, both left and right and fore and aft. Use your torque wrench to apply ½ the required torque the first time around, then ¾ torque, and finally full torque. On the final torque you should reach the reading on your wrench with one firm movement of the handle. Unless you have used a Permatorque gasket, you will have to retorque after the engine is hot.

If you find that you have leaks in gaskets after they are installed, soak some string with #1 Permatex and poke it in the affected area. You may have to loosen the part first to get the string in, but this method of patching a leak will sometimes work satisfactorily. Another use for this technique is on an old engine that is badly worn and that you don't intend to rebuild soon. Such engines have considerable blow-by which often damages gaskets, such as the pan gasket. To save pulling the pan, or other part, on a worn engine, you can use the string and Permatec treatment.

## ENGINE SWAPS

If you aren't doing a full-fledged restoration job, you may be tempted to install a modern engine in your old car. This will no doubt give you a more reliable engine, but such a swap doesn't guarantee trouble-free highway driving from coast to coast. The old drive parts, rear axles, and other components may be subject to failure at modern highway speeds and after high mileage. The metal in old parts may not be able to withstand the torque of a more powerful engine unless you use it carefully.

For some cars this kind of swap makes sense. If you can't find the necessary replacement parts for your old engine without paying a king's ransom, you may decide that authenticity isn't worth the cost. To guide you on such a job, here are some hints based on the experiences of other people, including Mike, at putting modern engines in old cars.

First, don't buy an engine at one salvage yard and a transmission at another. If possible, get both from the same vehicle. This will prevent a multitude of problems in adapting one to the other.

To install the engine and transmission, remove the fenders of the old car. Install the engine and transmission as one unit. Lower the engine down into the chassis, but hold the weight of the engine so it isn't on the chassis yet. Build your engine mounts from side to side first. Spend some time planning the arrangement of your engine mounts so they won't be in the way of other parts. Most cars today have cross members under the oil pan, which means that you have to pull the engine to remove the oil pan. You may want to take the pan off occasionally to check bearings or clean out sludge, so try to plan your mounts so that you have access to the pan. Check several cars, note how the engine mounts are installed, and compare mounts on old cars with new cars. You can adapt Detroit's methods to fit your own situation and yet have access if you plan carefully.

To level the engine you can use a carpenter's level across the air horn of the carburetor. If the carburetor is off, you can put the level on the intake manifold. Run the level across the engine first, that is, at right angles to the length of the car.

Don't try to get the engine in the exact center of the space available. Put it slightly to the right center. There it will allow more room for the steering components as well as provide better balance in the car. There are more components with weight on the left side of the engine, and the driver will also be on the left.

When you have the engine level, with the level at right angles to the frame, put a jack under the transmission so you can use it to level the engine from front to back. Build the rear crossmember.

Try to keep the elevation of the engine at a reasonable level so it won't drag the ground or hit any bumps that you drive over. Center the rear of the transmission as well as possible. It is all right to have the engine angled right slightly because the drive shaft will absorb the deviation from a straight line. Mike has put in some engines that angled right with respect to drive shaft, and they have run for 100,000 miles with no problems. The drive shaft itself must be reasonably straight so that the U-joints won't be in too much of a bind. You can get an idea on how to do this by sighting down the shaft of several factory cars. If the angle on your car looks excessive, change the front mounts until it looks right—no fancy geometry.

If your car has the possiblity of being a candidate for later authentic restoration, don't weld mounts for a swap engine to the frame. Instead bolt them on. And there is another reason for not welding old frames—the possibility of frame cracks. These frames are usually made of high carbon steel, so heat drives the carbon some distance away from the weld where it can cause that area to crack under stress. Mike learned this the hard way when he put an Olds 350 engine and automatic transmission in an old 1956 GMC pick-up. He welded some brackets to the frame, knowing that he would never restore the truck, then had continual problems with frame breaks which always occurred a short distance from a weld. He finally reduced the problem by using a stainless steel welding rod, altering the composition of the metal. Rather than welding an old frame and driving the carbon into a carbon "ridge," use bolts. Welding will probably just produce new cracks; bolt where possible.

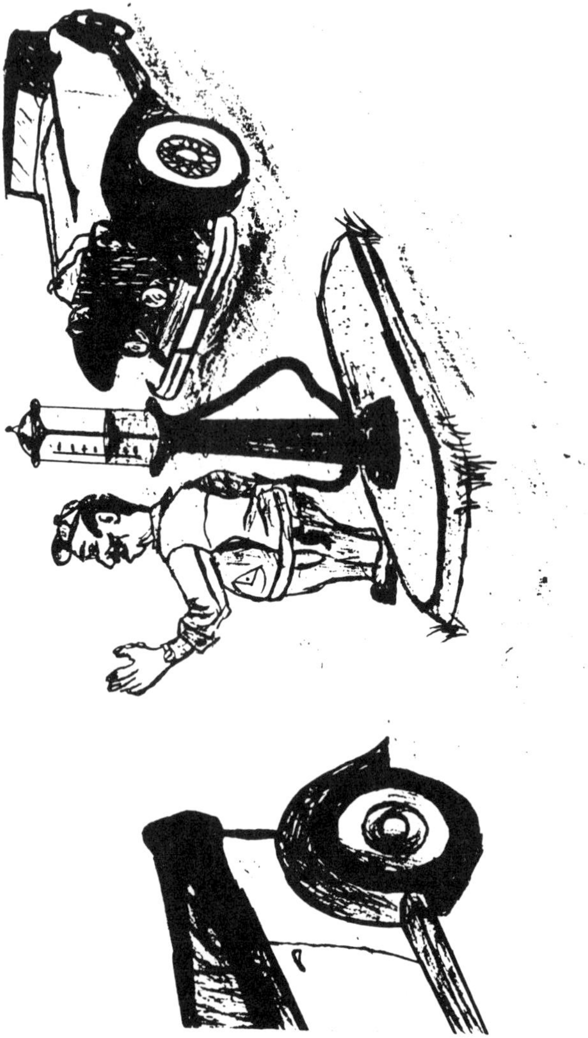

# Chapter 11
# Fuel Systems

With modern cars that are in daily use, fuel systems probably cause fewer problems than ignition systems. But for old cars, particularly those that have been abandoned for months or years, you will find that the fuel system adds its share of troubles. Some of these difficulties with old cars would never occur in your typical family automobile, so when restoring a car, you must treat every part of the fuel system with suspicion. A thorough checking of it will prevent the kind of situation that can later try your resolve to restore another car. A logical path to follow in examining the fuel system is that of the fuel itself, from tank to carburetor.

Before you start to work on the fuel system, *think safety*. Accidents with gasoline can happen in some almost unpredictable ways, so use care in handling it. *Don't* store the gasoline in glass bottles. Put it in a metal gasoline container, the kind that is sold in auto stores, or in a reasonable substitute. Some kinds of plastic are all right, but gasoline acts on others causing them to decompose and pollute the fuel. *Never* leave gasoline uncovered or in the sun. Mike once set a partially filled open can of gasoline near the door of his shop. A man walked into the shop, smoking a cigarette. Then he flipped the butt onto the floor where it briefly flared. A flame danced about six inches above the floor from the spot where the cigarette hit to the pan of gas about fifteen feet away. Mike stopped the fire by throwing a piece of tin across the can. This illustrates one fact about gasoline vapor; it is heavier than air, so it settles. Handle fuel with great respect, especially if you smoke or if anyone helping you smokes.

## GAS TANK

We will start with the gas tank cap. You may feel that any cap that fits your tank will work equally well, but there are two kinds of caps that can't be interchanged: vented and unvented. If the cap is missing on your car, you should determine whether the tank is vented by a separate pipe, as some are, or whether it needs a vented cap. Many late model cars vent through a charcoal filter and can operate with an unvented cap, so the typical new cap you buy will be unvented. But if you put one of these on a tank that has no built-in vent, you'll have problems. The car engine will probably start and permit you to drive a short distance down the road; then it will quit. If you wait a while, more air will seep into the tank and it will start again. Then the same routine. To avoid this kind of frustrating behavior, find out what kind of cap you should install before you locate a replacement. If your old car has a gas tank cap, it is probably the right kind, but not always. If your car shows the symptom mentioned above, try removing the gas tank cap and see if that cures the trouble.

When you get your car, there may be some old gasoline in the tank, but it probably should be drained out. Stored gasoline loses its more volatile fraction, the part that evaporates quickly and aids in starting your car in cold weather. If the car has been idle for an extended period, the gasoline may have turned to a jelly-like material in the bottom of the tank. You can remove this material by adding fresh gasoline, which acts as a solvent on the residue.

Another frequent problem with gas tanks on abandoned cars is rust. People usually see that the tank is almost empty before they park a car for the last time, and empty tanks rust. Most old gas tanks have a drain plug which you can remove to drain any old gasoline or condensed water. If the tank is rusty, take it to a car cleaning service and have it steam cleaned. If that doesn't remove the rust, put some large gravel or small rocks in the tank and agitate the tank until the entire inner surface has been worn clean. A tank that has rusted once will easily rust again, so you should keep it well filled with fuel after it is installed.

Some old tanks will have holes in them that require welding. This is a high-risk job. Take the tank to someone who has had experience at welding gas tanks. It is the kind of job that quickly separates the experienced and careful worker from those who are inexperienced or careless. Welders who work on gas tanks prefer to have a gasoline filled tank to one that is empty. The reason: liquid gasoline will burn if ignited, but gasoline vapor can explode.

One man that we know runs the exhaust from a car engine into the tank for many minutes before welding and during the welding process on the theory that carbon dioxide and carbon monoxide from the exhaust will displace the oxygen in the tank and prevent an explosion. Another fellow uses solder to patch gas tanks. He tins the hole and his metal patch first, then "sweats" them together. We prefer to take this job to a professional and let him use his favorite method. You can buy products that permit you to patch tanks without welding. If you decide to do it yourself, you can try one of these.

## GAS LINES

Old car gas lines are usually threaded together with couplings, similar to natural gas lines in house systems. When you remove one of these joints, make sure you put a piece of tape over the end of the line to protect it from dirt or other material that can cause serious problems later. Tape the fitting to the line so it won't be pushed along the line. Old lines frequently have fine pin holes that permit air seepage and prevent proper fuel pumping. To test for leaks, plug one end of the line and apply pressure to the other end, either by compressed air or by blowing on it. You can often locate leaks by listening for them, but if you immerse the line in water, you can check visually for air bubbles. Another way to test the line is to tape one end and suck on the other end. You can tell the line is leaking if you feel any air movement from the line into your mouth.

Many early fuel systems have a rubber flex line that carried the gasoline from the tank to the metal line located in the frame. These rubber lines sometimes collapse, stopping the flow of fuel. Some systems have a cut-off valve near the tank. If you can't get fuel from the tank to the fuel pump, check for a closed valve or a collapsed flex line.

If your old car is running but you have doubts about the fuel system, you can test the fuel line with a vacuum gauge (Fig. 11-1). First, run the engine until the fuel pump and carburetor are full of fuel. Then connect the vacuum gauge where the line enters the fuel pump. Make a reading on the gauge with the engine running. Then disconnect the gauge from this point and reconnect the line. Connect the gauge at the tank end of the line. If the reading at the tank end is lower than that at the fuel pump, there is a leak in the fuel line.

Some cars will have a filter in the tank over the pick-up tube. These frequently are plugged. If the filter on your tank is plugged, you will have to take the tank off the car to get to the filter, even if

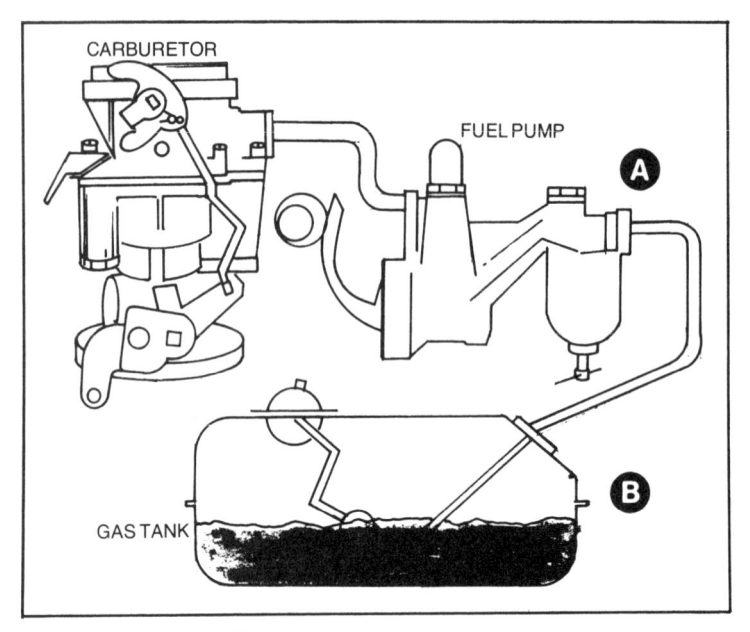

Fig. 11-1. Fuel system. To check for leaks in gas line, connect vacuum gauge at point A, then at point B. Readings should be identical.

the tank is perfect in other ways. People often try to avoid this job by applying compressed air to the line in the reversed direction of the fuel flow. This rarely works. Such filters aren't essential to proper operation of your fuel system, so you can simply remove a plugged filter. Filters that appear in the line *after* the fuel pump are more practical than those that appear before the pump.

## VACUUM TANKS

Some early production cars and many antiques will have a vacuum tank fuel system (Fig. 11-2). On these systems the fuel is transferred from the tank to the vacuum tank by air pressure. The vacuum tank is really a tank within a tank. The details of vacuum tank construction vary with different tanks. In a typical tank a line from the intake manifold runs to the inner tank where it creates a partial vacuum. This permits the normal atmospheric pressure to push gasoline from the fuel tank through the gas line up to the vacuum tank. A float in the inner tank, which is connected to a valve in the upper part of the inner tank, permits gasoline to flow into the tank until it reaches the proper level; then it cuts off the vacuum line from the manifold. The gasoline flows from there into the lower tank where it flows by gravity to the carburetor. Because gravity flow is necessary, the vacuum tank must be located high on the car's firewall. Some vacuum tanks have a petcock on the bottom so you can shut it off to work on the carburetor. If there is no petcock there, you will lose the gasoline in the vacuum tank each time you remove the line to the carburetor.

Vacuum tanks are often rusted and pitted for the same reasons that these problems afflict old gas tanks. The repairs are much the same as for a gas tank. Some restorers have used fiberglass materials to patch old vacuum tanks and make them work. But even veteran restorers say that the vacuum tank can be the Achilles heel of an otherwise successful restoration. One man told us he doubted if they *ever* worked well, even when they were new. We don't know about that.

Here is how one restorer solved a recurring vacuum tank problem. He had a 1931 LaSalle that ran perfectly—as long as the vacuum tank worked. Unfortunately, he couldn't keep the car going because the vacuum tank would interrupt the flow of fuel to the carburetor, usually at an embarrassing moment. He finally in-

Fig. 11-2. Many antique cars have a vacuum tank high on firewall to bring gas from tank in rear. Note oil can here, used to oil rocker arms in morning and at 50 mile intervals.

191

stalled an electric fuel pump under the seat of the car. He ran the electric line to the fuel pump through the ignition switch so the ignition switch would have to be turned on before the pump would work. When he turned on the switch, the pump would give out a click-click-click sound. This kind of sound would arouse suspicion in anyone who knows anything at all about 1931 LaSalles. In fact, it was downright uncharacteristic of *all* cars of that vintage. So the owner put a secret switch in the line between the ignition switch and the electric fuel pump. With the extra switch in the line he could start the engine first, then switch on the fuel pump, and the engine noise would mask the sound of the pump. From that time he had no more fuel line problems. A very effective solution to a nagging problem, but hardly an authentic restoration. If you see someone with a 1931 LaSalle who refuses to permit anyone else to drive it, you can guess why.

If you install an electric fuel pump on an old car, make sure you wire it through the ignition switch so it will be shut off with the engine. A man driving a dump truck once stopped at Mike's shop with a bad fuel pump. Mike connected an electric fuel pump in the gas line while the man, who was in a great hurry, found a hot wire to operate it. As the man left, Mike told him to disconnect the hot wire as soon as he stopped the truck, or to bring the truck back so they could wire it through the switch. But when the pump worked, the man forgot Mike's warning to come back and do the job right. Three weeks later, after stopping for lunch, the driver found that the starter wouldn't turn the engine over. He thought the starter had gone bad, so he got another truck to pull him. When he let out the clutch, the engine made a noise that worried him. Later inspection showed that a piston and rod assembly was bent and a chunk of iron was torn out of the block. What caused the destruction of the engine? The electric fuel pump kept pumping after the engine was shut off. Normally the carburetor needle valve would stop the flow of fuel when it was full, but this time the needle and seat finally gave way to the pressure on them, and the cylinders with intake valves open filled with liquid gasoline. This caused a hydraulic lock on the engine. The driver's impulse to hurry cost him hundreds of dollars.

**FUEL PUMPS**

If you suspect the fuel pump, or any part of the fuel system before the carburetor, loosen the fuel line at the carburetor and crank the engine. If gasoline spurts out of the line, the fuel system is working well enough to get the engine going. Experience with pumping rates of various cars will allow you to estimate if the flow of fuel is adequate, but it shouldn't take more than a few seconds to fill a pop bottle.

One of the symptoms of fuel pump problems is loss of power on acceleration. When the pump fails to supply enough fuel for a steady engine rate, choking the car may produce better running as the choke balances the air inflow to match that of the fuel.

Vapor lock can be another symptom of fuel pump problems, although this trouble isn't necessarily a sign that the pump is bad. Old cars were more subject to vapor lock than modern cars. One early remedy was to put clothespins on the fuel line. The clothespins acted as insulators, especially where the line ran close to a hot engine. Another solution is to change a metal line to a rubber line, but this can compromise the authenticity of your vintage car. If a metal line runs close to the engine, increasing the distance by bending the line away into the open will help. Any alteration that makes your engine run cooler will reduce the chances of vapor lock, so you should inspect the cooling system if vapor lock continues after you have checked the fuel pump. If everything else fails, you can add about 10% kerosene to the fuel during hot weather.

To service a fuel pump, disassemble it, recording the order of part removal, and wash the parts in kerosene. Blow the parts dry, except for the diaphragm. Fuel pump repair kits used to be available, but are not now unless you can find NOS parts. If you can find a new diaphragm, soak it in kerosene to improve flexibility before installing it. When you tighten the screws that hold the two halves of the pump together, hold the rocker arm to the end of its stroke. Tighten the screws gradually, moving from one to the opposite screw.

With an old car there is a chance that you won't be able to find either a repair kit or a rebuilt pump of the same model. One way to meet this problem is to find a rebuilt pump that is similar to the original pump. Take your old pump to a parts house and compare the available rebuilts to find the one that most closely resembles it. Choose one that is put together with screws, if possible, so you can take it apart easily. Remove the screws and pull the halves apart. The diaphragm will usually have a metal insert in the center with a spring-loaded arm that works it. You can probably transfer the diaphragm to your fuel pump.

Fuel pumps have two check valves, an input valve and an output valve. There are at least three kinds of check valves: a floating wafer, a neoprene flap, or a ball in a brass seat. Regardless of the kind of fuel pump or the make of car, these valves usually are interchangeable. You should have no difficulty substituting a valve from a rebuilt fuel pump to the original fuel pump. Drive the valves out of the rebuilt pump and press them into the pump that fits your car.

Many old cars will have no filter on the fuel system. You may want to install a filter to insure getting clean fuel to your carburetor, especially if you aren't doing an authentic restoration. If you have a weak system, it is better to install the filter on the side of the fuel pump which has higher pressure in it.

Fuel pumps can produce various symptoms from wasting gas by excessive pressure to a loss of power or constant dying. One delivery truck had a habit of stopping dead intermittently. After standing for a few minutes the truck would start again and run for an indefinite period of up to a couple of hundred miles before it would die again. Sometimes the next unscheduled stop occurred within a dozen miles. When mechanics finally took the fuel system apart, they found half of a flat washer in the fuel pump. When the truck would hit a bump, the washer would bounce up into the fuel hole, blocking it. When the truck stopped for a while, the washer would drop down again, and the fuel would flow until the truck would hit another bump. Apparently the piece of washer had been left in the pump at the factory. Moral: check your fuel pump, and other parts of the fuel system, for foreign objects.

## CARBURETORS

Before you start to work on any carburetor, here is a caution: *Never* use a magnetic screwdriver on a carburetor. If you do, you will magnetize some of the parts, such as screws, and they will pick up any particles of steel in the fuel. The particles will become magnetized and can adhere to small check valves, needle and seat, or other critical parts of the carburetor. Even if you have no magnetic screwdrivers among your tools, you should check any kind of screwdriver to see if it has become magnetized before you use it on a carburetor. There are many ways that tools can be subjected to a magnetic field, either around a car or in use with other equipment. For example, if you ever use a screwdriver near a television, radio or stereo set, the magnets in the speakers can magnetize it. To test your tools for magnetism, sprinkle some small steel shavings on a flat surface and see if the tool will attract them. You can sometimes demagnetize a tool by hitting it several times.

Most old cars have carburetors that are fairly simple. The usual problem with these carburetors will be an improper mixture, usually too rich, or an engine that won't idle. The symptom of the first problem is black smoke from the exhaust, usually evidence of a stuck float or needle valve. In the case of an engine that refuses to run at a certain speed, the problem is likely to be a stopped-up jet. The cure for these two kinds of carburetor problems is the same: disassemble and clean the carburetor.

Sometimes the dirt or other foreign particles that lodge in the carburetor and cause trouble can be so small that you can't see them. Such small pieces of metal or dirt can lodge under the needle valve and cause overflow. If your cleaning doesn't eliminate the problem, try tapping the carburetor lightly with a wrench. Hit it gently near the area where the fuel enters the carburetor. Sometimes the flow of gasoline will dislodge the particle so it will pass through the system. This technique can be used with any carburetor that doesn't appear to have been abandoned long enough to need a thorough cleaning.

In some cases you will find that the old carburetor has been damaged by corrosion or by physical damage. For a thoroughly authentic restoration you will want to match the original carburetor. But if you don't plan a completely genuine restoration, you can probably find a carburetor to fit your car. Throughout automotive history there have been so many kinds of carburetors produced that there are many models that have bolt patterns to match.

If you are trying for authenticity, but your carburetor has internal damage, you can probably fit the parts from another carburetor into your old carburetor. The internal parts of carburetors are much more interchangeable than those of other components. (The one common exception to this rule is the British S.U. carburetor found on M.G.'s and other English cars.) Even if the parts aren't identical, you can sometimes make them work. For example, if a float arm is too wide, you can snip it down. Or you can unsolder a float from one float arm and solder it onto another one. Or remove check valves from one carburetor to put into another, much the same operation that you would do with a faulty fuel pump valve.

If the float has holes in it, you can patch it with solder. When soldering brass floats, the heat will expand the air in the float so that some of it escapes before the hole is soldered. This leaves a partial vacuum inside the float. When you finish soldering the float, cool it slowly. If you allow it to cool too quickly, it may collapse. Some floats will collapse even if cooled slowly after soldering, but more will collapse if cooled quickly.

Some cars, fairly recent models, have composition floats. These appear to be similar to cork but of denser material. When they have been used for a long time, they absorb gasoline and sink, overflowing the carburetor. Such floats must be replaced.

A running car rarely has problems that are caused by the carburetor. Most carburetor troubles arise after the car has been standing idle for months or years. In such cars the gasoline will evaporate, leaving a gummy residue or permitting corrosion to occur. Dirt is sometimes a problem with old cars because the car has no filter or the filter was removed at some time in the car's history. All of these conditions suggest one remedy: clean the carburetor. But don't disturb the carburetor if it is functioning well.

When changing carburetors the fuel line (Fig. 11-3) may have to be repositioned, sometimes causing new problems. Make sure that any connections you make are leak proof. And that there are no joints over the distributor. One car owner installed a filter in his old car without noticing that the filter was positioned over the distributor. When he started the car, the line leaked gasoline onto the distributor. The next step was as sure as night and day—a spark ignited the fuel. When the gasoline started to burn, it set off the vapor that had already collected under the hood. The driver didn't have to open the hood to get at the fire. In addition to blowing the hood open, the explosion changed the shape of the valve cover. After installing a new valve cover, the car owner rerouted the fuel line before he tried to start the car again.

## FUELS AND EFFICIENCY

People who have trouble starting their cars with gasoline in winter sometimes add a more volatile substance to the carburetor. The typical choice is ether. Mike knew a couple of boys in high school who had built an old Chevy into what they called the "Ultimate Six." These fellows were extremely proud of their vehicle, looking down on the cars driven by other people at their school. Their attitude, of course, didn't make them candidates for any "most popular" awards. One frigid winter day the Ultimate Six wouldn't start. The brothers did what many others had done under similar circumstances, they poured some ether into the carb. When they hit the starter, there was an explosion that cracked the head on their pride and joy. Which brings us to a caution: If your old car

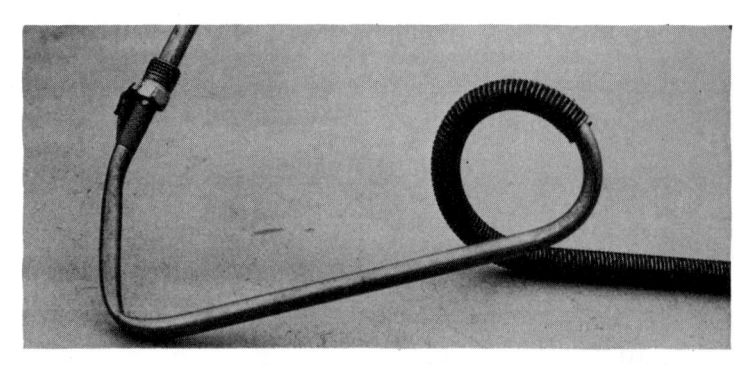

Fig. 11-3. If you install new steel tubing gas lines, slip a spring over line while making bends. Note kink at left where no spring was used.

won't start on a cold day and you are tempted to use ether, *use it sparingly*.

Gasoline mileage is rarely a big consideration for the car restorer, unless the car is driven to work. It is interesting to consider some of the practices of hot rodders of the 1950s and 1960s which may have become obsolete for most people. For example, some of that crowd used to pack dry ice around the intake manifold. The dry ice lowered the temperature of the fuel so that more raw gas would be drawn into the cylinder where the heat would vaporize it. The theory was that the extra fuel would give more power. Now the approach by most people, with today's gasoline prices, it to get *less* fuel into the cylinders. One way that Mike has explored is to use hot air by installing the air filter intake near the hot exhaust manifold. This method seems to give about 5% better gasoline mileage.

A similar technique was adopted during the depression years to save on gasoline, one that you may not encounter on antique cars but will likely find on production cars made after the early 1930s. It is a transfer box, a device that used heat from the exhaust gases to maintain the vaporized condition of the fuel in the intake manifold. This device can cause serious problems if there is a hole in the chamber walls. The car will act as if there is a stuck valve, making a popping noise. The engine will run but has no power. If your car has this transfer box and the engine has the symptoms mentioned above, check the box chamber for holes. These chambers are usually made of thin steel which must be brazed rather than electric welded.

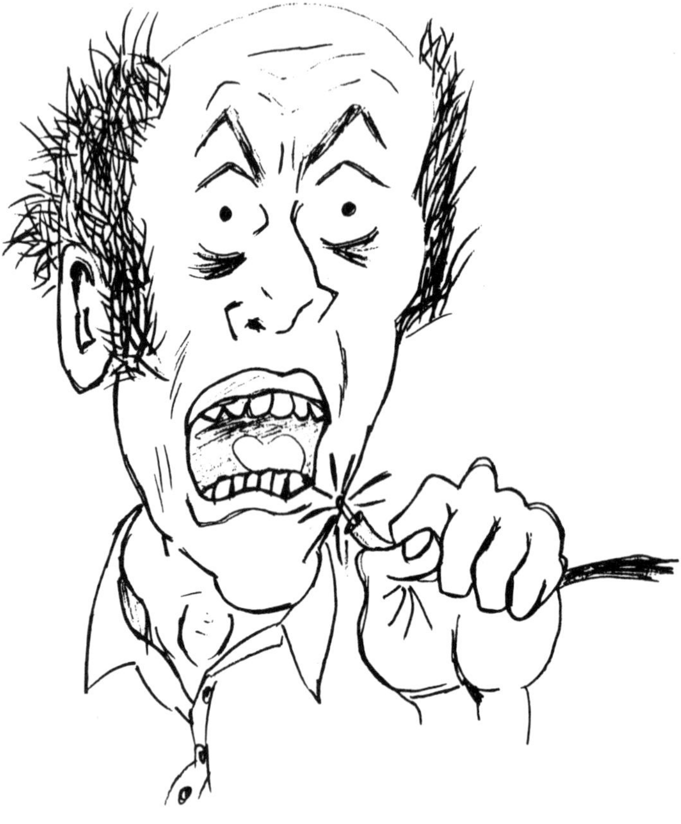

# Chapter 12
# Electrical Systems

Most mechanical repairs require a certain minimum tool kit, but you can service the electrical system of your old car with little more than a pair of long nose pliers. A VOM (volt-ohm-meter) is a desirable tool for checking the condition of the battery, voltage regulator, and the wiring, but for most electrical troubleshooting you can use some homemade electrical tools.

Some mechanics make their living working on cars with very little knowledge of how the electrical system works. Many, for example, don't realize that the points work in the low voltage circuit, although the rotor just above them operates at high voltage. You don't have to have a degree in electrical engineering to work on your car's wiring, but it helps to have a general understanding of how electrons behave in a circuit.

## SOME BASICS

You probably already know that voltage is measured in volts, current in amperes, and resistance in ohms. Ohm's law is the most essential law of electricity because it explains the relationship of voltage, resistance, and current in a circuit. It tells us that voltage is equal to current times resistance. It is usually expressed mathematically in the formula $E = IR$, where E is voltage in volts, I is the current in amperes, and R is the resistance in ohms.

If you examine this formula, you will see that, for a certain supply voltage, if the resistance is raised, the current must decrease. The relationship is easier for most people to see if we rewrite the formula in terms of current, as follows: $I = E/R$.

Observe that there are two ways to increase the current in a circuit. You can raise the voltage, which increases the electrical pressure that drives the electrons through the circuit. Or you can decrease that which impedes the flow of electrons, the resistance. To decrease the current you can reduce the voltage or increase the resistance. For automobile electrical systems the voltage is set at 6 or 12 volts by the car manufacturer, so changing that is not a real option. Unless, of course, the current through the system is low because of a low or dead battery.

If you can keep these relationships in mind, you should have no trouble understanding how a particular circuit works. To visualize electron behavior, look at diagram A in Fig. 12-1. It shows a typical circuit with a battery as the source and a resistive load. The load could be the filament in a lamp, for example. The arrows show the actual direction of electron flow, from negative to positive. A negative battery pole has a surplus of electrons, the positive pole, an insufficiency. In the battery the two poles are isolated from each other, and yet the surplus electrons are repelled from the negative pole and attracted to the positive pole. The potential difference, or voltage, forces the electrons through the load in the circuit and back to the positive pole. By convention, the current is considered to flow from positive to negative, but the reverse is the real direction it flows.

**TROUBLESHOOTING**

In addition to a dead battery there are three possible problems in electrical wiring: open circuits, short circuits, and points of high resistance. These problems are shown in Diagrams B, C, D, and E of Fig. 12-1.

An open circuit is just what the term indicates, a break in the circuit. The break can be caused by a blown fuse, an unplugged connection, or a broken wire. Broken wires can take many forms. The wires can be obviously broken, as happens if something catches the wire and rips it apart. But if the wire breaks inside the insulation because of frequent flexing, you will have to track it down with a test instrument. Diagram B shows a break in the ground lead, but a break anywhere in the circuit stops the flow of electrons.

A short circuit occurs when a conductor touches the opposite side of the circuit somewhere between the source and the load. A positive wire, for example, can touch the frame or other grounded part, bypassing the load. When a short occurs, the load is out of the effective circuit. Instead of the current limiting element, the load, the short circuit is composed of low resistance wiring, so the current flow in it is heavy. Because the positive to ground short offers negligible resistance, it steals current from the normal load, starving it. So the lights, or whatever load is designed into that circuit, won't work. The wire usually becomes the limiting element in a short circuit. When its ability to conduct current is exceeded, it gets hot.

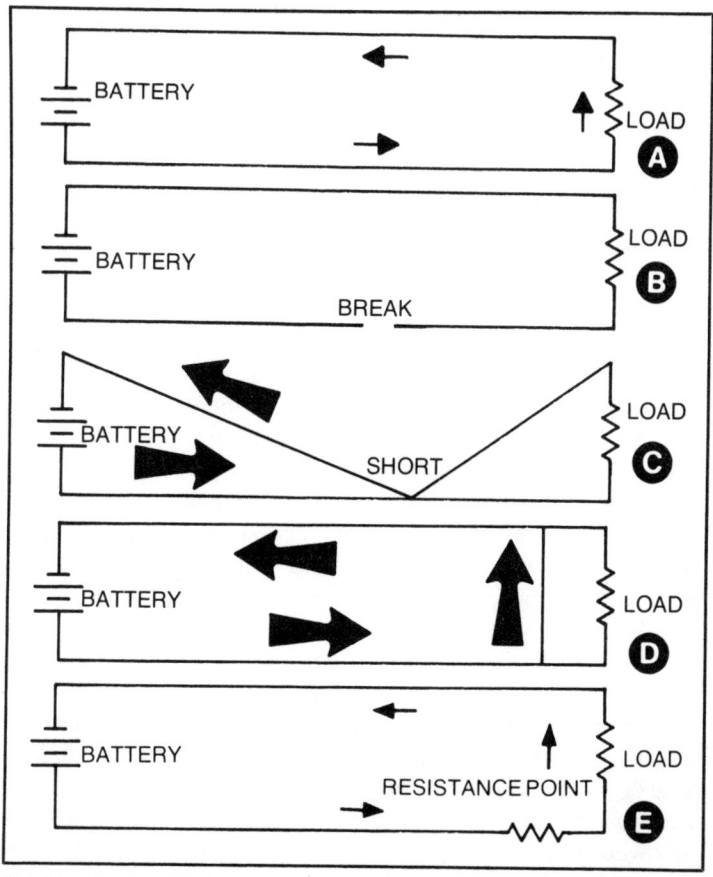

Fig. 12-1. Problems that can develop in simple auto circuits.
A) Simple circuit, normal current flow.
B) Open circuit, no current flow.
C) Short circuit, such as wire drooping onto frame. Heavy current flow in short circuit, no current through load.
D) Short circuit, conductor bridging load. Heavy current flow in short circuit, no current through load.
E) Resistance point. Resistance added by bad connection, corrosion, or other cause. Current flow reduced because of higher resistance in circuit.

If you go back to the formula for current, you will see that as the resistance approaches 0, the value of the current would appear to become infinitely high. In a practical situation this would never occur because a tremendously large current would quickly discharge the battery. And the wire would get so hot that its resistance would increase greatly, limiting the current.

Diagrams C and D show typical short circuits which are identical electrically but have different causes. In C the short was caused by a wire drooping onto the frame or ground lead. D shows a separate piece of wire or metal shorting out the load.

Resistance points almost always occur at connections. Corroded contacts in the connectors add considerable resistance to the circuit. To eliminate this possibility, check all points in the circuit where two wires join or where a wire bolts onto a part such as a starter.

Another way that resistance in a circuit can be increased is by partially broken stranded conductors. If some of the strands are broken and do not touch each other, the effective diameter of the wire will be reduced. The resistance of any material is inversely proportional to the cross-sectional area of the material. So when the wire diameter is reduced, its resistance increases.

Still another possible cause of a resistance point sometimes occurs after someone has tinkered with the wiring. This often occurs if the tinkerer failed to make an adequate connection when replacing connectors. This kind of resistance point can sometimes be located by a visual inspection. Look on any disturbed section of wiring with suspicion.

In some cases, resistance points can cause heating. For example, if half the strands of a wire are broken, the remaining strands must carry the current for the load. The total current will be somewhat lower than that of the undamaged circuit because the resistance of the damaged wire is added to that of the load. This kind of hot circuit won't blow a fuse. The total current will be less than that of the original circuit because the resistance of the damaged wire is added to that of the load. So if you see smoke but the fuse doesn't blow, suspect this kind of problem.

## TROUBLESHOOTING WITH METERS

There are two kinds of test meters that will help you troubleshoot the circuits in your car, an ammeter and a volt-ohm-meter—often called a VOM. Almost any small VOM will be adequate to check car wiring. You can make a useful current test meter from an old car ammeter and a couple of heavy wire conductors. Attach the wire conductors to the connection points on the ammeter and put alligator clip connectors at the free ends. Most small VOMs have a milli-ammeter built into the instrument, but they can be used safely only in a current range of micro to milli-amps. The heavy current present in automobile electrical circuits would cause immediate destruction of the meter unless it was properly shunted to match the circuit. It is much simpler to adapt a car ammeter, as described above.

In using the meters, remember that to measure current you must place the ammeter *in series* with the load (Fig. 12-2). When the meter is in series, every electron must travel through the meter, permitting it to measure that current.

To measure voltage, you must find the potential difference at two points in the circuit, usually across the battery, across the load, or across a part of the load if there is more than one load element in series. When you touch the leads of a voltmeter across the circuit, some current must flow through the meter, but not enough to load down the circuit and make the reading inaccurate. One of the differences between a cheap and an expensive VOM is the degree to which it loads the circuit. A cheap VOM may have an input impedance of only 1000 or 2000 ohms per volt, while a more expensive one might be rated at 100,000 ohms per volt on DC readings. A typical vacuum tube voltmeter, called a VTVM, would have an input resistance of perhaps 10,000,000 ohms per volt. This high input impedance permits VTVM's to accurately measure voltages in high impedance circuits without appreciable loading. VTVM's are also useful for measuring extremely small voltages, and their ohm-meters can measure very high resistances. Automobile electrical systems have low impedances, so any VOM will probably be satisfactory.

When you use your VOM, make sure you first switch the function switch to DC and to the proper voltage scale. The rule is this: use the scale with a maximum voltage reading that is *higher* than you expect to find in the circuit you are testing. Most small VOM's have a 10, 50, and 250 volt scale. Some have either a lower scale, a higher scale, or both. For a 6-volt car you would choose the 10-volt scale, for a 12-volt car, the 50-volt scale. Check the position of the pointer knob for the function switch *each time* you use the meter.

To use the ohm-meter, you must make sure you have switched off the circuit you are testing so that no current is flowing

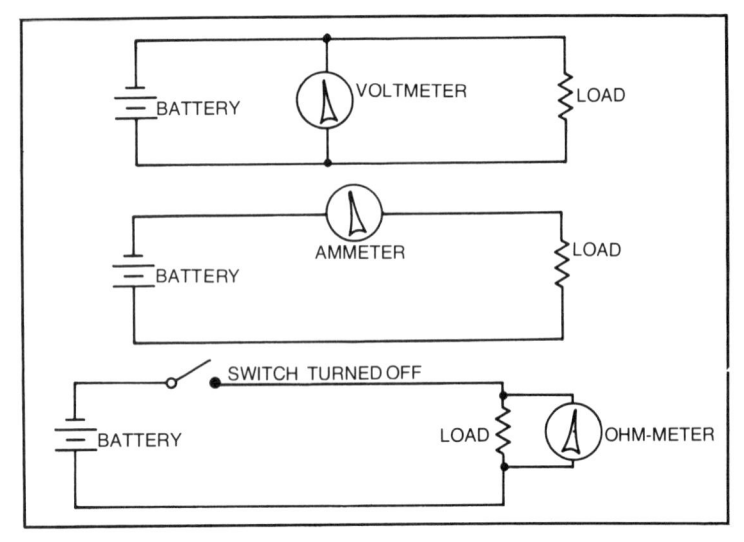

Fig. 12-2. How to use voltmeter, ammeter, and ohmmeter to read voltage, current, and resistance in electrical circuits.

in that circuit except the current provided by the battery in your VOM. You can use the ohm-meter to test the resistance of the load, the resistance of the wiring, or as a simple continuity tester. The car wiring should show no resistance at all unless it contains a ballast resistor or if the wiring itself is resistive. Spark plug leads are typically resistive in modern cars but not in most antique or early production cars.

To know whether you are getting the proper resistance, you can check the resistance of the load in your car and compare that with the resistance of the same kind of load in a similar car. But most of your resistance readings will probably be made to see if there are high resistance points in connections or in the wires themselves. When you use the ohm-meter as a continuity checker, you will need only an indicator, not an accurate meter. For this test even a defective meter will serve. Or you can make a simple continuity tester from a couple of batteries, a battery holder, a flashlight bulb, and a couple of test leads with alligator clips. By clipping the test leads to each end of the circuit that you want to check, you can quickly see whether you have an open circuit or a complete one. If the bulb lights normally, you obviously have continuity. If it glows dimly, there is increased resistance. If it doesn't glow at all, you have either a very high resistance or an open circuit.

Many mechanics prefer a simple test light to a continuity checker for car servicing. The test light consists of a lamp bulb, a ground lead, and a prod. Get a socket for a 12-volt bulb, an old ice pick or a screwdriver, an alligator clip, and some test wire (Fig. 12-3, 12-4). You can get a socket from the dash of an old car or you can buy a new socket at any auto parts store. If you use an old screwdriver for the prod, you should grind it into a point so you can penetrate insulation with it to test the conductor. Solder one lead from the socket to the prod, the other lead to a piece of test wire. The test lead should be at least 3' long to permit you to reach any point under the hood with one ground connection. If you don't have any test wire, you can use a single conductor from a piece of lamp cord. Solder an alligator clip to the end of the test lead. Tape the socket to the handle of the screwdriver or ice pick. To make a neater, more secure mounting, you can grind out a depression in the handle for the socket to fit into.

A test light has several advantages over other tools for checking car wiring. Some wiring circuits are too long for convenient continuity checking. For example, if you want to check the wiring to the tail lights, you can do it easily with a test light. Turn on the circuit and probe the wiring at various points to see if the test lamp lights. If it does, you know you have voltage at that point. As a precaution you should always start checking at the battery. Simply clip the alligator clip to ground and probe the ungrounded battery terminal. If the lamp doesn't light, you know that you either have a bad test lamp bulb, that the battery isn't grounded, or that the battery is down.

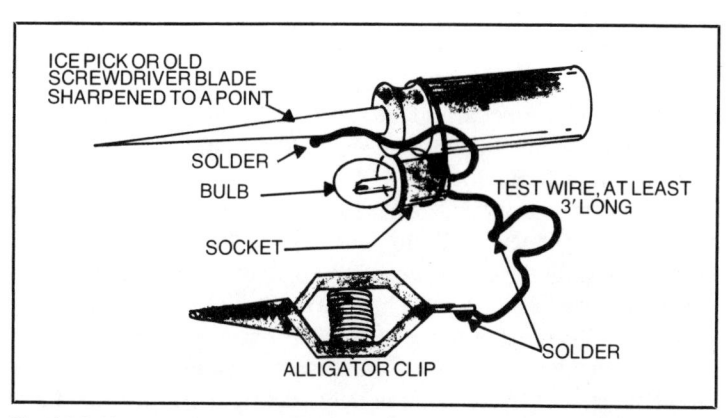

Fig. 12-3. Homemade test light. Tape socket to handle of old screw driver or ice pick. Solder electrical connections.

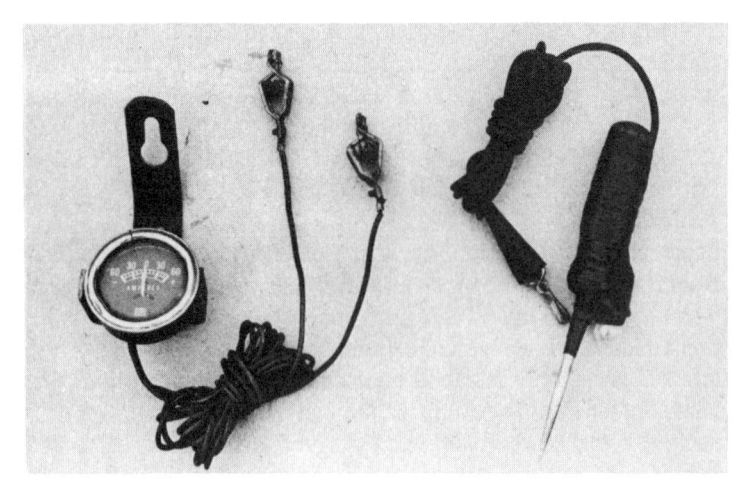

Fig. 12-4. Homemade test instruments. Old ammeter with test leads and test light.

You can use the test light to find resistance points. If the lamp burns brighter when the prod is placed on one side of a connection than at the other side, you know there is an abnormal resistance in that connection.

## HOW TO FIND SHORTS

If you car blows a certain fuse (Fig. 12-5) and you can't find the short, there are a couple of ways to proceed. One, not highly recommended for obvious reasons, is the "smoke" method. All you do is place a heavy wire or piece of metal across the fuse holder, then watch for smoke. To use this method you should have a sense of proper timing. Don't place the metal there and then forget it. Don't even leave it for several minutes while watching it. Ideally you should have someone place the jumper in while you watch the area where you expect to find the short.

The second method is to use an old car ammeter which will probably have a 60-amp scale. Prepare the ammeter as a test instrument by connecting leads to each of the terminals on the back. Then connect small alligator clips to the ends of the test leads. Tape over the connection on the back of the ammeter so they won't touch metal and cause a further short. To use this ammeter, clamp the alligator clips to the fuse holder terminals and turn on the circuit. If the needle is pegged on the meter, you know you have a direct short. But if the short is only slightly more than the fuse rating, the ammeter will give you time to check out various parts of the circuit, time you don't have before a fuse blows. You can carry the ammeter with you as you check the wiring, leaving it clipped to the fuse holders.

Shorts can be difficult to locate if they are intermittent shorts. Some may show up only after you have driven the car over a bumpy road. To locate one of these you should have a helper wiggle a short section of wire while you watch the ammeter. The procedure requires constant communication between the one watching the meter and the wiggler. Turn off the circuit involved, have the helper wiggle a section of wiring, then turn on the circuit and watch the meter.

This method of checking for shorts saves considerable time in cutting a wiring harness apart to try to find the short. If the short doesn't show up, turn on the lights and leave the ammeter in the circuit while the helper shakes various parts of the wiring until the short appears again.

If you don't have a surplus ammeter available, any electrical gadget that will work on 12 volts will do the job. It can be a headlamp or a small electric motor from a heater or a windshield wiper. The motor has one advantage over the ammeter—it makes noise when it runs. Using a motor you can work with the wiring and listen for the motor to start running when you jiggle the part of the wiring that is shorting. In selecting a device to substitute for the fuse, try to get something that will permit a heavier current than the normal load in that circuit so the normal load won't activate it. If you must use a device that draws a lower current, you should

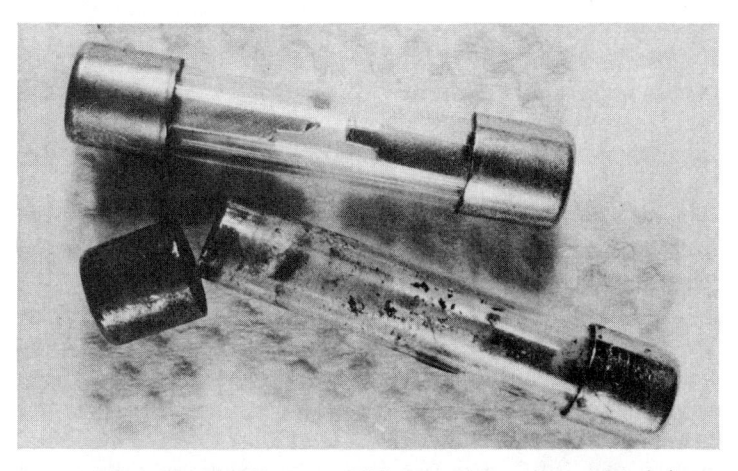

Fig. 12-5. Two ways that fuses can fail. Interior element is complete in lower one, but connection at end failed.

disconnect the load from the wiring. This will leave only the short to draw current and operate the device.

Some shorts don't show up as a blown fuse or a thrown circuit breaker. For example, headlights are rarely fused, so the short will simply prevent the lights from working, but the wiring will get hot. On many old cars you will find no fuse panel at all. On these cars the fuses are probably located in the individual lines. To check the fuses you will have to follow the leads for the circuit involved until you find a fuse holder.

While the foregoing methods will locate any minor working problems, you may have to do considerably more restoration work on the electrical system of your car. To guide you we will now present a run-down on how to do it, starting with the battery. See also troubleshooting chart, Fig. 12-6.

## BATTERY

When you check your battery, you should consider its temperature because a battery in a car out-of-doors on a cold winter day may not be able to furnish more than half the power it can on a warm summer day. Your first step in battery maintenance is to clean the battery. Accumulated material on it can easily discharge it. One way to test the cleanliness of a battery is to take a voltage reading from one pole of the battery to various points on the case. The case itself is a non-conductor so any voltage reading at all, even a flicker of the needle on your voltmeter, indicates leakage by contamination. Make sure you observe polarity when you use a voltmeter on a battery.

To clean the battery, mix a spoonful of baking soda into a pint or so of water and bathe the top of the battery with this solution. Be careful not to get any of the soda water *into* the battery. After the soda has neutralized the battery acid, flush the surface of the battery with clean water. Use this same procedure to clean the cable where battery electrolyte may have oozed along the cable from the battery. Cola drinks can be used for spot cleaning in emergencies.

Check the specific gravity of the electrolyte with a hydrometer. If the battery is fully charged, the reading should be from 1.280 to 1.300. A reading below 1.20 indicates a discharged battery. Specific gravity is the ratio of the density of a substance compared to the density of water, which is 1. Battery acid is a solution of sulfuric acid ($H_2SO_4$) in water. Because concentrated sulfuric acid is much more dense than water, the specific gravity of any sulfuric acid/water solution will be greater than 1. As a battery is discharged, some of the sulfuric acid is used up, the sulfate ion combining with the lead of the plates. So the ratio of acid to water in the solution is reduced, lowering the specific gravity. The measurement of the specific gravity is really a quick measure of the amount of acid left in the solution.

While the specific gravity reading can give an accurate rating of the battery's degree of charge under the right conditions, you must observe the temperature at which the reading is taken. The typical hydrometer is calibrated to give the readings mentioned above when the temperature of the solution is about 60° to 70° Fahrenheit. Some hydrometers are based on an 80° standard. Remember that the density of a liquid increases at lower than normal room temperature and decreases at higher temperatures. Any variation will have a slight effect on the reading.

One problem that sometimes arises with antique cars occurs when a car is stored in an unheated building for the winter and the battery becomes discharged. The freezing point of the electrolyte depends on its degree of charge. A fully charged battery isn't likely to freeze because it can withstand temperatures of $-75°$ F. or

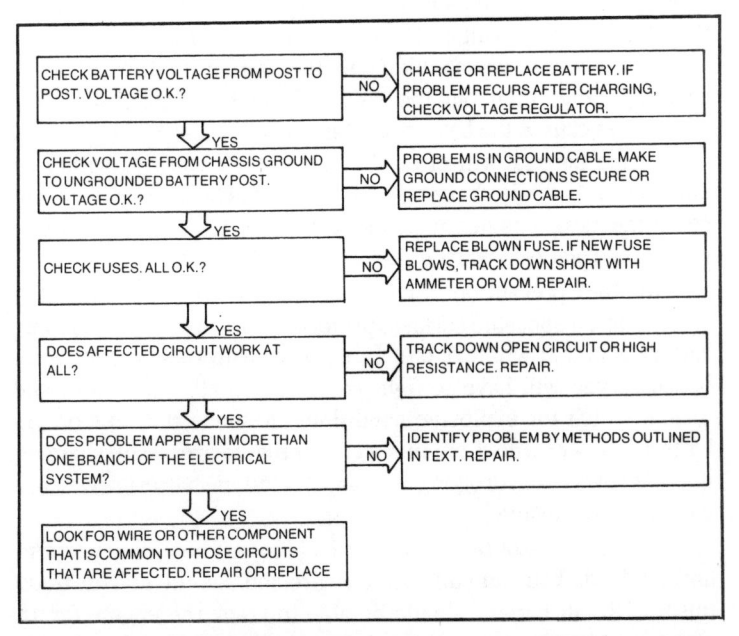

Fig. 12-6. General electrical troubleshooting chart. Use VOM or test light to check voltage. Old ammeter can be used to test for shorts as described in text.

lower. But a discharged battery can freeze at a temperature of 0° F. or even higher.

Even a clean battery will discharge itself if left unused for a long period of time. The rate of discharge depends on the temperature of the battery. High temperatures increase the rate of discharge. Old style batteries, with provision for adding water, should be checked frequently in the summer and water added as needed. Since chemical reaction speed increases with temperature, a battery used only in a hot climate can be operated with a lower specific gravity and perform satisfactorily. The lower specific gravity, or acid content, reduces the chances of self discharge.

The chemical activity in a battery supplies electrons for an electric current by the reaction of the negative spongy lead plates and the positive lead peroxide plates with the sulfate ions from the sulfuric acid. The reaction is a two-step process that releases water along with electrons. When you hook up a charger, you are passing current in the reverse direction to that followed by the discharge reaction. The charger removes sulfate from the lead sulfate compound and breaks down water to form sulfuric acid and return electrons to the spongy lead plates. In some old batteries the plates may be sulfated over so fully that the charger won't work. In this case you should leave the charger on it for a normal charging time, then tap the sides of the battery lightly. This sometimes causes the battery to start to take a charge. On the first charge the battery will often discharge itself quickly, within 24 hours or less. While charging such a battery, check occasionally to see if the battery is heating. An old battery will sometimes heat, causing the plates to warp and short out the battery.

Another precaution in charging old batteries is to place the battery on a disposable surface, preferably one that will absorb any battery acid that will leak out. Don't place batteries on your work bench or you will have to fight corrosion on all your tools. And finally, watch for explosive conditions. Remove the caps on old batteries and charge them in a well-ventilated area. The charging process releases hydrogen gas from the old-type batteries which is extremely explosive.

Another way of testing batteries is to see how they perform under a load. You can pull the coil wire and use the starter to do this. A 12-volt battery should be able to crank the engine for 15 seconds and maintain a voltage rating of at least 9.6 volts, a 6-volt battery, at least 4.5 volts. The theory of load testing specifies that the battery should be loaded to at least 3 times its normal discharge rate in amp/hours for 15 seconds. The cranking may or may not approximate this rate, but is an inexpensive way of applying a load. As such, it can give a rough indication of the battery's ability to perform. Mechanics normally use a carbon pile to apply a known load to the battery for a load rating test.

## CABLES

With any old car you should carefully check the condition of all ground cables or straps. The ground cable from the battery may lead to either the body, the engine, or the frame. Since the body and engine are almost always isolated from the frame by rubber mounts, there must be further ground straps that connect these members to the frame. If any ground cable or strap is in poor condition or is broken, it will interrupt the electrical circuit.

Sometimes a poor or broken ground strap can lead to mysterious behavior. One man we know once thought his car had been invaded by evil spirits that were lurking in the carburetor because of an electrical problem. When he tried to start the car, he could smell something getting hot. Upon inspection he found that the choke cable was red and smoking. The problem proved to be a broken ground strap between the engine and the frame. The only conductor that touched both of those members was the choke cable housing. The housing wasn't heavy enough to conduct the current demanded by the starter, so it got red hot.

Corrosion is a major problem with cables and at the clamps. Clean the clamps, using a soda solution, and inspect the cable itself for broken strands. Broken strands reduce the cable's ability to conduct current, raising its resistance. When this occurs, the cable causes a loss of efficiency in the electrical system because some of the energy is converted to heat.

Old 6-volt systems must operate at a higher current flow to do the same amount of work. The power in a direct current electrical system is measured in watts. It is equal to the voltage, in volts, multiplied by the current in amperes. So a 6-volt system must carry twice the current of a 12-volt system to maintain the same power ability. Remember this when you work on 6-volt cars, and don't substitute a cable from a 12-volt car for an old 6-volt cable. One way to use cables from 12-volt cars is to use a doubled cable, putting 2 cables in parallel.

If you have another car with the same voltage rating, you can start your old car by using a jumper cable. If you have no jumper cable, you can use a quick, one cable hook-up, but only if the two cars have the same battery pole grounded. Drive the car with the good battery against the front end of the other car, making firm bumper contact. Then bridge from the ungrounded pole of one battery to the other with any good conductor, such as a bumper jack or a length of Romex house wiring cable.

When you use any kind of jumper cable hook-up, you should be aware of possible danger. If the dead battery has recently been used to crank the engine and is hot, there may be enough liberated hydrogen in it to cause an explosion. Avoid making sparks near it. Hook up the cables in a sequence so that you hook to the ground connection on the car with the good battery last.

## GENERATORS

To check the generator, remove the cover band and see if it looks clean inside. Look for bits of thrown solder, which are a sign of loose connections between the armature winding and the commutator segments. See if the commutator is dirty or rough looking. Check the level of the mica between the commutator segments, particularly noting if it is higher than the segments. Any of these conditions can cause low generator output.

On many old cars you will find that the cover band has been lost. In these cases the generator will have been subjected to flying dirt or grease. To clean the commutator many mechanics use a piece of sandpaper held against the commutator with a finger. This practice will clean the commutator but can be a bit dangerous. A better method is to keep an emery board, such as women use to file their fingernails, on hand. This stiff emery board can be inserted and held against the commutator without pressing your finger into the generator. A quick cleaning of the commutator by this method is frequently all that is needed to get a sluggish generator working.

If you remove the armature on your generator, you should clean and pack the bushings with grease before reassembly. Also check the bushings for excessive wear. If your car is very old, the generator may have bearings that support the armature shaft instead of bushings. These should be cleaned in kerosene, then packed with grease. If the cleaned bearings are gritty when rotated, replace them.

Most auto parts stores stock several sizes of bushings for generators. Some generators have small diameter shafts for which the correct size bushing is not directly available. In this case, you can buy a double set of bushings and fit the smaller bushing inside the larger one to bush down to the smaller shaft size. If the inside bushing is too small, you can hone it to fit the shaft. This kind of bushing down can be repeated for parts other than generators or starters if you can find two bushings that fit together.

If you suspect serious problems with your generator, you can easily check it for an open armature. This test can be performed with your test light and the car battery. Connect one pole of the battery to one side of the commutator. Connect the alligator clip on your test light to the other pole of the battery. You may have to use an adaptor to do this because most alligator clips are too small to connect directly to the battery post. Make sure you have a good connection by touching the test light probe to the opposite battery pole to see if the bulb lights. Then touch the probe to the side of the commutator not connected to the battery. If the bulb doesn't light, the armature is open.

When you reassemble the generator, check to see if the brushes rest evenly on the commutator. If they look worn, replace them. Worn brushes are often a sign of weak brush springs which have probably been weakened by excessive heat. Replace the springs when you install new brushes.

After cleaning your generator you can check it by connecting a battery of proper voltage to the generator main terminal and frame. Ground the field terminal. If the generator runs like a motor, at a smooth, steady rate, it is good. (Note: this will *not* work with an alternator).

After working on your generator and installing it again, it should be polarized so its polarity will match that of the battery. When you have connected all electrical leads in the system, put a jumper across the field and battery terminals of the regulator for a second or so. This permits battery current to correctly polarize the field.

The steps outlined above will solve most generator problems (Fig. 12-7). If more reworking is required, it will probably be more practical to replace the generator. For authentic restorations you will want to make an exact replacement, but for less ambitious jobs you can probably find a substitute generator that will work equally well. The main problem here is to find one that can be adapted to the mounting arrangement on the engine.

If you choose to rework a car of recent manufacture, it may have an alternator instead of a generator. Alternator diodes can be fragile. For example, if you do any electric welding on a car with an alternator, as a precaution it is a good idea to unhook the main battery terminal wire from the alternator. If you don't, you could blow the diodes. This is unlikely if you ground the welder at a point

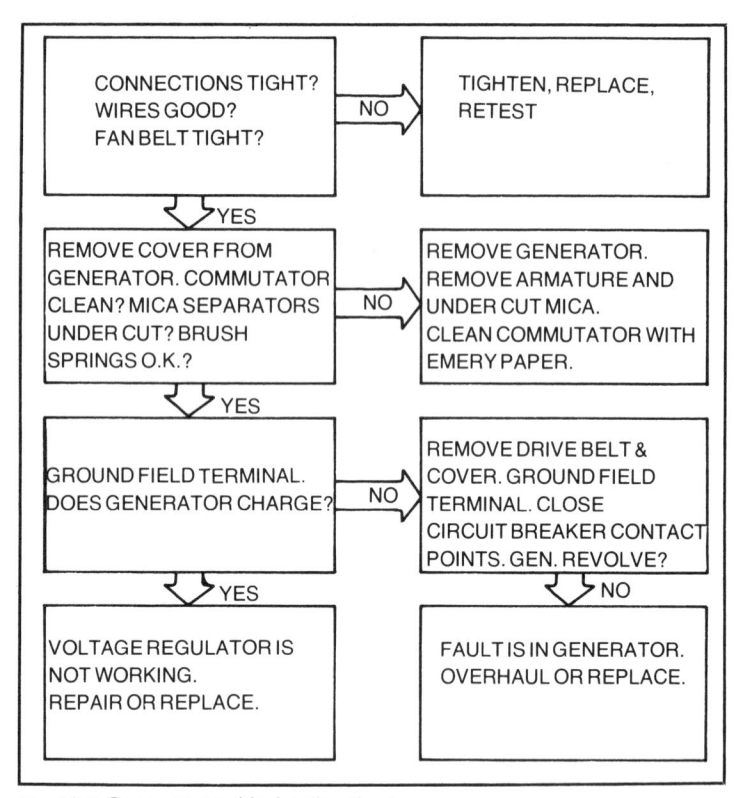

```
┌─────────────────────────┐      ┌─────────────────────────┐
│ CONNECTIONS TIGHT?      │      │ TIGHTEN, REPLACE,       │
│ WIRES GOOD?         NO ─┼─────▶│ RETEST                  │
│ FAN BELT TIGHT?         │      │                         │
└───────────┬─────────────┘      └─────────────────────────┘
            │ YES
┌───────────▼─────────────┐      ┌─────────────────────────┐
│ REMOVE COVER FROM       │      │ REMOVE GENERATOR.       │
│ GENERATOR. COMMUTATOR   │      │ REMOVE ARMATURE AND     │
│ CLEAN? MICA SEPARATORS  │ NO ─▶│ UNDER CUT MICA.         │
│ UNDER CUT? BRUSH        │      │ CLEAN COMMUTATOR WITH   │
│ SPRINGS O.K.?           │      │ EMERY PAPER.            │
└───────────┬─────────────┘      └─────────────────────────┘
            │ YES
┌───────────▼─────────────┐      ┌─────────────────────────┐
│ GROUND FIELD TERMINAL.  │      │ REMOVE DRIVE BELT &     │
│ DOES GENERATOR CHARGE?  │      │ COVER. GROUND FIELD     │
│                     NO ─┼─────▶│ TERMINAL. CLOSE         │
│                         │      │ CIRCUIT BREAKER CONTACT │
│                         │      │ POINTS. GEN. REVOLVE?   │
└───────────┬─────────────┘      └───────────┬─────────────┘
            │ YES                            │ NO
┌───────────▼─────────────┐      ┌───────────▼─────────────┐
│ VOLTAGE REGULATOR IS    │      │ FAULT IS IN GENERATOR.  │
│ NOT WORKING.            │      │ OVERHAUL OR REPLACE.    │
│ REPAIR OR REPLACE.      │      │                         │
└─────────────────────────┘      └─────────────────────────┘
```

Fig. 12-7. Generator troubleshooting chart.

near where you are welding and if the welding is done at some distance from the engine.

## VOLTAGE REGULATION

The charging rate of the generator is determined by the condition of the battery. A fully charged battery will have almost the same voltage as the generator, so the charging current will be low. But if the battery becomes discharged, the charging rate goes up. To quickly check the performance of the voltage regulator you can discharge the battery slightly and see if the regulator permits a heavier charging current. Most old cars will have a separate starter button so you can easily use the starter to discharge the battery. Leave the ignition key turned off and use the starter to turn over the engine for 15 seconds or more. This will drop the battery voltage. Then turn on the key and start the engine. You should notice a higher than normal charging rate as indicated on the ammeter. After a few minutes the charging rate should fall, as the battery reaches higher voltage. When the battery is in good condition, the charging rate will appear to be at zero.

If your battery is discharged and the ammeter shows no charging, the trouble may be in the generator or the regulator. A common problem is a bad ground connection for the regulator. To test this possibility, make a secure ground connection with a test lead or cable and connect the other end to the base of the regulator. Run the engine at a speed that is about equal to about 20 or 25 miles per hour on the road in high gear. If there is no charging, connect a ground wire to the field terminal on the generator. This eliminates the regulator from the system. Rev up the engine again; if the ammeter shows charging the regulator is at fault.

Most old cars have a voltage regulator with 2 coils that operate electromagnets; later cars have 3 coils. The two-coil regulators have one coil that operates the regulator and a coil that works the cut-out. Regulators with 3 coils have an extra current regulator. The purpose of the cut-out is to prevent reverse current flow from the battery into the generator when the car isn't running. One man who had an older car had a regulator with a defective cut-out which would not permit charging. He overcame the problem by inserting a matchstick under the points to force them together while he was driving the car. He would remove the stick when he stopped, before he shut off the engine. Eventually he forgot the stick and shut off the engine without removing it. When he remembered it, the regulator and generator had been badly damaged by excessive current.

The 2-unit regulator is usually found on very old cars which have 3-brush generators. Three-unit regulators are found on more recent cars that have 2-brush or shunt-wound generators. When you inspect either kind, notice the condition of the contact points. Badly burned points can indicate a shorted generator field.

As with all other electrical circuits, bad connections and other resistance points can cause trouble in the charging circuit. If your light bulbs burn out frequently, the problem is probably high voltage. The high voltage can be caused by a bad regulator, but it can also be caused by poor connections in the regulator and battery circuit which offer high resistance points to the flow of current into the battery. This condition will force too much current through the lights, burning them out. It would probably cause point damage first, so with either condition, check for resistance. An old discharged battery can also cause such problems. Make sure that all connections offer no resistance.

## STARTERS

To test the starter circuit, turn on the headlights and hit the starter switch. If the lights go very dim, then get stronger after you release the switch, the trouble is either a weak battery or a starter that draws too much current. If the lights go out, there is probably a loose connection or a high resistance connection at the battery. If the lights don't dim at all and the starter does nothing, there is probably an open circuit in the starter hook-up. To check the starter solenoid, short it with a heavy cable. If the starter turns, replace the solenoid. If the starter makes no effort to turn, check the line to the solenoid with a test light. If the light glows, the starter is bad. If the starter makes a noise but doesn't turn the engine, the engine may be locked. Remove the spark plugs and try again. To check the engine further, try to crank it by hand. If it doesn't turn, the trouble is in the engine (Fig. 12-8).

Sometimes the problem with a starter is mechanical instead of electrical. The starter motor may spin, but it doesn't turn the engine. On old cars this means a defective spring on the starter gear. Later cars, which have a starter drive with loose balls that are jammed into a tapered space and lock the drive so it rotates in one direction only, can also show the same symptom. In this case the culprit is usually dirt that prevents free ball movement.

On some late model GM cars the starter solenoid grounds through the brushes on the starter. These can refuse to work even though the circuit to the solenoid is complete and the solenoid is good. The problem is caused by brush wear. When the brushes are badly worn, the plastic brush holders rest on the armature, preventing good brush contact. If you suspect this problem, have someone use the starter button or key while you rap the starter at the brush end with a ball peen hammer. If the starter works at that, you can be pretty sure that the brushes are bad and should be replaced.

To disassemble the starter, remove the solenoid, or switch, if attached to the starter. Take off the cover band. Then take out the through bolts and separate the commutator end plate, the field frame, and the drive end. Note: on some starters the brushes are attached to the end plate; if so, unhook the brushes. If the commutator is rough, worn, or out of round, it should be turned down on a lathe. Take it to a machine shop and tell them to remove as little material as possible.

After you have had the commutator turned down, you may find that the mica separators are flush with the commutator segments.

If so, the mica can hold the brushes away from the commutator. To correct this, you must undercut the mica.

To make an undercutting tool, grind the excess set off the teeth of a hacksaw blade so that the teeth are flush with the sides of the blade. Next, cut off the end of the blade at about a 30° angle so that the toothed section extends beyond the back of the blade. This makes the teeth the leading edge of the blade. Tape the other end of the blade heavily to protect your hand.

Install the armature assembly in a vise with the commutator section accessible for your saw blade. Don't overtighten the vise or you will damage the armature. Saw the mica separators until they are cut away to about 1/32″ below the surface of the commutator (Fig. 12-9). Gently sand the commutator with fine, #00, sandpaper to remove any burrs left on it. Blow it clean to remove any copper dust that may have been left by the sawing or sanding.

Clean and lubricate any Bendix-type drives with light engine oil. Reassemble the starter. These steps will correct most starter problems.

## LIGHTS

As mentioned earlier, headlights are rarely fused. On some cars there is a wire that runs from the ammeter to the fuse panel, by-passing the switch, that supplies current for the brake lights, turn signals, and perhaps other lights.

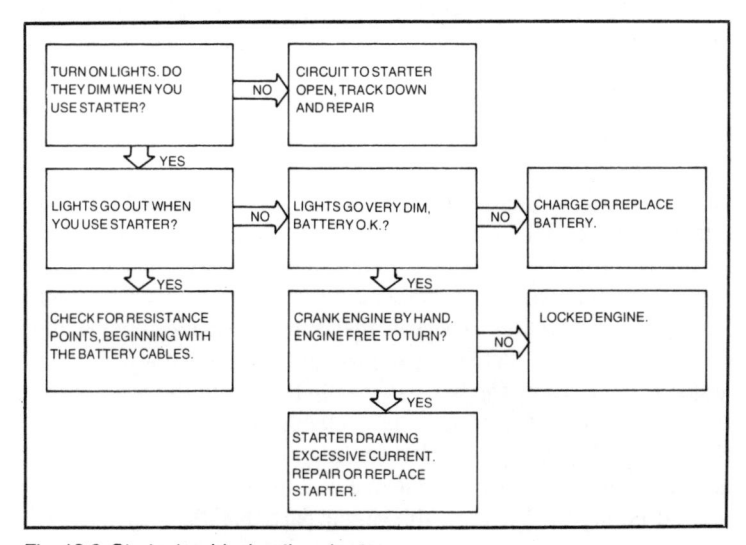

Fig. 12-8. Starter troubleshooting chart.

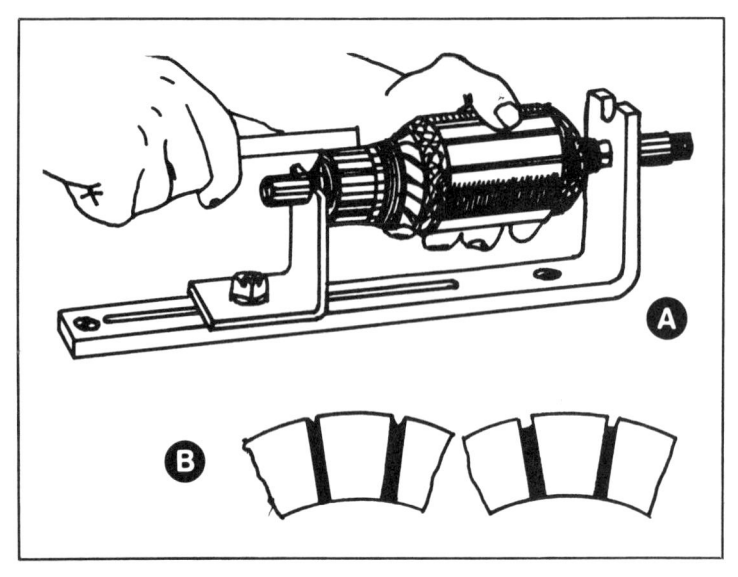

Fig. 12-9. Repair of starter commutator. (A) Undercutting mica separators on the commutator. (B) Mica should be undercut cleanly and squarely.

Rear lights usually cause more trouble than headlights. This is especially true for cars that have been used in parts of the country that have freezing temperatures in winter. In cold weather water and mud are often thrown onto the rear wiring. When the vehicle is parked, this icy mud and water quickly freezes, encasing the wiring in ice. The next time the car is driven, the ice melts just enough to fall free from the frame or other car part to which it was anchored. If the piece of ice is heavy enough, it will break loose some of the wiring as it falls. Cars from cold climates should be carefully inspected for this problem.

Unsatisfactory ground connections are a frequent cause of dim lights. For example you may notice that a parking light at one corner of the car is dim. This situation almost always means a poor ground connection, but it can also be caused by a positive high resistance connection. You can test the wiring by clipping the ground lead of your test lamp to a ground connection that you know is good and touching the hot wire to the lamp with the prod. If the test light glows, the trouble is probably a bad ground for the parking light. This problem sometimes occurs even when the ground lead from the car light makes a good connection with a ground point. In that case the metal part that the ground wire connects to is not grounded. A fender, for example, may not be properly grounded to the frame. The cure here is to run a separate ground wire to a ground point on the frame.

Another frequent problem with old cars is a defective dimmer switch. The most common cause of dimmer switch malfunction is corrosion, particularly on cars that haven't been driven for years. The cure is simple. Sit in the driver's seat and work the switch vigorously from one position to the other with your foot. You will probably be able to quickly wear off the corrosion on the brass contacts. As soon as you have bared enough metal for good conduction, the switch will start working. To further clean the switch, get a spray can of TV tuner cleaner from an electronics store. You can use the cleaner on any bad electrical connections on your car, including points under the dash. If you use this material in a confined space, avoid breathing the vapor.

Cars that are very old usually have wires that appear to be colorless. Even if the wiring was color coded when new, it has faded or is stained with dirt and grease so badly that you can't identify each wire by color. If you have such a car and have to trace out the circuits, you should mark each circuit as you identify it with colored tape or other means.

If your car is modern enough to have a wiring harness, or clusters of wires, you can probably find a wiring diagram for it in a large library. The wiring on early antiques will be simple enough that you can probably make the proper connections even if you can't find a diagram for your model.

Remember that the heavy wire that runs from the battery to the wiring circuits will go to the ammeter first. By appearing in the early part of the circuit, the ammeter will show any current flow being used by the car's electrical system. The power to the regulator and the headlights is typically taken off the ammeter, without going through the switch. But the current to the rest of the wiring, that is to any device that can be turned off by the switch, is carried by a wire that goes from the ammeter to the switch.

If your old car was produced before World War II, it probably doesn't have sealed beam headlights. Early headlights were subject to damage from moisture and dust that could enter the housing and coat the reflector. When you work on one of these cars, you must remove the lens and clean it and the reflector. Install a new bulb. Try to do the work on a day of low humidity or in a heated room. When you install the lens, seal it against moisture and dirt by running a bead of clear silicone rubber caulking material around the edge.

## DASH GAUGE PROBLEMS

If you notice that a dash gauge isn't working, check to see if the others are also defective. If they are, there is probably a break in the supply voltage from the battery. To check the voltage at various points under the dash, you can use the ignition key as a ground point.

One possible cause of dash gauge problems, as well as with general ignition problems, is a bad switch. You can check this by bridging across the switch terminals with a conductor. To remove the switch, you can make a simple tool from a piece of choke cable. Use the end of the cable with a knob on it. The stiff wire of the cable can be used to depress the springs in the switch. Turn the key to the accessory position and insert the choke wire into the tiny hole on the front of the switch. Turn the key left and right while applying pressure with the choke wire. When you find the point where you can depress the inner parts with the choke wire, jiggle the key back and forth while you continue to push on the choke knob. When the inner parts can be depressed, you can lift out the key and the lock tumblers. This is a necessary first step to removal of the switch assembly, necessary because when the tumblers are in the switch, the chrome ring that holds the switch in the dash can't be unscrewed. The ring is threaded like a nut so that you can unscrew it and pull the switch out the back of the dash. Removal of the headlight switch is somewhat similar, but you should first disconnect the battery, a useful precaution when working on *any* part of the electrical system. In removing the light switch, reach under the dash and depress the small chrome button on the rectangular box, pulling outward on the switch knob with your other hand. The knob will come out, permitting you to remove the ring that holds the switch on the dash.

The principle of operation for most dash gauges is similar. The circuit for fuel and oil pressure gauges is usually identical, with a slightly different hook up for temperature gauges. The gauges contain two coils which are mounted at right angles to each other, one angled to the left of the vertical, the other to the right. The position of the needle in the gauge is controlled by the balance of current flow in the two coils (Fig. 12-10). When the coil on the left carries a much higher current than the one on the right, the needle assembly is attracted to the left by the electromagnetic effect of the left hand coil. For example, if the fuel or the oil pressure is low, the variable resistance at the sending unit is low. Since the sending unit's lead goes to the gauge circuit between the two coils, it provides a low resistance path to ground for the current that travels through the left coil. The coil on the right gets very little current, so the needle stays at the low end of the gauge dial. Then as the oil pressure increases, or the gas tank is filled, the resistance in the remote unit increases, driving more current through the coil on the right, attracting the pivoted armature to which the needle is attached. The resistance unit in the gas tank is operated by a float on a lever arm that moves a contact over the variable resistor. Some cars have a different circuit for the fuel gauge. In one variation the resistance is greatest when the tank is

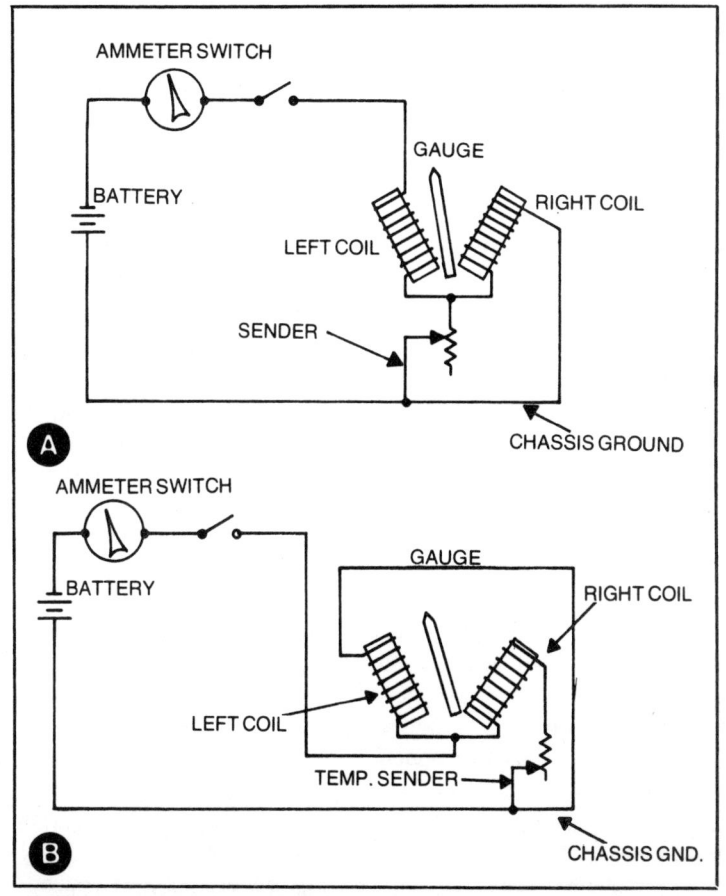

Fig. 12-10. General wiring diagrams for most dash gauges. (A) Circuit for oil pressure or fuel gauges. As resistance in sender increases, more current flows through right coil. (B) Circuit for temperature gauges. As resistance in sender decreases, more current flows through right coil.

221

empty. As the tank is filled the resistance decreases, permitting more current to flow through the gauge coils, causing the needle to show a higher reading.

The typical temperature gauge has a negative temperature coefficient resistor. This unit has high resistance at low temperatures, low resistance at higher temperatures. The right coil is grounded through this resistor so that when the resistance in the sender drops, more current flows through the right coil, making the needle show a higher reading.

To check the sending unit on the temperature gauge, remove the wire from the unit on the engine block and ground it while someone watches the gauge. Since you are removing the resistance from the circuit, the needle should move. If it doesn't, the trouble is in the wiring or the gauge itself. Check out the wiring and connection points before you remove the gauge.

If the trouble is in the oil pressure readings, remove the sender at the engine and screw in a manual gauge. You will probably have to adapt a manual gauge with a short piece of high pressure hose and select a fitting that matches the threads in the block. If the manual gauge shows oil pressure but the electrical gauge shows none, check out the wiring. If the wiring is good, the problem is with the gauge itself or with the sender.

**PRIMARY IGNITION CIRCUIT**

The primary ignition circuit includes the coil primary, the contact points, and the condenser in the distributor (Fig. 12-11). The coil will normally be marked as to polarity. The wire from the ignition switch should be connected to the pole marked "Battery." The other pole should be connected to the wire that goes to the contact points in the distributor, the pigtail lead. Some coils are marked with a "+" or a "−." On these, run the wire from the ignition switch to the "+" pole. (If your car has a positive ground, the connections will be reversed).

Some cars have a ballast resistor in the primary circuit that can cause problems. The ballast resistor keeps the coil cooler at low rpm because at these speeds the current flows long enough in the primary circuit to heat the resistor, increasing its resistance. This limits current flow. At high speeds the current flow duration is so short that the resistor doesn't have time to heat. Here the full voltage appears across the coil winding, producing higher secondary voltage when it is needed. This resistor can change resistance with age, or even burn out. If it burns out, the primary circuit is open, stopping the engine. If you try to start the engine again, it may run as long as you depress the starter button, then die. This symptom can occur in cars that have a bypass circuit for the ballast resistor. The bypass circuit is intended to permit full current flow when starting the car. When the starter switch is released, the bypass goes out of the circuit, and only the ballast resistor is left.

Much of your checking of the primary circuit can be a visual inspection (Fig. 12-12). While you are inspecting the primary wiring and the points in the distributor, you can also check the distributor cap for cracks. Some cracks will appear as a gray or dull line. Such cracks prove a short circuit path to ground when moisture condenses in them.

When you work on the distributor, you should be aware that many old distributors have more open spaces in them than modern ones. These sometimes have clearances great enough for small parts, such as screws, to fall down inside the distributor. If you drop a screw into one, *get it out*. You may have to remove the distributor and shake it. We know of one case where a man dropped

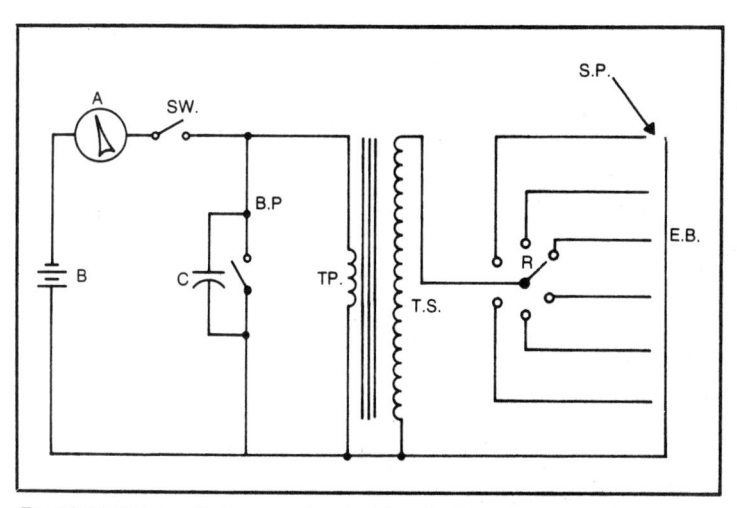

Fig. 12-11. Schematic diagram of car ignition chart.
B  - battery
A  - ammeter
Sw - ignition switch
C  - capacitor, usually called a condenser
B.P.- breaker points
T  - transformer, or coil
T.P.- coil primary, low voltage side
T.S.- coil secondary, high voltage side
R  - distributor rotor
E.B.- engine block
S.P.- spark plug gap

223

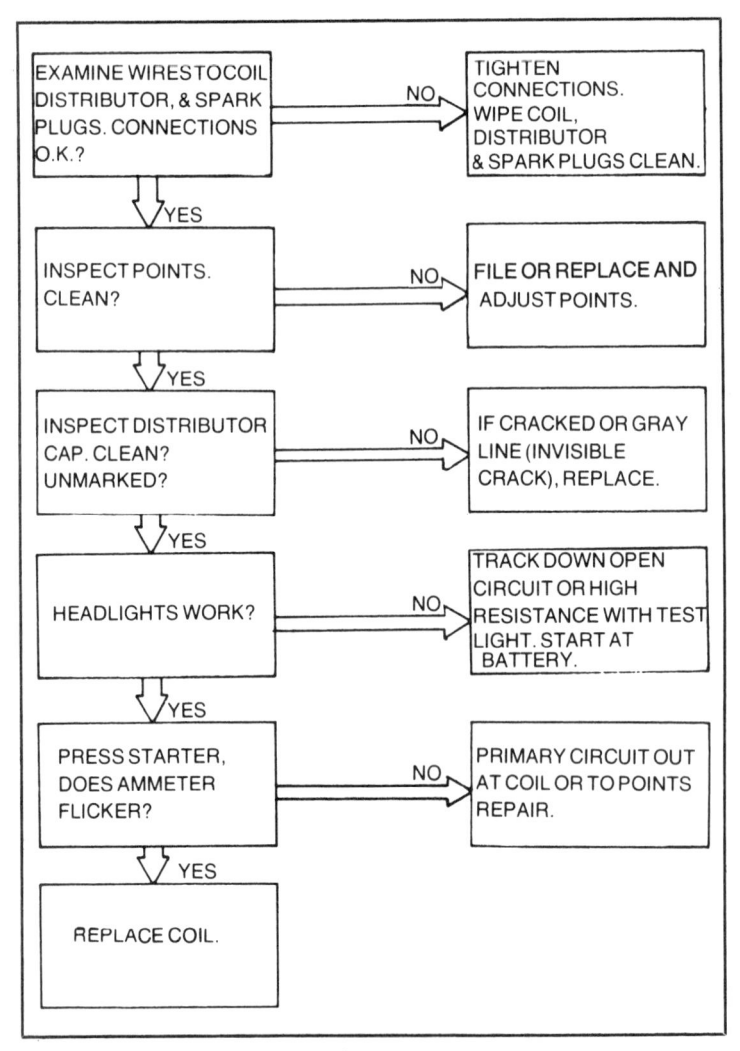

```
┌─────────────────────────┐
│ EXAMINE WIRES TO COIL   │         ┌─────────────────────────┐
│ DISTRIBUTOR, & SPARK    │   NO    │ TIGHTEN CONNECTIONS.    │
│ PLUGS. CONNECTIONS      │────────▶│ WIPE COIL, DISTRIBUTOR  │
│ O.K.?                   │         │ & SPARK PLUGS CLEAN.    │
└────────────┬────────────┘         └─────────────────────────┘
             │ YES
             ▼
┌─────────────────────────┐         ┌─────────────────────────┐
│ INSPECT POINTS.         │   NO    │ FILE OR REPLACE AND     │
│ CLEAN?                  │────────▶│ ADJUST POINTS.          │
└────────────┬────────────┘         └─────────────────────────┘
             │ YES
             ▼
┌─────────────────────────┐         ┌─────────────────────────┐
│ INSPECT DISTRIBUTOR     │   NO    │ IF CRACKED OR GRAY      │
│ CAP. CLEAN?             │────────▶│ LINE (INVISIBLE         │
│ UNMARKED?               │         │ CRACK), REPLACE.        │
└────────────┬────────────┘         └─────────────────────────┘
             │ YES
             ▼
┌─────────────────────────┐         ┌─────────────────────────┐
│                         │         │ TRACK DOWN OPEN         │
│                         │   NO    │ CIRCUIT OR HIGH         │
│ HEADLIGHTS WORK?        │────────▶│ RESISTANCE WITH TEST    │
│                         │         │ LIGHT. START AT         │
│                         │         │ BATTERY.                │
└────────────┬────────────┘         └─────────────────────────┘
             │ YES
             ▼
┌─────────────────────────┐         ┌─────────────────────────┐
│ PRESS STARTER,          │   NO    │ PRIMARY CIRCUIT OUT     │
│ DOES AMMETER            │────────▶│ AT COIL OR TO POINTS    │
│ FLICKER?                │         │ REPAIR.                 │
└────────────┬────────────┘         └─────────────────────────┘
             │ YES
             ▼
┌─────────────────────────┐
│ REPLACE COIL.           │
│                         │
└─────────────────────────┘
```

Fig. 12-12. Ignition troubleshooting chart.

a screw into a distributor and didn't bother to retrieve it. The screw later jammed the distributor mechanism, destroying it.

Old cars that have been left out in the weather for years can have some unusual electrical problems, including some at the distributor. Here is one possibility that Mike found on an old pickup truck. The truck wouldn't start, but everything checked out all right. The truck had been running a few days before, which confused the issue. The problem was in the weights in the distributor that work by centrifugal force. The truck had been shut off after running normally. The weights, which had become rusty and corroded from the weather, had jammed in the outside position. Locked in that mode they had changed the timing enough to prevent the engine from starting.

If the points were open when your old car was last driven, they will likely be corroded badly. The points may be whitish or even black, indicating corrosion. You should remove all the corrosion and rust from every part in the distributor. When corrosion builds up on points, it is impossible to accurately set them. A quick repair can be made by filing the points with a point file. Don't use sandpaper because bits of sand will act as insulators. If you can't find specifications for the proper point setting, you can use this rule of thumb: set V-8 engine points at 0.015″, 6-cylinder or smaller engines at 0.020″.

Although filing may repair corroded points, you will probably have to replace badly corroded and worn parts. Points for a specific car may be hard to find. Since you may not be able to get the exact replacement points, try to adapt another set. Remember that in mounting points the main requirement is to make sure the base part of the point is anchored to the plate and that the cam on the shaft will open the points. Another requirement is that the wires that lead to the points must reach, but that is rarely a problem. With so many kinds of points on the replacement market you should have no trouble finding a set that can be adapted to your car.

While you are working on the points, don't forget to lube the cam lobe. If it isn't greased, it will wear the part that contacts it, reducing the gap and slowing the timing. The point setting controls the dwell angle by the number of degrees in which the points are shut.

When you replace points, you should also replace the condenser. The purpose of the condenser is to store the electrical charge that builds up on its plates while the points are open. It prevents arcing on the points which could quickly destroy them. Also it promotes faster collapse of the field in the primary of the coil.

## HIGH TENSION WIRING PROBLEMS

Antique cars will have copper conductors in the high tension wiring, but more recent cars may have carbon conductors to reduce radio noise. Cars that have a rubber boot on the end of the spark plug wires often have wiring problems that are caused by a mechanic. In time the boot can become bonded to the plug. Then, during a tune-up, the mechanic will grab the boot or the wire back of the boot and twist it sharply to break it loose from the plug. This puts a stress on the wiring near the boot, often cracking the conductor. The spark will bridge the gap, but in time it will widen the gap by breaking down the conductor. After a thousand miles or so the break becomes bad enough to cause misfiring. If your car has carbon wiring, you should be suspicious of this kind of misfiring.

Spark plugs themselves can cause considerable trouble. Spark plugs have undergone much refinement, although the earliest ones were more exotic in that they had platinum electrodes (Fig. 12-13). The early plugs had porcelain insulators. Later, mica and glass were tried before aluminum oxide was introduced. Platinum is a bit expensive for most applications today. The first resistor plugs were introduced by Chrysler in 1948.

Some special plugs cause unique problems. For example, in the early 1940s, Packard and Chevrolet among others used a miniature plug of smaller diameter than current plugs. These had a bad habit of blowing the porcelain out, usually denting something that you didn't want dented.

A new plug will fire when about 10,000 volts is applied to the terminal. After use, the voltage requirement climbs to 15,000, even after cleaning. But if you file an old plug so the points are square, this drops back almost to that of a new plug.

Your typical old car will have a worn engine that will quickly foul the plugs. In a typical old 6-cylinder car at least two or three cylinders will be using oil. If you don't want to overhaul the engine, you can install plugs with hotter ratings in the bad cylinders. For example if the car was designed to use Autolite A-42 plugs, you could substitute A-52 in a cylinder that shows an oily plug. If the condition is extreme enough, you can go to an A-82 plug. You should check the plug periodically to see if your choice was right. Long distance highway driving in hot weather can damage the plug, but this isn't likely to happen on an antique car that you use only for short runs. If you permit anyone else to work on the engine, make sure you warn the mechanic about the use of plugs with different heat ranges so he won't switch plugs accidentally.

If you have a plug fouling problem and can't find a hotter plug for your old car, you can increase the voltage to the plug by adjusting the plug wire. If the car has boots on the plugs, it will be easy; if it doesn't have them, you will have to use a piece of rubber tubing. Pull the boot off the plug slightly so that the wire conductor is spaced some distance from the plug terminal. Pull it out far enough to cause the engine to misfire, then push it in just enough to correct the misfiring. The voltage must build up to a higher value to bridge the gap you have created, making the plug fire even in an oily cylinder. This stops the fouling without resorting to a special plug.

Old cars with 6-cylinder flathead engines often had a reputation for starting problems. One reason: the location of the spark plugs in the top of the head. Each plug on these engines has its own basin which can hold water around the plug. To compound the problem, old cars often have a hinged hood, with the hinge running right down the center of the hood. Water can go through the seam by the hinge, where it will hit the head and plugs. Some will pool around the plugs and splash onto the plug insulator. Moisture on the insulators provides a short circuit to ground for the high voltage energy, robbing the plug itself. The cure for a wet engine is to wipe it dry. You should keep the plug insulators wiped clean. You can also spray the wiring with an ignition spray that prevents the problem.

If you decide to paint the engine, remove the plugs. People often spray engines with paint without removing them. After painting, the engine will start and idle in a normal way, but it will lose power at highway speeds. There is often lead or other metallic material in paint that can provide a short circuit for the spark. The problem shows up more noticeably when the engine is under load. The moral is clear: *don't* paint the plugs.

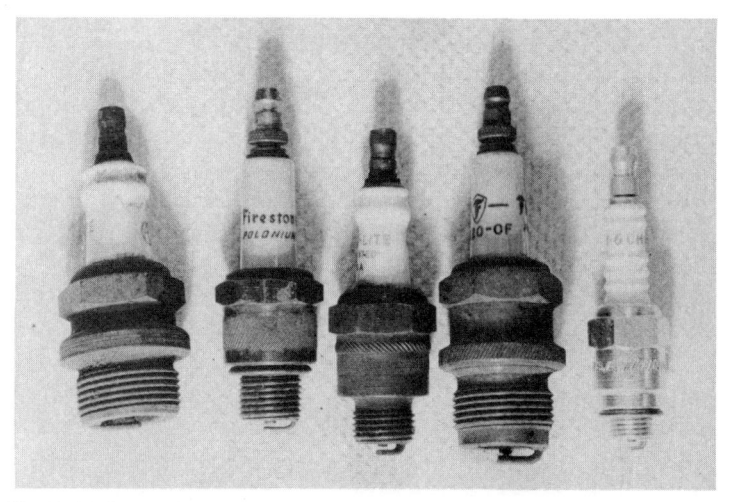

Fig. 12-13. Some of the various sizes of spark plugs used in vintage cars.

Dirt on the plug insulators causes problems in more ways than one. Any foreign material offers the possibility of conducting current, but it also adds to the surface area of the insulation. Increased area in any material means lower resistance, and the increased surface can also harbor more moisture.

You should periodically wipe off all parts in the high tension circuit, the plugs, distributor cap, and coil tower. In the early days of the automobile, perhaps the time when your car was made, service station attendants routinely did some of the maintenance as a free service to their customers. The wiring on the old cars is more open and a bit more subject to problems from dirt or moisture than that of new cars, but a quick cleaning now and then will keep it working right.

People who live near the Granby Crossing, a crossroads in Missouri, still talk about a service station owner named Clyde. During the days of the Depression Clyde serviced cars and gave instant ignition check-ups along with selling you gas and oil. His speed at electrical diagnosis was sensational. His tools were his bare hands. He would grab the spark plug terminals, one at a time, and tell you if the proper voltage was getting to each one. Occasionally a young man would imitate Clyde's technique, but the method never gained popularity. Clyde said that 15,000 volts didn't hurt, it just gently tingled.

COOLING SYSTEM

# Chapter 13
# Cooling Systems

We call it the cooling system, but a better name would be the heat regulating system. Most people know what happens to an engine that runs too hot, things like the rings welding themsleves to the cylinder walls, the bearings failing, and, finally, the entire engine going into the condition known as melt-down. But the other side of the coin is an engine that runs too cool. A cold engine is inefficient because the gasoline doesn't vaporize completely and combustion temperature is too low. Also, there are other problems. The pistons may not seal properly, letting exhaust gases blow by the rings into the crankcase. Exhaust gases contain considerable water vapor, which condenses in the crankcase and forms acids which produce excessive engine wear. Then there is one really serious problem with a cold-running car—in cold weather you can get *cold* driving one.

When you consider that a car engine produces enough heat to warm a house of average size in winter, you can see that cooling job is a formidable one. The design of cooling systems has been refined over the years to keep pace with the heat output of larger engines, but the basics are the same as for early cars. The main components of a modern cooling system are the engine block, the water pump, the radiator, the hoses, the thermostat, and the fan. If you rework an antique car, you may not find a water pump or a thermostat. Early water-cooled systems relied entirely on the natural circulation process known as thermosiphon (Fig. 13-1), developed by Jonathon Dixon Maxwell who built the early Maxwell cars. The hot water rose to the top of the system because of the principle that hot fluids rise and cooler fluids descend.

Modern cooling systems also work with the help of natural circulation, but they include a pump, located at the front of the engine block, to force the coolant through the system. The water pump has a vaned wheel, called an impeller, which fits closely inside the pump housing. When the fan belt turns the impeller, water is trapped in the vanes and forced into the block by centrifugal force. The water then circulates through the passages in the block and up to the entrance to the upper hose, where the thermostat is located. The thermostat controls the rate of circulation through the upper hose and the radiator. By its control of coolant flow, the thermostat is the prime regulator of the car's heat regulation system and extremely important to proper operation.

## THERMOSTAT

Antique cars may not have thermostats, but the chances are that the car you rework will have been designed to use one. The thermostat is actually a temperature-controlled valve. When the coolant is at air temperature, the thermostat is closed. If you start the car, the water can circulate through the block because of a bypass tube that is located near the thermostat. This bypass lets hot water return to the pump while the thermostat is closed, so that the engine will not develop hot spots in the block. But the water cannot get through the valve to the radiator hose. As the engine warms up, the coolant gets hot and heats the thermostat bellows, which warms the liquid sealed inside the bellows. As the liquid in the bellows vaporizes, it produces a pressure inside the bellows

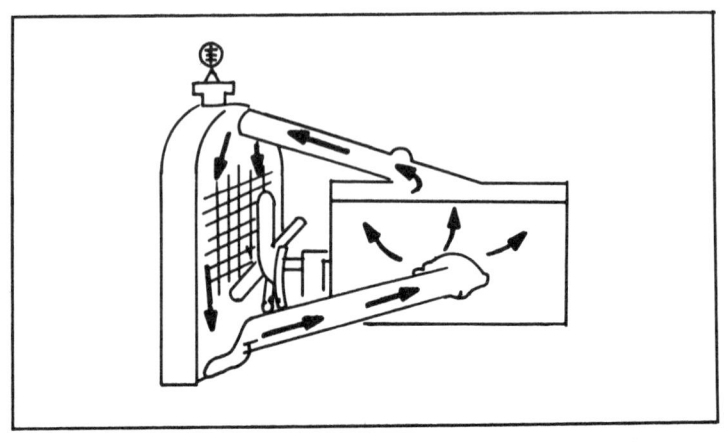

Fig. 13-1. Simplified diagram of thermosiphon method of cooling used on early car engines.

that opens the valve. Then the water can move through the whole system.

When thermostats get old, they sometimes stick in one position and the valve can no longer do its job. Most of the time thermostats freeze in the open position. A thermostat that is permanently open permits relatively cool water to circulate through the radiator, making the engine take longer to reach proper operating temperature. But if a car has been abandoned and the cooling system dry for a time, the thermostat can stick in the closed position.

Many people find that their car is overheating and simply remove the thermostat in an attempt at a quick fix. This almost never helps, and it can aggravate the problem in some cars. One reason is that the water can circulate too fast in many modern cars when the thermostat is removed, so fast that the radiator cannot do its job. With most old cars you will probably have no trouble running the car without a thermostat, but if the car came out with a thermostat, you should make every effort to find the right one for it.

If you can't find a new thermostat for a rare car that you are restoring, you can easily check the old one. Suspend the thermostat in a coffee can of water by means of a cord tied to a pencil across the top of the can. Place a thermometer in the water and apply heat. A 180° thermostat should start to open when the thermometer shows 170°-175°. It usually won't be fully open until the thermometer reads about 25° above the temperature rating of the thermostat.

## COOLANTS

As you know, a discussion of coolants in use today can be covered by few words about the use of ethylene glycol antifreeze. But if you are going to work on an old car, you should be aware of other materials that could have been poured into the radiator. For example, suppose you find a car that was running during the days of the Great Depression and you remove the radiator cap to find an oily gunk in the upper tank. Your normal conclusion is a cracked block, but a strip-down shows no visible cracks. Where did the oil come from? A former owner probably used kerosene as an antifreeze. You can remove the residue with hot water and detergent. But, you ask, why kerosene? In the 1930s it cost about ten cents a gallon.

Some people tried even more questionable additives. One old Ozarker says he would pour a half gallon or more of honey in the radiator of his 1928 Chevy to protect it against freezing. Antifreeze cost money and honey was free if you could find a wild bee tree. One hopes he used it only during mild winters. Although sugar can reduce the freezing point of water, a 1:3 mixture of sugar and water, by weight, will reduce the freezing point only about 2° C. or about 3½° F. The use of such unusual materials suggests that a Depression car that was operated in a poor section of the country is likely to have special problems due to improper maintenance.

When you find a choked cooling system, the culprits are usually rust and scale. But here, again, the car may have been the victim of someone's home remedy. During those same old hard times many motorists got their stop leak additives from a cylindrical carton on the kitchen shelf, the oatmeal box. While oatmeal would indeed retard the leaks, it also frequently stopped up the system. This kind of material may be easier to remove than scale, but the chances are that you will have to rod out the radiator or have the job done at a special shop.

If your vintage car was owned by someone who had a regular job during the Depression, it was probably protected by a mixture of alcohol and water. Alcohol made an effective antifreeze while it was in the system, but its boiling point was unfortunately low. Motorists who added alcohol in the fall, and then neglected to check their coolant level later, often found a frozen radiator on a cold morning in mid-winter. The alcohol vaporized at normal running temperatures, leaving the water to freeze. Also denatured alcohol had other disadvantages. One man told us the story of Melvin, a high school friend, who borrowed his father's car for a mid-week night date. The car stalled on a lonely road, and Melvin had to get the girl back home. The engine seemed hot, so Melvin decided to check the radiator. He had no flashlight, so he removed the cap and lit a match to look down into the upper tank. *Wham*. When Melvin came to school next day, he was eyebrowless and bald above his forehead. Such were the perils of using antifreeze before ethylene glycol arrived on the market.

After you restore your car, you can get just about all the information you need to know about coolants from the back of a plastic antifreeze bottle. Modern ethylene glycol antifreezes have the advantage that they protect against boil-over as well as against freezing. For example, in a modern car with a 15-pound pressure cap, a 50% mix of water and antifreeze can protect the cooling system from under 30° below 0° to above 250° Fahrenheit. A new solution of antifreeze also contains rust inhibitors and anti-foam ingredients.

Modern stop leak preparations work better than oatmeal, but they should be used only as a last resort. Stop leak additives usually make good insulation and for your car's cooling system you need heat *transfer*, not insulation. So if you want to do a top notch job in restoring an old car, try to fix all the radiator leaks *right*.

## HOSES

You will almost certainly have to replace all the hoses on any old car that has been stored for a number of years (Fig. 13-2). Even if the car has been used recently, you should carefully inspect the hoses. Typically they will be hard and brittle, suggesting early failure. Or, you may find that some of them have soft spots where oil was spilled on the hose and has caused deterioration. In use soft hoses can collapse and impede the flow of coolant or they can blow up like a balloon. Lower radiator hoses on modern cars have springs in them to prevent collapse.

If the hoses pass your first inspection, remove them and check their interior walls. If the walls are crumbly, replace them. Particles from the walls of old hoses can be washed away from the hose and deposited in the heater or radiator core, causing a blockage.

To replace an old hose you will often need only the inside diameter of the hose and the length because early hoses were almost invariably straight sections of tubing rather than the convoluted shapes used today. Check the end of the hose to see the number of plies. Most red heater hose has 3 plies, black, 2 plies. Two-ply hose is generally considered a 2-year hose; 3-ply hose is much more durable.

## FAN BELTS

Most old cars will have a single fan belt, and the same rule that applies to hoses goes here too: expect to replace the belt. But you may find no belt at all, and so you must measure the correct size of belt to buy. If the car is very old, it will probably require a much wider belt than those used on cars today. You can estimate the correct width by measuring the pulley widths. To get the correct length, make sure the adjustable pulley is near the position that will accept the shortest belt length and run a piece of string around all the pulleys, then measure the length of the string. Or just go to your local auto parts store and see if they have a listing of the proper size for your car.

If your car is an antique, it may require a flat belt. A Model T Ford, for example, will need a flat belt that is 1-1/8" wide and 1/8" thick. The length will vary from 23" for a 1909 model to 32" for the last T's made. For other antique cars the width of flat belts varied from 5/8" to 2", and the length from about 25" to more than 40". These flat belts were sometimes made from fiber-reinforced red rubber. If you can't find a replacement flat belt for your vintage car, you can make one from fiber belting leather. Cut a strip to the right length, then join the ends with belt lacing. The belt lacing can be attached by driving it into the belt ends with a hammer.

Fig. 13-2. Straight upper hose on this antique car is typical of the easy-to-replace hoses on old cars.

If the car has a fan belt, inspect it carefully. Check the inside of the belt for glazing, a hard shiny look. This is evidence that the belt is too loose and slipping. If you see any breaks on the inside surface, get a new belt.

To adjust the fan belt tension on a typical old car, look for the movable pulley which is almost always on the generator. You can usually slide the generator in or out by means of a slotted mounting bracket, the adjusting strap, but you must loosen the locking bolt on the adjusting strap and the two pivot bolts. Another method for belt adjustment consists of an adjustable width pulley. This kind of pulley has a threaded shaft so that one side of the pulley can be screwed into position and held there by a lock nut. To adjust belt tension you simply loosen the lock nut, reset the side of the pulley, then tighten the lock nut. A variation of this method of belt adjustment is a pulley whose width is made variable by adding or removing shims located between the two halves of the pulley.

When you install a new belt, the tension should be made slightly greater than that of an old belt to allow for belt stretching. You will find published recommendations for how far you should be able to depress the belt with your finger, but the suggested figures vary from about a quarter of an inch up to an inch. The correct amount of deflection depends on the span length between pulleys and on how hard you push. We recommend up to ¾" for old cars that have greater than average distance between pulleys. One way to learn to judge the proper tension is to use the finger test on a car, such as a new one, that you know has been set with a strand tension gauge. Although there is some variation in how different manufacturers set their belts, it is usually not a significant difference. Once you get the feel for proper belt tension you can use your judgement with the finger test.

Even if an old belt seems to be in good condition, it's a good idea to find a replacement and carry it with you. Mike once restored a 1941 Dodge and retained the old belt. Then he and his wife took a 100 mile trip, during which the fan belt broke. The breakdown occurred miles from nowhere and Mike's car club was responsible for a skit and a parade at their destination. They were late for the parade, of course, simply because Mike failed to observe Murphy's law.

Don't use grease or oil to silence a sqealing belt. Grease acts on the rubber to make it swell and fail prematurely. Noise probably means maladjustment, so check the tension. And don't use a notched belt on power steering; it can cause annoying vibrations.

## WATER PUMP

If your restored car overheats, check out the water pump along with other cooling system components. On very old cars the vanes of the impeller may be badly corroded, a condition that reduces the pump's efficiency in moving water through the system. To check the pump's action, remove the lower heater hose at the heater end and hold the hose so that the end is in a vertical position with the water level at the open end. Have someone start the engine and watch the water in the end of the hose. If it doesn't move, the pump is defective.

A rattling noise from the front of the engine can mean a loose shaft in the pump. Stop the engine and try to shake the fan blades from front to back. If the blades can be moved ⅛" or more, the pump should be replaced. On a modern car, with a clutch fan, it may be the fan bearings that are worn. To check the pump further, look for leaks around it. The best way to check for water pump leaks is to stop the car and let it stand until the engine is cool, then look. Use a light to inspect the area of the block near and under the pump. Leaks will usually be around the shaft vent hole rather than at the housing gasket. Such leaks can be an ominous sign for several reasons. A leak can wash the grease out of the bearing, causing it to fail, and if water can leak out, air can get in. When air is fed into the cooling system, corrosion will increase, the system will overflow, and foamy water is *not* an effective coolant. Also, as the bearings become more worn, the fan will develop more end play so that it can finally move forward into the radiator or its shaft will break.

## RADIATOR

The radiator transfers heat from the engine coolant to the air by passing the coolant through the core. The radiator also contains two tanks, one above and one below the core. The most common kind of radiator core is the tubular core used on modern cars. Some older cars may have a different kind of core, the cellular core (Figs. 13-3, 13-4). You can usually identify the kind of core by removing the radiator cap and looking down into the upper tank. If you can see the openings of vertical tubes, the radiator has a tubular core. The tubes have a flattened cross-section so that air can flow around them. The tubes are held in place by thin horizontal sheets of metal, the fins. These horizontal fins are often formed into a wiggly design so that they not only space the tubes but also add extra surface area to dissipate the heat. Check to see that they are attached to the tubes; if not, they will cut down on heat transfer and the engine will overheat.

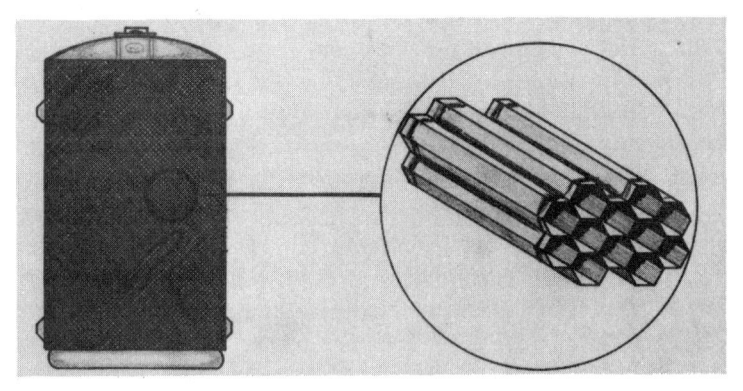

Fig. 13-3. Handmade cellular radiator found on some old cars.

A cellular radiator core is much more complex. The only straight paths on these cores that you can follow with your eye are the horizontal ones from front to back, the air paths. Coolant flows down around all sides of these air tubes. On some cellular cores the pattern of horizontal air tube openings is rectangular, on others the visual effect is that of a honey comb. Such radiators were once hand made and are far more expensive than the simpler tubular radiator.

The first step in radiator restoration is to blow the bugs and dirt out of the air passages. If you have access to an air hose, put the nozzle behind the radiator and blow from the engine side to the front. If you don't have an air hose, you can use a water hose with a triggered nozzle at the end. If there is an oily or greasy dirt in the fins, use a grease solvent, then flush with water.

If you have any doubt about the condition of the radiator, it's a good idea to back flush it before you start the engine. Old cooling systems usually have a considerable amount of scale that may have collected in the radiator, clogging at least some of the passages. By forcing water through the radiator in a direction that is opposite to the natural flow, you can often remove this rust or scale. Remove the clamps that connect the radiator hoses to the engine block and aim the upper hose to one side so the dirty water will go onto the ground. Connect your water hose to the lower radiator hose. You can make a simple adaptor which will act as a reducer from the large diameter radiator hose to the water source. Get several short pieces of radiator hose of various diameters and insert one inside the end of another and clamp the two together (Fig. 13-5). Get a hose repair fitting from a hardware store and attach it to the end of the smaller radiator hose. You can then screw your garden hose into the end of the adaptor and clamp the large end of the adaptor to your radiator tank (Fig. 13-6).

Another method is the long hose way. Attach a long large diameter hose to the lower tank of the radiator, make sure the hose is long enough to reach above the radiator cap. Fill the hose with water until the radiator is full. Then while the hose is full, use an air hose to shoot jets of air into the water. Use care in any flushing so that you don't apply too much pressure to the radiator.

While flushing the radiator, you can also flush the engine block and the heater, but remember to run the water against the direction of natural flow (Fig. 13-7). For the heater the natural flow is from bottom to top, so you attach your flushing hose to the top heater outlet. Even if the radiator is open there is a good chance the heater core will be clogged because it carries a more restricted flow of water and is shut off for much of each year.

If your attempts to back flush the radiator don't do the job, take the radiator or heater to a special shop and have them rodded out. Sometimes that is the only way to unstop a badly plugged core. Such shops can also patch any leaks in the cores or tanks.

## LEAK DETECTION

If your cooling system has a leak, check the radiator and heater carefully. If the car has a modern pressurized system, you

Fig. 13-4. 1924 Chevrolet with cellular rdiator.

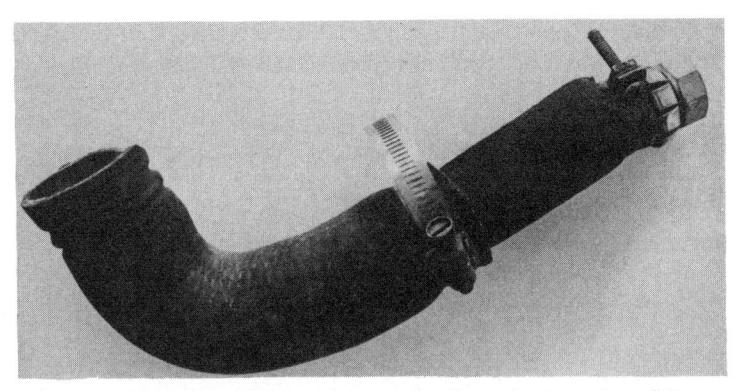

Fig. 13-5. Homemade adaptor which can couple garden hose to radiator or block.

can use a radiator pressure checker to test the cap to see if it holds at its rated pressure. If the cap releases below or above the marked rating, replace it. The cap should maintain the proper pressure in the system so that the coolant won't boil out because of low pressure. After testing the cap, put the tester on the radiator in place of the cap and pump up the system to the rated pressure, or, if the cap tested low, to the pressure held by the cap. Be careful not to apply more pressure to an old car with many miles on it. Watch the gauge for at least a couple of minutes to see if it holds. If there is a pressure drop, make sure the rubber on the tester is sealing properly. If the seal is good, you must look for the leak that allowed the pressure to drop. Start the car and watch the gauge to see if the pressure continues to rise. If it does, pull off one spark plug wire at a time, at the distributor cap, until the pressure increase stops. This will tell you which cylinder is leaking exhaust gas into the cooling system.

If you don't have a pressure tester you can test for exhaust gas leaks another way. Remove the fan belt that drives the water pump. Remove the thermostat and replace the housing. Fill the system with water until it is flush with the top of the thermostat housing. Start the engine. There should be no movement of water so if you see bubbles coming to the surface of the water in the thermostat housing, you know there is a compression leak. Disregard any minor splashing of water caused by engine vibration. To locate the cylinder that is producing the leak, remove the spark plug wires, one at a time, until you identify the faulty cylinder.

If you find a compression leak, try the easiest cure first, such as tightening the head bolts. Make sure you use the proper tightening sequence for the engine you are working on. If you don't know the right order, you can probably find a numbered diagram in a repair manual at your local library.

Next, if this doesn't help, remove the head and inspect the gasket. Check the head itself with a precision straight edge to see if it is warped. If necessary, have it resurfaced at a machine shop.

### CRACKS IN HEAD OR BLOCK

If the trouble is a cracked head or block, you will probably have to have the crack welded (Fig. 13-8). But even then, you should use some kind of sealer because of hairline cracks that form along the weld. Avoid the kind of sealers that stop leaks by forming masses of rabbit pellets; these sealers can stop up more than just the leaks.

A good sealer need not be expensive. On Mike's first job as a mechanic, a woman brought a 1956 Pontiac with a leak to him for repair. The first examination indicated that the head gasket was bad, but when Mike pulled the head there was a 3″ crack which ran about ¼″ to ½″ under the head surface of the block. The woman didn't want to spend much money on the old car so she sold it to Mike for $25. He went to a drug store and got a quart of water glass,

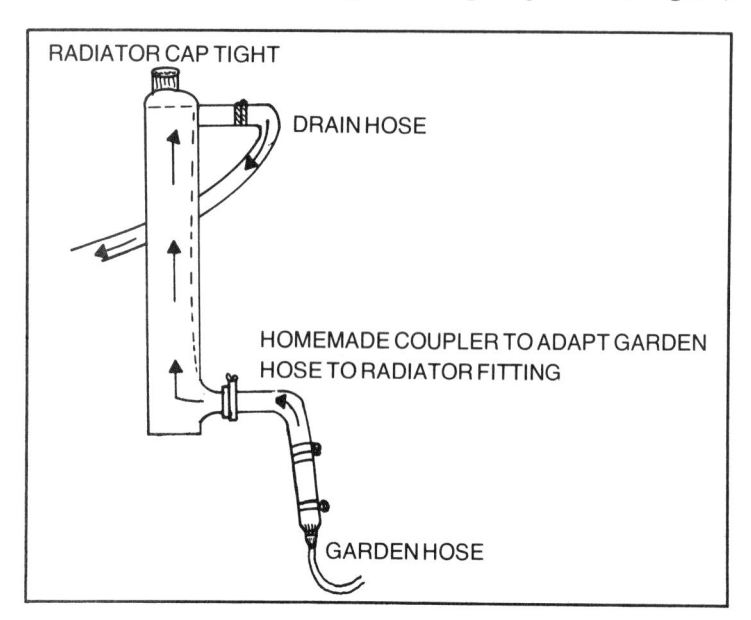

Fig. 13-6. Using the homemade coupler and a water supply from a garden hose to back flush a radiator.

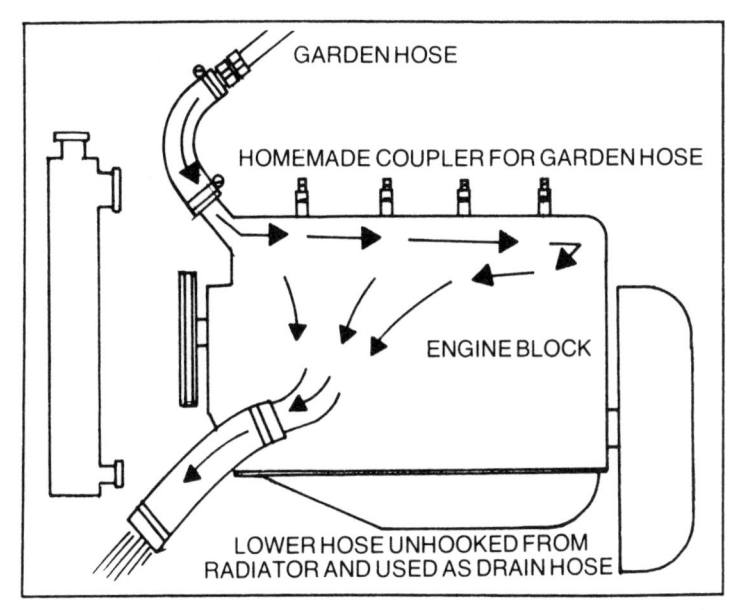

Fig. 13-7. Using the homemade coupler and garden hose to back flush an engine block.

an egg preserver. He added this to the coolant until the leak stopped. Mike has tried several kinds of block sealers and has found only one that works as well as water glass. The best commercial brand may be slightly better, but its price is much better, too. But don't use water glass for radiator leaks.

## OTHER HEATING PROBLEMS

Suppose you do the routine checking and find no problems but your car still overheats. What do you do then? On very old cars there is a chance that someone has tinkered with the design of the system. One possibility: the original radiator may have been replaced with a smaller one of insufficient capacity. Check this out with members of a car club who might know someone with the same model car that you have.

The possibilities of component swapping are almost endless. One man bought an old Renault Caravelle which had had an engine replacement. The original engine for the Caravelle was the same power plant used in the early Dauphines, with the radiator at the front of the engine where it could receive air from the vents in the rear quarter panels of the body. But the replacement engine had been taken from a later model, the Renault R-8. This engine had the radiator at the extreme rear of the car. Soon after buying the car the owner blew his engine and had to get another, so he found a wrecked R-8 and bought the engine. A short time later he blew the second engine. With the cost per mile escalating too fast for comfort, the man decided to investigate the problem before sticking still another engine in his car. Inspection of the two body styles convinced him that the R-8 engines were designed to be used only in bodies with reverse air flow cooling, such as the R-8. This points up the fact that careless substitution of components can lead to unexpected problems.

Another possible cause of overheating: wrong engine timing. A car that is timed too slow will have no pep and will run hot, but timing that is too fast can also cause heating. If an engine is timed too fast, there will usually be some pinging, such as you get with cheap gas, particularly on old engines with carbon build-up.

Improper air/gas mixtures can also cause an engine to run hot. You can get an excessively lean mixture if there are vacuum leaks below the throttle plate or if someone has tampered with the carburetor jets. Or if the mixture is too rich, carbon can form in the engine and some of it may be trapped under the valves. A valve with carbon under it can't seat properly and so heat isn't properly transferred to the head. Instead, hot spots occur. Still another cause of heating is oil that is drawn into the combustion chamber.

Fig. 13-8. Engine block which has had a crack welded.

These problems, which produce a hot running engine, can cause the engine to run on, or "diesel," after the ignition is shut off. Dieseling is made worse by a too fast idle. There is a common misconception that bad timing itself can cause the engine to run on. Many people come in to Mike's shop asking to have their timing set. Mike checks it and tells them the timing is all right. But, they say, the engine runs on. Mike then explains to them that when they shut off the key the ignition is *off* so the timing has no effect after that.

Some cars, such as the old Dodge and Plymouth flathead sixes, have heat distribution tubes that can rust and cause trouble. These tubes ran from just behind the water pump to the rear of the block so that they could carry water to the hottest parts of the block under the exhaust valves. When the heat distribution tube in an old engine rusts away, it can clog the passages and cause the engine to develop hot spots. This often causes scuffing of the rings. To replace the tube, remove the radiator and water pump. Then, using a stiff piece of wire with a hook on it, fish out the tube or the pieces of tube.

## TEMPERATURE GAUGES

Sometimes when you think a car is running hot the trouble is in the heat indicator rather than the engine. Here is how one motorist was fooled by a gauge during the early days of the import car invasion of the U. S. He took his two year old 1958 Renault Dauphine to a dealer for a water pump replacement. After leaving the dealer's shop, the Dauphine owner noticed that the temperature gauge stayed on cold. At first he was delighted with the efficiency of the new water pump, but then he remembered that the owner's manual suggested closing the roller blind over the radiator if the car ran cold. True to the manual, he pulled the blind. But the temperature gauge stayed on cold. When he drove into his driveway and shut off the engine he could hear the water boiling in the radiator. He opened the blind and drove the car until the boiling stopped, then started checking to see what was wrong. A call to the dealer brought a snap diagnosis by phone: the temperature gauge in the instrument panel was bad. He asked the dealer if the mechanic could have done something to cause the problem. No, the dealer said, impossible. Then, while checking over the engine, the owner removed the temperature sending unit. As he studied it, he noticed the inscription, "12 V." He then remembered that his 1958 car had a 6 volt electrical system. Remembering that a 1959 Renault, which had a 12 volt electrical system, was undergoing engine work at the same time his car had been worked on, he returned to the dealer's shop and found the six volt sender from his car still lying on the bench. After the mechanic on duty had switched senders for him, the car's temperature gauge worked perfectly.

Even when properly installed, gauges and sender units are notorious for causing trouble. They can signal trouble when there is none or they can say "Go" even though there is steam coming out of the radiator. As a mechanic Mike hears more about the latter problem. If your car has a faulty gauge, start toubleshooting by checking the connection at the sender. Look for burnt spots or worn insulation on the wire. Have someone watch the instrument panel while you ground the lead to the sender. If there is no movement or light change, the problem lies in the wiring or in the instrument panel. If grounding the wire makes things happen in the panel, the trouble is with the sender.

Some antique cars have the vapor pressure temperature gauge. This gauge has a metal case with dial and a capillary tube with an immersion bulb. The immersion bulb is mounted in the engine head where the water temperature is highest. The capillary tube connects the bulb to the dial on the car's dash. The bulb contains a fluid, usually ether, whose vapor pressure expands evenly with an increase in temperature. As the gas is forced up the capillary tube, it goes into a curved bourbon tube. One end of the tube is attached to the edge of the dial where it is connected, by a linkage, to the dial needle. As pressure is applied, the tube straightens from its curve, moving the needle.

To test this kind of gauge for accurate calibration, drain the cooling system and unscrew the bulb from the block. Place the bulb in a pan of hot water with an accurate thermometer. The gauge should give the same reading as the thermometer. If it doesn't, look for a replacement. Such gauges are almost impossible to repair.

## AIR COOLED ENGINES

Except for the old Franklins, the VW, and the Corvair, very few cars with air cooled engine have been sold in this country. Apparently most people have a degree of prejudice against the use of air cooled engines on automobiles. Herbert H. Franklin was convinced of the superiority of air cooled engines, so surely convinced that for many years he refused to play down the air cooled feature of his cars. Finally, in 1922, he compromised enough to permit a phony radiator design that made the Franklin car look more conventional. Early Franklins won many performance and economy tests against water cooled cars. One of the secrets of the early Franklin success was their power to weight ratio and that depended, in part, on air cooling. Another reason for the commercial success of the Franklin car was Herbert H. Franklin's personal interest in quality control.

Instead of casting a line of cylinders in a solid block with water jackets around it, Franklin made free standing cylinders with fins on each for cooling. By this method the Franklin car avoided the need for water jackets, pumps, radiators, and several gallons of water. The same weight saving advantages no doubt appealed to the designers of the VW and the Corvair.

Air cooled engines have fewer cooling parts to malfunction but they are subject to some of the same kind of problems that trouble water cooled engines. Cleanliness is important. While there is no radiator to choke up, the cooling fins must be kept free of dirt and trash that will insulate them from the air. All air passages must be kept open. And the fan belt should be inspected regularly, as owners of early Corvairs soon learned.

Regardless of the kind of cooling there is one part of the cooling system that people seldom consider as such, the oil. Oil is pumped to the head of overhead valve engines and carries away some of the heat from the valve area. If you permit the oil to get low it doesn't have as much capacity for heat dissipation.

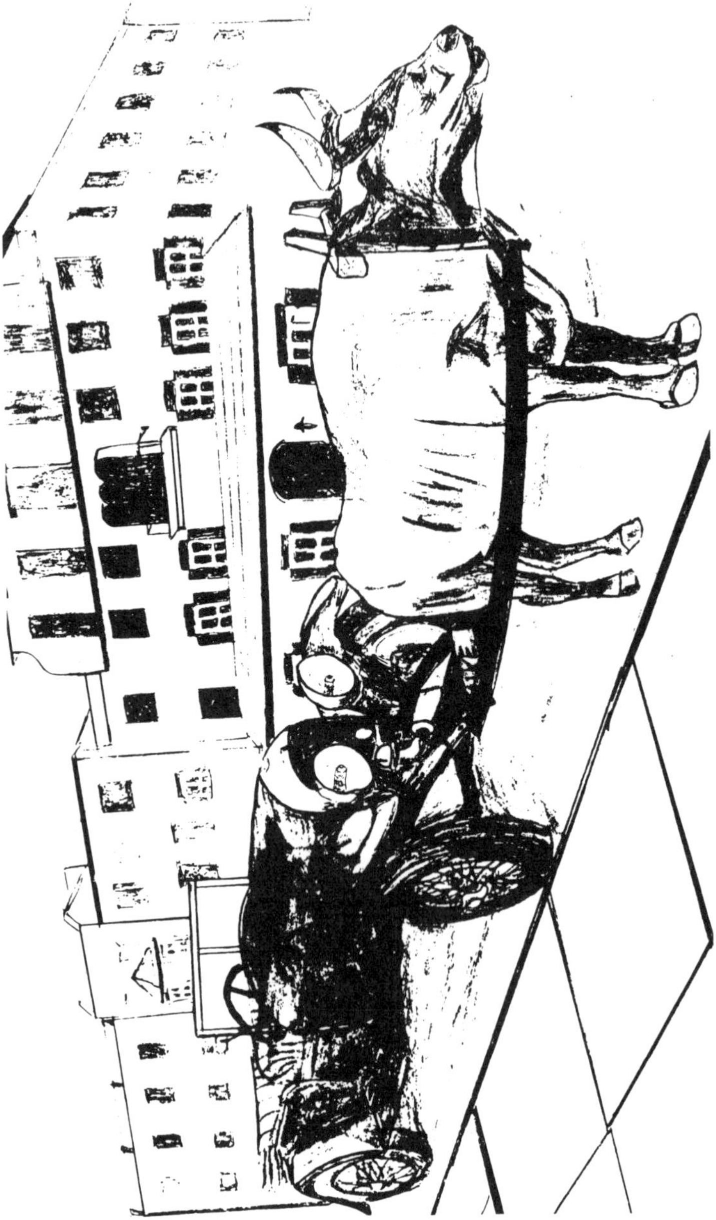

# Chapter 14
# The Power Train

The most important item in the power train is the engine, which we have already discussed. Gasoline engines must be operated at a certain speed to develop adequate horsepower and torque to drive the car, so some kind of variable gearing is necessary. Early cars had chain drives, similar to the bicycles which they replaced. Various other methods have been used to transmit power from the engine to the drive wheels, including a friction drive. Many early cars made use of this principle because of its simple construction. The most popular was the Cartercar, which used a friction wheel that was driven at a 90° angle by a revolving disk that was coupled to the engine. When the friction wheel ran near the center of the disk, its speed was reduced but power ratio increased. When the driver wanted to move to a higher gear, he moved the wheel toward the edge of the disk. As he did, there was a gradual change of gear which provided smooth acceleration.

Another type of early power train was the planetary transmission as used in the Model T Ford. This one has survived in the automatic transmissions of today.

In addition to allowing the engine to run at an optimum speed, the power train must provide a means of engaging power gradually. This job is done on most modern cars by a torque converter, on older cars and those with manual transmissions by a clutch. In the typical conventional drive system, the clutch is followed by a transmission which changes the gear ratios. In low gear the crankshaft may turn about 12 times for each wheel revolution, in second gear, about 8 times, and in high gear about 4 times. With an automatic transmission the ratios may be different.

Behind the transmission, the drive shaft transfers power to the rear end, or differential, which in turn drives the rear wheels. The drive shaft contains two or more important components which permit it to move out of a rigid line when the back wheels hit a bump, the universal joints.

While there are many other possible arrangements, an overwhelming majority of old cars will have the kind of power train described above. We will assume that your car is so equipped.

## CLUTCH AND FLYWHEEL

To deliver power, an engine must run at several hundred rpm or more. An engine will start at 100 rpm but won't keep running at that speed, much less pull a load. The clutch permits the engine to run independently of the transmission and, by disengaging the two, allows the driver to change gears in a manual transmission.

The first problem for anyone who has never driven a car with a manual transmission but who is restoring a car with one is to learn how to drive it. The transmissions on old cars may not be synchronized and so require more skill than modern manual shifting cars. Even people who are used to manual transmissions can damage the gears in a non-synchronized unit. In one case that we know of, a neophyte drove a car with a non-synchronized first gear only across town and damaged it by forcing the transmission into low gear while rolling. Downshifting with such cars requires a certain amount of practice to get engine speed and gear speed synchronized. The art of double clutching is worth learning. Put the clutch pedal down and shift to neutral, then, with the clutch pedal up, accelerate the engine to the make the clutch shaft run at the proper speed, then push the clutch pedal down again to shift. Or, to be safe, try to avoid downshifts except when the car is stopped.

The clutch works by forcing a friction disk against the flywheel at the back of the engine. The movable part of the pressure plate moves backward to disengage the flywheel, or forward to engage it. When you depress the clutch pedal, the pressure plate moves backward and disengages from the disk. The pressure plate housing is bolted to the flywheel and moves all the time that the engine is running. Inside it is the steel plate that matches the friction surface of the clutch disk. When the pressure plate is in the engaged position, the steel plate is held to the friction disk which is held to the flywheel by spring pressure. The clutch disk, between the pressure plate and the flywheel, moves too. When the pedal is depressed, it activates the throw-out bearing through the throw-out arm, moving the fingers on the pressure plate and releasing the clutch disk.

The single-plate dry clutch is the kind used by most manufacturers of automobiles, but two other kinds have been used extensively, the multiple disk clutch and the wet clutch. The multiple disk clutch has, as the name implies, several friction disks instead of one. And the wet clutch runs in oil. Dodge Brothers built cars with multiple disk clutches, and Hudson cars were noted for a wet clutch.

### CLUTCH REMOVAL

To remove the clutch you must first disconnect the transmission from the engine. Disconnect the universal joint at the rear of the transmission, the speedometer cable, and all gearshift linkages. Support the transmission while you remove the cap screws that attach it to the clutch housing. When you are removing the transmission, avoid letting it sag when you are taking out the last screw. Use guide pins in the screw holes so the transmission will slide straight back. This will avoid damage to the clutch.

Various kinds of clutches will require slightly different procedures in removal. Following is a typical one. Before removal, mark the pressure plate housing and the flywheel so you can install the parts in the same position with respect to each other. When you unscrew the bolts that hold the pressure plate to the flywheel, loosen each bolt about a half turn at a time so you won't distort the plate. Pay particular attention to which side of the friction disk faces the engine. These disks can be installed incorrectly, with the sides reversed, causing the springs on the disk to hit the bolts on the flywheel.

When you have removed the pressure plate from the flywheel, inspect each part for wear or damage. If the clutch disk is worn, the flywheel face and pressure plate are likely to be scored and need remachining. Pressure plate rebuilding is a job for a specialist.

This is a good time to give special attention to the flywheel. Most old car engines will be used conservatively, but if you rework a flathead V-8, you may be tempted to rev it up occasionally. Check the flywheel to see if it has a burnt appearance from a slipping clutch. Inspect the surface carefully; you will probably see that it has a checkered look. Such checks are really small breaks in the flywheel. If you see this condition, replace the flywheel. Flywheel horror stories abound in the history of cars, stories of flywheels exploding at high speed, sending pieces up through the floor boards and amputating the legs of front seat occupants. While this kind of accident usually happens at race tracks or where cars are hot-rodded, don't take a chance with a questionable flywheel.

The clutch facing is likely to be worn and need replacing. Clutch disks are normally sold as a unit, with the facing installed, but in earlier times you could buy bulk facing. In most cities you can still find a parts house that has been in business for many years and will have some old stock. Replace the facing the way you would a riveted brake lining, by drilling out the old rivets and installing the new facing with new rivets. Make every effort to keep the facing free of oil or grease.

When you replace the clutch, you should use a centering tool. The main driver gear from an old transmission makes an excellent pilot shaft to guide the clutch.

The clutch pedal should have about 1" to 2" of free play before the levers that actuate the clutch mechanism are moved. By examining the clutch coupling to the fork that operates the throw-out bearing, you can determine how to make the adjustment. Typically there will be an adjusting nut on the rod that pushes against the fork. The acutating rod should have a clearance of ⅛" to ¼", which will provide the proper amount of slack in the pedal.

**TRANSMISSION**

As mentioned earlier, a gasoline engine cannot develop full power at low engine speeds. When a car is stationary, its inertia must be overcome before the car will begin to move, so much more power is needed to get the car rolling than to keep it going after it is started. Also, the car requires much more power to drive it up a hill or to accelerate than to cruise at a constant speed on the flats. On the other hand, a gear that would be appropriate for starting or hill climbing would require a far higher engine speed and greater gas consumption than would be desirable for cruising.

Because of these conflicting requirements, some kind of variable speed transmission is necessary. A standard 3-speed transmission varies the engine revolutions per wheel revolution from a ratio of 4 in high gear to 8 in second gear or to 12 in low gear. Automatic transmissions make the gear ratio selection without the aid of the driver by mechanical, hydraulic, or electrical control.

When two gears mesh, the speed of the driven gear is determined by the speed of the driver gear and by the number of teeth on the gears. If a gear with 14 teeth drives a gear with 28 teeth, the second gear will rotate at ½ the speed of the driver gear. In any change of gear size and speed, there is also a change in torque. Torque is the power to twist or turn something. For example, a certain amount of torque is required to remove a screw on a bottle cap. Torque is measured in pound-feet, which shouldn't be confused with the units called foot-pounds, which are used to measure work. In the two gears mentioned above the second gear rotates at the ½ the speed but will turn with about twice the torque as the first gear. (Some energy will always be lost to friction.)

Early transmissions achieved a gear change by means of sliding gears which moved on a shaft until they meshed with other gears. Most modern transmissions have the gears in constant mesh to avoid gear clashing during shifts. Power enters the transmission through a main drive on the clutch shaft. The power is transmitted to a countershaft gear or cluster gear. The cluster gear has, in addition to the gear that is engaged to the main drive gear, three other gears on the shaft. The smallest of these is the reverse gear. The next to smallest gear on the shaft is low gear. On a sliding gear transmission an idler gear is added to change the direction of rotation of the drive shaft. Second gear is larger than low gear. High gear is achieved by locking the drive system straight through from the main drive gear shaft to the drive shaft behind the transmission.

Many of the old sliding gear transmissions have weak bearings on the countershaft, probably because the manufacturers expected the car to be driven in high gear nearly all the time. Such transmissions are relatively trouble free unless abused by poor shifting habits or unless the car had considerable use in the lower gears where the cluster gear shaft would have had undue pressure on it. If you disassemble such a transmission, check to see if the bearings look weak. For many occasions where you will drive an old car, such as parades, the lower gears will be used much more than in average driving. If the bearings are weak, you should be aware of it, but there is little you can do except go into high gear whenever possible.

If you have to repair your transmission, try to find a detailed drawing of it. An exploded drawing will be helpful in locating and identifying parts. To completely renew your transmission is a major repair job, requiring you to disassemble, clean all parts, and replace those that are worn or damaged. In many cases you can save this kind of time-consuming work by finding a satisfactory transmission on a parts car.

## TRANSMISSION TROUBLE DIAGNOSIS

The most common complaint about transmissions is noise. Sometimes the transmission is blamed for noises that occur at some other point in the car. For example, some "transmission" noises continue when the clutch is disengaged, proving that the noise comes from the engine instead of the transmission. On the other hand, if the noise occurs when the car is in neutral but stops when the clutch is disengaged, it is the transmission or power train. If the noise occurs only when the car is moving, check to see if it occurs in just one gear or in all gears. A noise that persists in each gear can arise from trouble in the rear end. But if only one or two gear positions are involved, then you should map out the transfer of power through your transmission, then examine any gears that are under load during the noise.

The kind of noise can also help you to identify the cause. A humming noise may indicate slightly worn gears, but if the noise gradually becomes more of a growl, then a grind, you should start looking for another transmission. Transmission bearing problems begin with a hissing sound but progress to a thumping noise. If your transmission appears to have rattles in it, the trouble may be gears that are loose on the shafts, loose clutch parts, loose bearings, or loose gear shifter forks. In fact, rattles are always hard to pinpoint because the sound could be carried from one part of the car to another.

A new transmission normally is a bit stiff to shift but quickly breaks in and improves in shifting. Later, the effort to shift gears may increase due to poor lubrication, a bent shifter fork, improper linkage adjustment, or even a malfunctioning clutch. If the car has a vacuum gear shifting mechanism, the trouble is likely to be caused by vacuum leaks or a damaged piston or valves in the vacuum cylinder.

Gear clashing is a symptom of a synchronizer that fails to work right. A broken synchronizer spring is a likely cause if the trouble occurs suddenly. But a clutch that doesn't fully release can cause the same kind of trouble. Of course gear clashing can occur on any non-synchronized gears if the driver doesn't take measures to avoid it.

Another troublesome symptom of transmission problems is the failure of the car to stay in gear. In some cases the car slips out of gear only under stress, such as when traveling a good rate of speed and the wheels hit a rough place in the road that vibrates the whole car. This could be an indication of loose coupling in the power system between the engine and transmission. If the transmission is out of line with the engine, this can happen at any time. Other possible causes of high gear slippage are too much main gear shaft end play, worn bearings, damaged synchronizer, worn notches on the gearshift lever detent ball notch assembly, or poorly adjusted linkages. If the car shifts out of second, look for too much clearance between the gears, excessive main shaft end play, worn gear teeth, defective synchronizer on main shaft or in second speed gear, or maladjusted linkage. Finally, if the car slips out of low or reverse, check the sliding sleeve for loose fit, the countershaft for excessive end play, or the linkage for improper adjustments.

If your car locks while shifting gears, killing the engine, it may be because the transmission is locked in two gears at once. To test for this condition, depress the clutch and start the engine. If the engine runs while the clutch pedal is depressed, the transmission is locked. *Don't* try to push the car while in this condition or you will damage the transmission. Sometimes you can relieve this condition by shifting back to the original gear. The problem is caused by a faulty interlock system—worn detents, for example. A bent shifting fork will do the same thing. You can sometimes live with this condition by making sure you give the transmission time to move completely out of one gear before you force it into another one.

As you can see from the above symptoms, poor adjustment of the gearshift linkages can cause the car to slip out of any gear, so these should be checked first. Linkages on column-mounted shifts are especially subject to wear and misadjustment.

If your transmission leaks oil, check the oil plug first to see if it is tight. Next, check the oil level; it may be too high. Next, check the gaskets to see if they are present and in good condition. If these easy-to-fix conditions all give a negative test, the problem is with the oil seals or the oil slingers which protect the seal from excessive oil pressure.

## DRIVE SHAFT AND UNIVERSAL JOINTS

Since the rear axle moves up and down on the suspension, a car must have some provision for the drive shaft to bend and to shorten or lengthen. These functions are served by the universal joints and slip joints (Fig. 14-1). Many kinds of universal joints have been used, particularly before the early 1930s when most car manufacturers went to joints with needle bearings. One early type consisted of two yokes connected by doughnut shaped disks of leather or belting material. Such joints required no lubrication. Maintenance for these fabric or leather units consisted of occasional belt tightening or disk replacement.

Another type of universal joint was housed in a ring shaped cover with lubrication plugs located 180° apart. To oil the joint, you remove both plugs and screw a grease fitting into one of the holes. Rotate the joint so that the other hole is at the top. Use a hand gun to put gear oil into the lower fitting until it comes out the top. Replace the top plug, then rotate the joint until the fitting is at the top. Remove the fitting and replace the plug.

Some universal joints on old cars have leather boots. These should *not* be filled with grease because the pressure caused by movement of the joint while full can rupture the leather.

If the car goes from neutral into gear with a jump, suspect the universal joint. To check the joints, shut off the engine and put the car in gear. Rock the car forward and backward, listening for a clunk from the drive train. To confirm the diagnosis, go under the car and grasp the drive shaft near the U joint that you suspect. Push against it and look for unnatural movement. If there is any noise or side play, replace the joint.

The car you restore will probably have either an open drive shaft with a universal joint at each end or it will have a torque tube. The torque tube is an enclosed drive shaft with one universal joint near the transmission. But there have been an endless variety of numbers and kinds of universal joints used during the automobile

Fig. 14-1. The slip joint on a power train with Hotchkiss drive permits the drive shaft to change length.

age. One man we know took a 1961 Buick Special to a garage because of shuddering vibration in the drive train. The mechanic who checked it said that both universal joints were good so the trouble was in the differential. The Buick owner didn't want to spend much money on the old car so he said he would just drive it until it quit. Later he took it to another garage for a second opinion. That opinion was immediate.

"Universal joint," said the mechanic who looked at it.

"But another mechanic told me they were both good."

"Both are. One ain't. This car has four."

This incident points up a big advantage to restoring your own car. You will know the car better than the average mechanic would know it.

Since universal joints are often faulty, we will go through the replacement procedure for the most common type, that on a car with a Hotchkiss drive system, the open drive shaft with two universal joints.

You can do this job without any special tools, just a wrench, a hammer, a punch, and a pair of pliers. If you have an old pair of diagonal wire cutting pliers, you can make a good lock ring remover by grinding off the point.

Before you start on a universal joint replacement job, check the alignment of the joints with respect to each other. Make sure you replace them with the same alignment.

Begin by removing the bolts in the U joint near the rear end. Slip the drive shaft forward and down, then out the rear. The drive shaft is thicker at the end where the U joint fits it. Any damage to the drive shaft tube can cause vibration in the car, so don't clamp the shaft in a vise.

Remove the lock ring from the outside of the caps on the cross. If you don't have an old pair of diagonal pliers, as mentioned earlier, you can use a screw driver for this job. Push inward with the blade against the ring.

Get a large socket from your tool box, one that is just slightly larger than the caps on the U joint cross. Place the socket under one end of the yoke to receive the cap and use a punch to drive the cross down (Fig. 14-2). If the cross is no good you can hit the projecting arm of it. Get the cap off one side, then the opposite side. With the caps off you can easily remove the cross (Fig. 14-3).

To install a new cross, notice that there may be different size caps on the two parts of the cross. The hole for the grease fitting should go on the drive shaft side of the joint. Before you try to install the cross, check the caps to see that the needle bearings are in the right position, standing vertically around the inside wall of the cap as you look down into it. The grease should hold them, but occasionally one or two will fall down and block the cap from going all the way onto the cross.

Raise the cross through the hole in the yoke to put the cap on, then drive it down, using a socket just slightly smaller than the end of the cap (Fig. 14-4). Put the lock ring in the space above the end of the cap then reverse the joint and pull the cross out of the cap, but not far enough to lose out the needle bearings. Then put on the second cap.

Put the lock ring on the first cap installed, then drive that end down until it seats against the lock ring. You should now be able to install the opposite lock ring.

Check the centering by trying to twist the cross. If the joint is stiff, tap the cross toward the last cap installed. If the caps are too close together, the cross can rub on the caps themselves instead of on the bearings. In extreme cases the joint won't take grease. Keep tapping the joint in each direction until it is centered and free to move.

## DIFFERENTIAL

Cars turn corners, so differentials are necessary to permit the outer drive wheel to make more rotations than the inner one. A

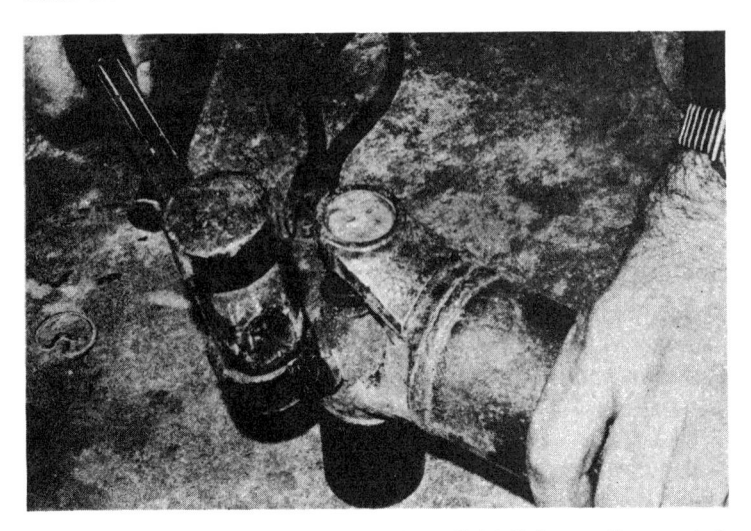

Fig. 14-2. Driving the cross out of a worn universal joint. Note use of large socket below yoke.

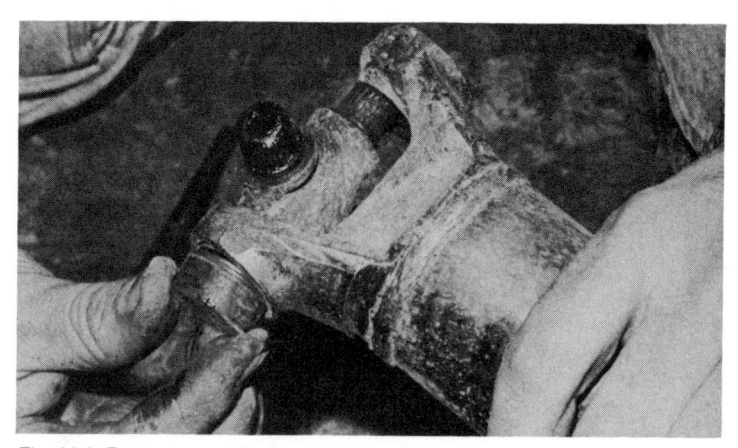

Fig. 14-3. Removing cap from cross in old universal joint.

pinion gear on the end of the drive shaft meshes with a large ring gear that drives the individual wheel axles through two differential pinion gears that mesh with the side gears on the axles. The differential pinion gears do not normally rotate on the pinion shaft, but when the car turns a corner, the pinion gears rotate, transmitting more motion to the outside side gear than the inner side gear, permitting the outer side gear and its axle to turn more rapidly.

One aspect of rear end design that changed considerably during the 1920s and 1930s is the type of main pinion and ring gear. The earliest differentials had spur bevel gears, with straight gear teeth. The drive shaft entered the differential case at the center, even with the axles. Later the spiral bevel gear was developed, permitting gear contact between more than one pair of teeth at a time. With more teeth in contact, the gearing was quieter and lasted longer, but, again, the spiral bevel differential placed the drive pinion at the center of the differential.

Some early engineers saw that they could lower the body, and with that the center of gravity, by running the drive shaft lower. The first solution to this problem was the well-known worm gear, which was often used on trucks. In the worm gearing used on the typical truck the drive shaft entered the differential housing at the top. The Stutz Bearcat was notable among cars that used the worm gear with the drive shaft at the bottom.

In 1927 Packard introduced a new kind of gears for the pinion and ring gear, a kind of gear in which the teeth are cut in a way similar to the spiral bevel gear but with the pinion gear angled so that the drive shaft can be lowered. The name for the new kind of gearing, *hypoid*, quickly became known to service station attendants, sometimes to their dismay. Many lube men put the same kind of lubricants in hypoid rear ends they had been using in other cars until they learned that the older oils were sure death to a hypoid gear. Hypoid gears work under extreme pressure, so that the lubricant was wiped off the gear teeth unless it was formulated to withstand the wiping action. This is just one of many instances of car engineering development that was dependent on the work of oil company chemists. A hypoid lubricant works not only for rear ends with hypoid gears, but for others as well.

## DIFFERENTIAL AND REAR AXLE DIAGNOSIS

Old timers tell us that before 1930 cars had more rear end trouble than later. Whether those problems were due to poorer gear design or to the lubricants available then, it's hard to say. But, it is said, one frequently hears a motorist worrying that he feared that his rear end was going out. During depression days the significant cost of replacing a rear end made this worry prevalent on everyone's mind, so that any noise that occurred while the car was moving brought concern for the differential or rear axles.

Actually, much of the noise that is ascribed to rear end problems never turns out that way. One innocuous problem that is often mistaken for rear end problems is tire noise. This kind of

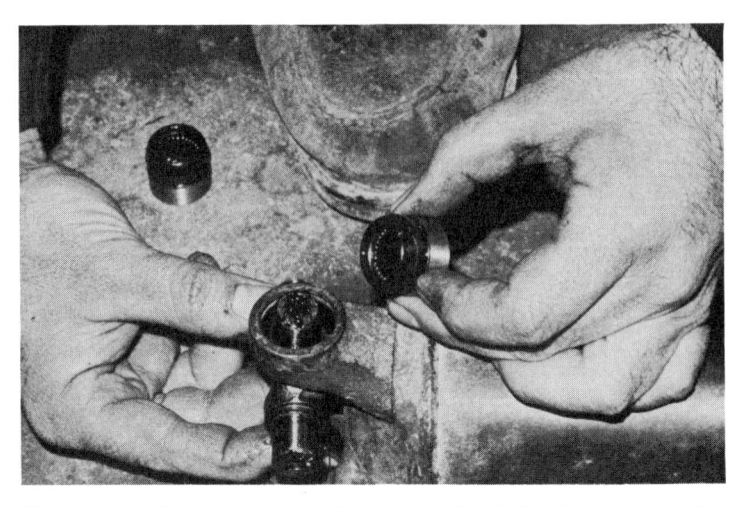

Fig. 14-4. Installing new cross in universal joint. Needle bearings are packed in grease around inner wall of cap.

noise sometimes arises on trips over unfamiliar roads because of differences in pavement surfaces. If a noise can be linked to a change of tires or a change of road surface, the tires should be suspected. To test for tire noise, try driving the car on several different road surfaces and see if the noise persists. Or, if you have extra tires, switch tires.

As mentioned earlier, universal joint problems can be misdiagnosed as rear end trouble, so the universal joints should be checked before condemning the differential. Even a bad muffler has sometimes been the culprit for unusual noises that caused concern for the rear end.

To test for rear end problems, check to see if the noise is constant on a straight road or if it appears while rounding a bend. Also try to determine if the noise is more evident when the car is coasting or when the car is accelerating. If acceleration makes it more noticeable, the ring gear is probably set too far back from the drive pinion. But if the noise grows louder while coasting, the opposite is probably true, and the gears should be moved farther apart. These problems usually occur only after a differential has been serviced and the pinion replaced.

If you hear noise only when the car is rounding a curve, the trouble is likely to be in the spider gears which might be tight on the pinion shaft, or in the side gears being too tight in the differential housing. Too much backlash in the gears can also produce this symptom.

The first symptom of a rear end problem is likely to be a humming noise. Some gears produce this kind of noise for a long time without getting significantly worse, but it usually indicates improper ring gear and pinion adjustment, which should be corrected. Use the acceleration-coasting test to determine the kind of adjustment needed. A growling noise indicates excessive wear has already occurred, and a knocking noise means that replacement of parts must be made.

To check the power train for backlash, put the car in high gear, raise one back wheel off the floor, and twist the wheel to see how much free motion it has before resistance occurs.

Sometimes you may want to determine the car's axle ratio. If it has a Hotchkiss drive with an open drive shaft, this is easy to do. Mark one rear tire and the drive shaft with chalk marks so you can count the revolutions of each. Put the car in neutral and push it forward while someone counts the revolutions on the drive shaft and those of the rear wheel. If the drive shaft rotates four times while the wheel rotates once, the axle ratio is 4:1. Make several trials and calculate the ratio to the nearest tenth.

## REAR END REMOVAL

If the rear end proves to be defective, and if you can find a parts car, complete replacement is the easiest cure. Jack up the rear end of the car, remove the rear wheels, and disconnect lines or rods. Disconnect the shock absorbers at the bottom end. Take the bolts out of the rear universal joint, and remove the drive shaft. Place a jack under the rear end assembly to hold it. It's a good idea to use an extra support for this if you have it. Then remove the U-bolts on the springs. Now you can lower the rear end and remove it. To replace the new rear end, simply reverse the procedure listed above. If your car has hydraulic brakes, you will have to bleed the lines after replacing them. Also you should check the differential for oil and add hypoid lubricant if needed. The wheel bearings should also be greased.

The most difficult part of this job is getting the four U-bolts on the springs loose. These bolts are usually rusted badly, and the nuts are frozen to the bolts. To get them loose, spray the bolts with WD-40 and let it soak in. If you can back the nuts off a few turns, squirt some WD-40 on the bolts above the nuts and tighten the nuts again. Squirt on more WD-40 and back off the nuts again. Keep moving them up and down until you can get the nut off.

To eliminate this part of the job, as well as disturbing the brakes, you can use an alternate method of rear end replacement. This method removes the gears and axles without disturbing the housing. Jack up the rear end and remove the wheels and brake drums. On most cars there will be four bolts that connect a retainer, backing plate, and axle housing. Remove the nuts (if the parts are held together by studs) or bolts, and slide the axle out.

If the car has a Hotchkiss drive, the next step is to remove the rear U-joint. For cars with a torque tube, unbolt the tube at the transmission and let it down. Then remove the ring of bolts in the center of the rear end housing. Watch here for the possibility that a copper washer was used under the nuts to prevent leaks, particularly on the bottom half of the housing. The copper may be jammed into the bolt threads, making the gear carrier difficult to remove. Use a knife blade or a screw driver to clean out the threads. Slide the gear carrier out the front of the housing. This carrier will be heavy, so use care in removing it. Clean the gasket area, install a new gasket, and slide the new gear carrier into place.

Replace the parts in reverse order to their removal. If the copper washers are badly damaged so they will not seal the case, spread some #1 Permatex sealer around each stud in the lower half of the housing. If you have leaks and don't want to do the job again, loosen the nuts slightly and wrap a Permatex-soaked string around the full circle of bolts and tighten the nuts again.

On some cars, including most Chevrolets, the procedure is different. On these there will be no nuts holding the axle at the wheel end of the housing. Instead, the axle is held in by horseshoe clips on the axle gears in the pinion carrier. The procedure for these cars is to remove the cover at the rear of the differential housing. Keep a pan handy to catch the grease. Rotate the ring gear until you can see a bolt head that fits a ½" wrench. The head of this bolt will be to your left as you stand behind the differential, and the bolt will set in the gear carrier horizontally. Note that this bolt head is smaller than the other bolts heads you will find in the differential. Remove the bolt. Then slide out the pin that is held by the bolt. This pin is usually quite free and will slide out easily. Caution: once the pin is free, *don't* rotate either axle or the pinion gears will roll out too. Slide both axles inward toward the center of the differential and remove the horseshoe clamps on the axle gears. Then slide the axles out of the housing. Now slide the pin back into the gear carrier and insert the bolt to hold the gears in the differential.

From this point the procedure is the same as for the type of rear end mentioned earlier. Go to the front and remove the ring of bolts in the center of the rear end housing, and so on.

These two procedures cover most cars, but there are exceptions, such as the Model T Ford. But the procedure for almost *any* job on a Model T is different from other cars.

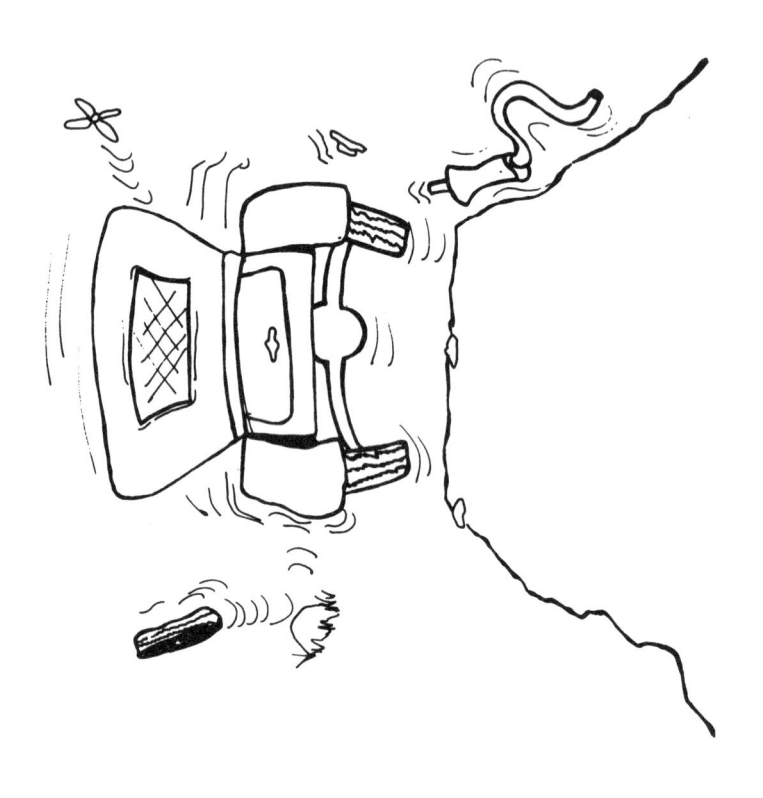

# Chapter 15
# Other Chassis Components

Even though your vintage car may never be driven on long trips, you should make sure its suspension and brake systems are in good condition. Front suspensions cause more problems than rear suspensions for two reasons: most of the weight of the car is on the front, and the front end is complicated by the steering mechanism. Rear suspensions rarely need more than a change of shock absorbers or, occasionally, a broken spring leaf replaced.

## FRONT END DESIGN

Most antique and early production cars have solid front axles; on later production cars the front wheels are suspended independently. Regardless of the type of suspension, the wheel hubs run on ball or roller bearings which, in turn, run on the spindle shafts. The spindle and steering knuckle are made in one piece which is supported by a kingpin. The kingpin is supported by the axle in beam axle cars, or by the upper and lower steering knuckle supports in cars with independent suspensions.

There are three kinds of front axles that have been used extensively throughout the history of the automobile, the Lemoine, the Elliot, and the reverse Elliot (Fig. 15-1). Modern cars use the reverse Elliot, in which the spindle is attached to a yoke which fits above and below the end of the axle. Antiques, such as the Model T, usually have the Elliot axle, in which the yoke is on the axle. The car you rework will almost surely have one of these two kinds of axles.

## FRONT END INSPECTION

Jack up the car so that the weight is off the wheel at the side you want to check. Grasp the wheel at the 12 o'clock and 6 o'clock positions, top and bottom, and try to shake the wheel, pushing on one hand while you pull on the other. If there is movement, have someone watch the suspension parts near the wheel to see which parts are worn. If you have no helper, set up a mirror so that you can see the suspension members and watch the mirror as you shake the wheel. Listen for clunking noises while you shake. Try to determine if the slack is in the suspension parts or in the wheel bearing. If you suspect the wheel bearing, remove the hub cap and dust cap. Tighten the wheel bearing to the point that all the slack is out. Note that you are not adjusting it for use, but at this point you are tightening it all the way to eliminate its movement while you test the other components. Grasp the wheel again and shake it. Any slack now must be coming from the kingpin itself. Make this test on both wheels.

## REPLACEMENT OF KINGPINS AND BUSHINGS

If you find that the kingpins are bad, the next step is to replace them. Remove the nut that adjusts the wheel bearings. Pull the nut, the washer, and the bearing. If it is a ball bearing set-up, pull the race and the bearing. Next, pull the wheel assembly. If the brake drum is rubbing on the brake shoes, back off the brake adjustment to get the wheel assembly free. With the wheel off the car, undo the brake line from the backing plate. If there is enough slack, you can leave the brake line connected. Next remove the backing plate. There are usually four bolts that attach the backing plate and the brake shoe assembly to the spindle. After removing them you can

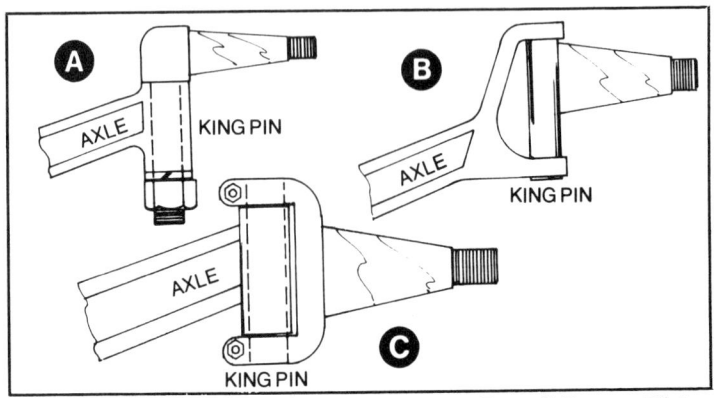

Fig. 15-1. Three kinds of front axles. (A) Lemoine. (B) Elliot. (C) Reverse Elliot.

slide the backing plate off over the spindle. On some cars these bolts also hold the steering linkage or the arm that connects the tie rod to the two wheels. When you have removed all connections from the spindle, it will move freely. On most cars there are two bushings in the spindle; on others the bushings are in the axle. On the usual arrangement the bushings are positioned above and below the axle with a vertical pin through them.

Check the kingpin to see how it is fixed to the axle. There will probably be a center bolt, a lock pin, or other similar arrangement. See if there is a nut on the lock pin. If there is, remove the nut and drive out the lock pin, driving it in the direction opposite the nut. If the lock pin is a simple tapered one, with no nut, find which is the larger and which is the smaller end of that pin. Hit the pin from the small end to drive it out. The kingpin itself may be difficult to remove. In that case, get a punch that is smaller than the diameter of the kingpin, but as near to the same diameter as possible without overlapping it. Hit the punch with the heaviest hammer you can use. It's a good idea to wear goggles for this step because the kingpin is hardened steel and can shatter. Using a punch nearly the same diameter as the kingpin reduces the danger of flying pieces. Before striking the punch, put a jack stand or other firm block under the axle to prevent it from moving when you strike the punch. The kingpin should be driven out with as few blows as possible because continued hammering will mushroom it. To help jar it loose, strike the axle where the kingpin fits through it with a hammer. Strike the axle from one direction, then move the spindle and hit it from the opposite direction. It sometimes requires as many as 20 or even more blows to the axle to break the kingpin free. After hitting the axle, try the punch on the kingpin with a heavy hammer. Don't hold the punch with your hand. A punch holder is ideal for this job, but you can use pliers to hold it if you use a heavy cloth to protect your hand. Note the specification of a *heavy* hammer. The heavier the hammer used, the fewer the number of blows will be needed to remove the kingpin and the less mushrooming will occur.

When the kingpin comes out, you can slide the spindle off and clean it at your wash vat for matching to a new one, unless the parts are easily available. Next, drive the brass bushings out of the upper and lower arms of the spindle. Use a punch or other similar tool. It makes no difference which direction you drive them; they will come out in either direction. If they don't come out easily, you can drive a tapered punch or a nail in the space between them and the spindle arm to collapse them.

When you install new bushings, make sure the grease hole in the new bushing lines up with the grease hole in the spindle. If you forget to do this, it will probably be impossible to remove the bushing without damaging it. But you can select a drill bit with the same diameter as the grease hole in the spindle and drill a new hole in the bushing.

Try the kingpin to see if it fits the new bushings. If the bushings are made of brass, you will probably have to hone the new bushings to fit the kingpin. Plastic bushings usually fit the kingpin. To hone the bushings, use a solvent as you work, and check frequently so you will hone the bushings just enough to allow the kingpin to turn freely in the bushings. It is possible to use a brake hone to do this job if you don't have a standard hone. The king pin may have a slightly different diameter at its two ends, so make sure you check each end with the bushing that will hold it. Also check the fit with the kingpin fully inserted into the bushings. When inserted the full length, there may be a difference in fit to that with only one end inserted in its bushing. An improper fit at full insertion can occur if your hone has gone into one of the bushings at a slight angle. At final assembly the kingpin should move freely in the bushings, but there should be no slack in the fit.

Check the axle to see if there are any rough places or burrs from the hammering. Clean these off with a file, but use the file sparingly so you won't change the angle of the surface. To install the spindle, make sure the thrust bearing goes below the axle, and any shims that might be needed to take up slack go above the axle. Rest the spindle on the axle, then drop the kingpin into place and slip the bearing in the bottom and push up on the spindle. See if you can slide one or more shims in the top. Push the kingpin back up and work the shims into position. You can reach down into the bushing with your finger to align the shim(s) with the hole, but be careful not to cut your finger on the thin metal shims. Your finger will tell you when the shim is properly aligned. Hold the kingpin next to the spindle and examine it. The kingpin will have a notch in it that should line up with the hole in the axle that holds the lock pin. Sometimes this notch is at the mid-point from top to bottom, of the kingpin. If it isn't at the mid-point, you must be sure to start the kingpin in the axle in the right direction to make the off-center notch line up with the lock pin hole in the axle. Start the kingpin into the bushing and tap it lightly to install it. No heavy blows here; you might damage the new kingpin. Check to see if the notch in the kingpin is positioned to make a full round hole for the lock pin.

When the notch is fully visible in the hole, insert the lock pin. The ends of the kingpin will be protected by either a rubber O ring or an expansion plug dust cover. If it has expansion plugs, install the lower one before putting the spindle on. For the top plug, hold the plug over the top end of the kingpin and strike it with a ball peen hammer to flatten it and lock it in place. As an added safety precaution, use a chisel to nick the edge of the spindle and bend a bit of metal over the top of the plug.

Install the parts now in the reverse order of the procedure followed in removing them. Put the steering linkage on, the backing plate, and so on. On most cars the yoke is on the spindle, as described here, but remember that on some old cars the yoke is on the axle. In other words, the axle on antiques appears to be split with the spindle fitting between the split ends.

If you find that the kingpins must be replaced and your local parts store doesn't carry kingpins for your car, don't give up. Sometimes you can find another kingpin that has the same measurements. Mike once had to repair a 1933 International truck that had a broken kingpin, and, since this was a low production model, no 1933 International parts were available from his parts man. Mike started comparing and found that a Jeep kingpin fit the International perfectly. In this case, although the kingpin was broken, the bushings were good, indicating that the parts were not excessively worn. Considering this, and that the kingpin for the truck was no larger than that for a Jeep, it would seem that the breakage was caused by a design error. It simply wasn't large enough to do the job on a truck.

## STEERING LINKAGE

If you are reworking an antique, make an *especially* careful check of all the steering components and front suspension parts (Figs. 15-2 through 15-4). Several years ago Mike attended an antique car show, and while heading back to his motel he saw a beautifully restored Model T in the ditch. Mike and his companions stopped to help the driver, figuring that he had stopped at one watering hole too many. But the driver was sober. His car had gone out of control because the rear end of the wishbone that stabilizes the front end had dropped loose. The wishbone is held by a ball socket at that point, and the socket had worn out. Even though you may drive your car only at low speeds, a car that goes out of control at a crowded parade could be disastrous.

Have someone wiggle the steering wheel while you check to see if there is any movement in any of the ball sockets. If an arm moves, the part it is connected to should also move. Older models often have adjustments. For example, an adjusting screw with a large screw slot in the end may be held by a cotter pin. Remove the cotter pin and, with a screwdriver socket in your rachet, tighten the adjusting screw by twisting it clockwise until the slack is out. You may have to back it off slightly to replace the cotter pin. These adjustments are found on the drag link that connects the steering box to the left front wheel and on the ball socket that connects the left front wheel to the tie rod and at the end of the tie rod.

Next, check the adjustment of the steering gear. Wiggle the steering wheel and see if there is any slack in the wheel before any part of the steering mechanism starts to move. If there is, you can tighten the steering gear. Most steering gears have an adjustment screw on the top of the gear box. This screw usually has a ⅝" lock nut on it. Jack up the front of the car far enough to raise the wheels off the ground. Hold the screw while you back off the lock nut a few turns, then tighten the screw. To get the adjustment right, turn the steering wheel through its full rotation from lock to lock. When the steering gear is properly adjusted, you should be able to feel a resistance in the wheel at the middle of its rotation. For example, if your steering wheel has four turns from lock to lock, you will feel a resistance at two turns. This is designed into the steering gear to make the car more easily steered in a straight ahead direction. Lock the lock nut while holding the screw.

## HOW TO MAKE A PRESS FIT

Grease is often recommended as an aid in making a press fit between ball joints and other press fit items. We haven't found this to be very helpful. White lead is better. If you have to make a press fit, here is how to do it with "tools" you are likely to have at home. Place the part that goes inside the other part in a freezer, or in the freezer compartment of your refrigerator. Leave it there long enough to reach the temperature of the freezer. Then heat the other part with a hair dryer. Remove the inner part from the freezer

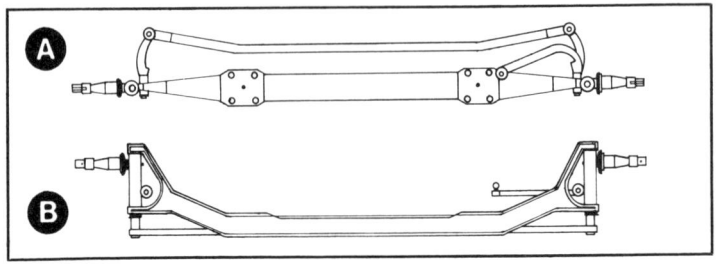

Fig. 15-2. Steering components on an Elliot axle. (A) Top view. (B) Front view.

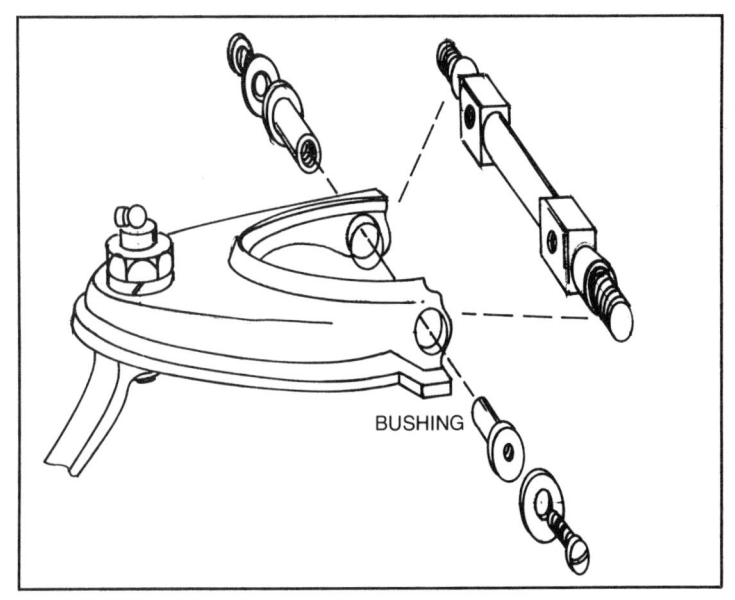

Fig. 15-3. The upper inner control arm bushings are one of the first parts of the front end to show wear. If they are bad, proper alignment is impossible.

and press the two together. The hair dryer gives just the right amount of heat for this; a torch produces too much heat and does more harm than good.

## SERVICING REAR LEAF SPRINGS

Springs can be broken or begin to sag because of overloading, loose U-bolts, tight shackles, or bad shock absorbers (Fig. 15-5). To examine the springs for sagging, the weight of the car should be on them. Look for cracks. If the main leaf is broken, the damage can usually be found easily. Check to see if the axle will move with respect to the spring. The main leaf is connected to the spring hangers on the frame, placing the axle in position.

If a leaf other than the main leaf is broken, you can see it only at the edge of the leaf. Visual inspection may not be good enough to find a cracked leaf because the crack can be filled with grease. Run a screw driver along the edge of the leaf to see if you can feel a line in the leaf with the blade of the screw driver. Even if you don't feel it, the blade will clean off the grease and dirt so you can make a better visual inspection.

In the case of a cracked leaf, the leaf, or the whole spring must be replaced. On older cars you can usually replace just the broken leaves. If the suspension appears weak, with the car body riding too low, you may have to remove the springs and take them to a spring shop to have them re-arched.

If you did not do a complete strip down on your car but need to remove the springs, here is the procedure. First clean the threads on the U-bolts that hold the springs to the axle. Run a thread chaser up the part of the bolt that extends beyond the nut, then soak the threads with WD-40. Give the solvent a day or more, if possible, to soak into the threads and attack the rust.

Jack up the car and place jack stands, or any other solid support, under the frame directly in front of the points where the rear springs are attached to it. Place a jack under the rear axle and raise it enough to disconnect the shock absorbers. Lower the jack until only the rear axle is supported by it.

Even with WD-40 you may have to use considerable force to break loose the nuts on the U-bolts. Remove the bolts or pins that connect the spring assembly so you can remove it from the car.

There are normally two parts that hold the leaves of the spring together: the rebound clip and the center bolt. Remove the rebound clip first. Some rebound clips are simply made of bent

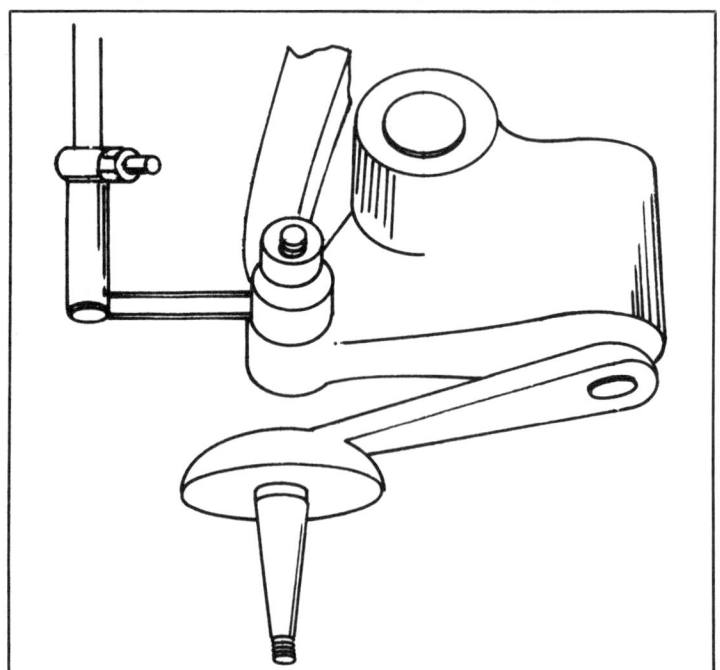

Fig. 15-4. Top view of knee action suspension used on early 1930s GM cars.

metal; others have a bolt through them that must be removed. Install one or two C-clamps on the springs to hold them together while you proceed. One end of the center bolt will protrude without a nut or other hexagonal part on it. Hold it with a pair of lock-jaw pliers while you remove the nut and the other end with a wrench. When this bolt is removed, you can unscrew the C-clamps and allow the spring leaves to separate. A spring that measures, say, about 4" thick when installed will expand to about 8" when the bolts are removed and the clamps removed.

When replacing leaves, observe proper orientation for each leaf. The center bolt is normally offset, so you must install each leaf with the longer reach, from center bolt hole to the end, in the proper direction. It usually isn't necessary to buy new springs. You can probably find a spring in a salvage yard with leaves of equal width to the one you are repairing. If a leaf is too long, you can shorten it by cutting it with a torch. A main leaf, for example, can be used to replace the shorter leaves on your spring. The torch will leave a rough edge that must be ground off to permit the leaf to lie flat against the rest of the spring. In working with the leaves, make sure you don't get any oil or grease on them. Oil permits excessive movement between leaves and causes springs to weaken and sag.

If the spring has sagged but there are no broken leaves, you can either replace it or have the springs re-arched.

Measure the diameter of the old center bolt, usually 5/16" or ⅜", so you can buy a new center bolt that will fit your spring. Note that the center bolt must be installed by starting it through the spring from the side nearest the axle. For example, if the spring goes above the axle, you will feed the bolt through the shortest leaf first. Place your C-clamps on the springs to apply pressure and force the leaves close enough together to get the center bolt through (Fig. 15-6). As soon as you can, start the nut on the end of the center bolt; do this as insurance against the C-clamps slipping loose. But continue to use the C-clamps, along with the center bolt, to gradually tighten the leaves and bring them closer together.

When you have installed the center bolt and tightened it, replace the rebound clip. The purpose of this clip is to prevent the main leaf, which is attached to the frame, from taking the brunt of the stress when the wheel hits a big bump. The clip makes the whole spring work as a unit, preventing breakage.

Next, check the spring bushings. Many old cars had brass insert bushings, either a threaded or a smooth bore bushing with a fitted pin. Later model cars have rubber bushings which never need lubing. If you are working on an old car with brass insert bushings, check the bushing at the end of the spring that is anchored to the frame. Note that the other end is supported by a hanger. Some makes of cars put the hanger end at the front of the spring; others, at the rear.

## SHOCK ABSORBERS

The first shock abosrbers worked by friction, metal against metal. On those models the life of the shock absorber was short. Another early type consisted of a spring, weaker than the main spring, that worked to hold the body down while the main springs held it up. Claude Foster developed the first direct-acting shock absorber in 1904, a device with a leather or cloth strap that gave a one-way action. He called his product the Gabriel rebound snubber, named after the name of his company which made musical horns. He later developed a shock with a metal arm which gave rebound action in both directions.

No early cars offered shock absorbers as standard equipment. Hudson introduced direct-acting shocks in 1932, followed by Auburn, REO, and Chrysler. Early shocks could be serviced by adding fluid without removing the shock from the car. In 1937 Gabriel introduced the sealed shock absorber, bringing in the age of the disposable shock absorber.

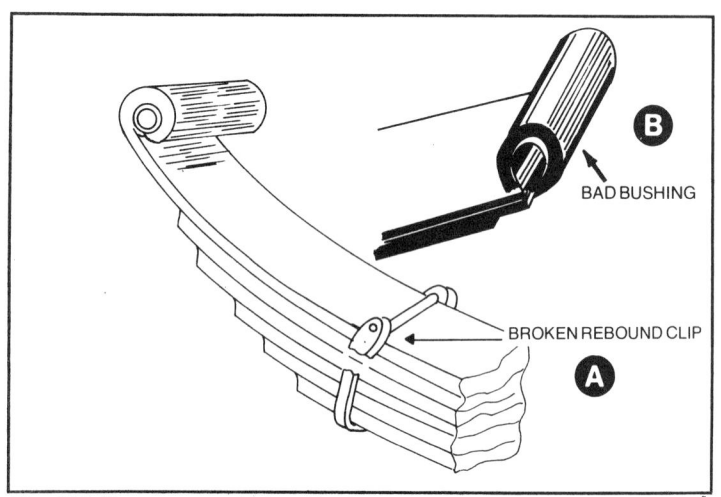

Fig. 15-5. Two common faults of leaf springs. (A) A broken rebound clip will permit the leaves to shift, weakening and breaking them. (B) If the bushings are worn, the shackle bolts will vibrate and rattle. Badly worn bushings can cause alignment problems.

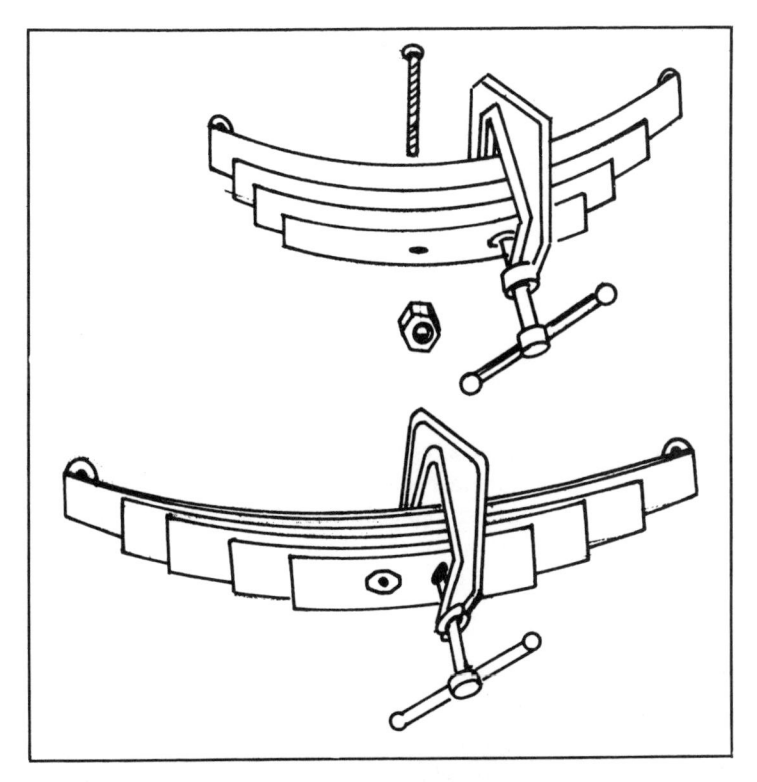

Fig. 15-6. To reassemble a set of leaf springs, use a C-clamp instead of the center bolt to tighten the leaves together. When installing the bolt, make sure the round head is on the axle side. Tighten the bolt, then install the rebound clip.

The shock absorbers on your car are probably one of two kinds: a hydraulic cylinder mounted on the frame with a lever arm attached to it and bolted to the axle (Fig. 15-7), or the telescoping shock absorber used on most cars today. One unusual type of shock absorber is the rotating vane shock which sometimes has as internal thermostatic spring. The spring varies the adjustment of the shock absorber according to temperature and so compensates for changes in viscosity of the fluid.

Bad shock absorbers can give a rough ride, produce noises, sway, poor handling, and even broken springs. To check the shocks, bounce the car at each corner and note the rebound motion. If the car body continues to bounce after you release it instead of coming to rest immediately, the shocks are worn.

If the shock absorbers fail to control the car, check to see if they are the lever arm kind of shock. This kind can usually be refilled. Clean the body of the shock with diesel fuel, or other solvent, and a brush. Some of these shocks have a filler plug. Such units can be filled to capacity without damage to the shock, but if there is no filler plug, then you must fill the unit through a relief valve. In that case, fill the unit, then remove a couple of tablespoons of fluid to provide expansion space inside the shock absorber. To fill these shocks you can use a suction pump of the kind used to fill transmissions and differentials with oil. If you have no such pump, you will have to remove the shock absorber to fill it.

If your shocks are badly worn and replacement shocks are not available from your parts store and you can find no repair kits, take the parts to a hydraulic jack repairman and see if he can match them. If you can't find repair parts locally, check with your local car clubs for the addresses of parts suppliers for your make of car.

For cars with bad telescopic shock absorbers, the problem is one of finding the proper replacement. With so many different lengths of shock absorbers on the market, you are almost sure to find one that fits your car.

## MECHANICAL BRAKES

If your car is an antique or early production model, it will probably have mechanical, instead of hydraulic, brakes. Some mechanical brake systems use cables (Fig. 15-8) to activate the brake shoes, some have rod and clevis pin connectors, while still others have a combination of rods and cables.

Until the 1920s most cars had brakes on the rear wheels only, but during the 1920s 4-wheel brakes gained in use. Until the late 1920s most brakes were of the external contracting band type, with the drum inside the band. Since the brake shoes were exposed to the air, these brakes had good heat transfer to the cooling air, but, being in the open, they were subject to damage from road grit. You can easily recognize this kind of brake by the wrap-around brake bands with their return springs located in the open, usually on top of the drum.

The internal expanding shoe brake came into general use in the late 1920s and was used almost universally from about 1930 until the era of the disk brake. It consists of two or more shoes hinged at one end and with a cam or similar activating device at the other end.

Regardless of the kind of car you have, its brakes will have certain parts at each wheel such as the external band or internal shoes, anchor pins, and a leverage linkage. When you first get the

Fig. 15-7. A single-acting shock absorber. Filler plug is at upper rear, almost out of sight here.

car and try to apply the brakes, you will probably find that some parts move only with great resistance or not at all. Make the usual sketches of how they are put together and disassemble them for a restoration.

If the car has a cable system, the cable housing will usually have protected the cable from the weather, but any grease in the housing will probably have hardened. Remove the cables from the housings, labeling each section, and clean them with steel wool and a solvent such as kerosene or diesel fuel. Clean the housing with solvent. Coat the cables with fresh grease before installing them.

Rod-operated brakes require similar treatment, cleaning and removal of rust from working parts. With either kind of brake there is a good chance that the brake band or brake shoe return springs will have to be replaced. It would be nice to be able to go to a parts store and order them by name, but this of course, is impossible. You can probably order the parts from specialists in antique car parts, but if you save the springs and check them against every kind of spring available for other purposes, you can surely find some that will work.

One special problem with mechanical brakes is to get the brakes equalized. Examine the brake system carefully to find the method of adjustment for this purpose. Some cable systems, for example, have a single cable running part of the way to the rear wheels, then an equalizer. The cable to the rear wheels may be looped through the equalizer which is made like a yoke with a tightening bolt. By loosening the bolt, you can slip the equalizer to left or right on the cable that connects the brakes of the two wheels until an equal pull is exerted at each wheel.

The parts on mechanical brakes may change dimensions slightly with significant changes of temperature, as from winter to summer, so inspections should be made if the car is used under changing conditions. Assuming that you have inspected the brakes and put them in good working condition, here is a typical brake adjustment procedure for cars with mechanical brakes.

1. Set the hand brake to the full release position.
2. Jack up all four wheels.
3. Remove clevis pins from brake rods at each wheel.
4. Tighten the adjusting screw until you feel drag at all four wheels. Back off the adjustment just enough to prevent drag when brakes are cold.
5. Adjust the pedal to cross shaft so as to obtain a clearance of ⅛" between the lever and the clevis pins.
6. Adjust the length of the brake rods so that when all backlash is removed, and clevis pins are installed, the length is about 1/32" short of an exact fit. You can estimate this setting. Just make sure you don't get the rod so short that it actuates the brake pedal.
7. Set the hand brake lever in first notch. Turn the wheels and test to see if the drag on all four wheels is equal.

Fig. 15-8. Cable-actuated mechanical brakes.

8. Road test the car to see if the brakes work effectively without pulling the car to one side.

## HYDRAULIC BRAKES

If you get an old car that has been standing for many years, the brake lines may be clogged with the granular remains of old brake fluid. The best way to restore the brakes is to remove the lines, measure them, and install new tubing. If the lines appear to be in good condition, clean them with a solvent such as alcohol. Replace lines that have been bent. Carefully inspect the flexible lines near the wheels for deterioration.

Wheel cylinders will undoubtedly be pitted and so must be honed. The rubbers should be replaced, but honing is usually more important than getting new rubbers. In some cases the old cylinders will be frozen with old brake fluid and must be replaced.

In any work that you do on hydraulic brake systems, maintain the utmost cleanliness. Any oil left from the honing process must be removed or it will attack the rubbers, causing them to swell. Even if the brakes are working perfectly and all you need to do is to check the level of the fluid in the master cylinder, clean the outside of the master cylinder meticulously. Carefully remove the plug and inspect the fluid level. The typical measurement from the fluid level to the top of the opening is ½". This corresponds to a level that is ⅞" below the uppermost interior surface of the reservoir (Fig. 15-9).

If you have to open the hydraulic line to replace parts, the system must be bled to remove the air from the system. To bleed the system, attach a rubber tube to the bleeder screw near the upper part of the backing plate and back off the adjusting cams. Place the end of the hose in a jar or can of brake fluid, keeping the end of the hose below the surface of the fluid. Have someone pump the brake pedal with the bleeder screw open. Check the level in the master cylinder at short intervals while you do this so that you can prevent it getting low on fluid and causing more air to be pumped into the system. Perform the bleeding operation at each wheel until no more bubbles emerge from the fluid in the jar. Close the bleeder valve while the rubber tube is submerged.

The procedure described above is the standard method of bleeding brake systems as outlined by repair manuals. Here is a much quicker way to do it. Have someone pump the brake pedal to apply pressure, then hold the pedal while you loosen the bleeder screw at a wheel. When brake fluid starts to come out, close the screw. Do this for each wheel and the job is done. You will spill a small amount of brake fluid at each wheel, but probably no more will be wasted than by the standard procedure.

To adjust the brakes, jack up the wheel and turn the brake shoe adjusting cam until the brake lining is tight against the drum, then back off the cam until the wheel is free. Do this for each wheel. Then road test the car to see if the brakes work effectively without pulling the car to one side.

## BRAKE LINING REPLACEMENT

The brake lining on old cars is usually riveted to the brake shoes, and when the lining wears thin, the rivets often score the drum. You can remove minor marks on the drum with emery cloth, but if the scoring is significant, the drum must be turned.

Remove the old lining by punching or drilling out the rivets. Wash the shoes in solvent before installing new lining. Then place the lining on the shoe and rivet the two center holes. To complete the job you must clamp the lining against the shoe while installing the remaining rivets. A brake lining clamp use in combination with a C-clamp is ideal for this job.

If your car is a late production model, it will probably have shoes with bonded brake linings. Even if it has riveted linings, you may find that shoes with bonded linings are available for it.

## TIRES FOR OLD CARS

Several tire companies are specialists in providing tires of all sizes for antique, classic, and production cars. Tire availability is no problem, but the cost of low-production tires is greater than that for tires on your late model family car.

If you want to put wide strip whitewall tires on your nicely restored old car and can't find them, you can sometimes adopt a more modern tire to your purpose. Try to find a tire with two or three white stripes that will fit the wheels. Then take the tires to a tire shop and have the black rubber strips between the white lines ground off. Tires of this kind usually have a wide white rubber section under the black dividing strips, so by grinding off the surface black material and you have a tire with a wide whitewall that will look more authentic on an old car.

Another way to get the wide white wall effect is by a wide, thin, white piece of rubber that snaps into place behind the rim. The tire bead holds the rubber in place. These sometimes stick out from the tires and can be ripped when the tire strikes a curb.

Some car owners have achieved the wide whitewall effect with white paint. There are several low-cost methods such as this

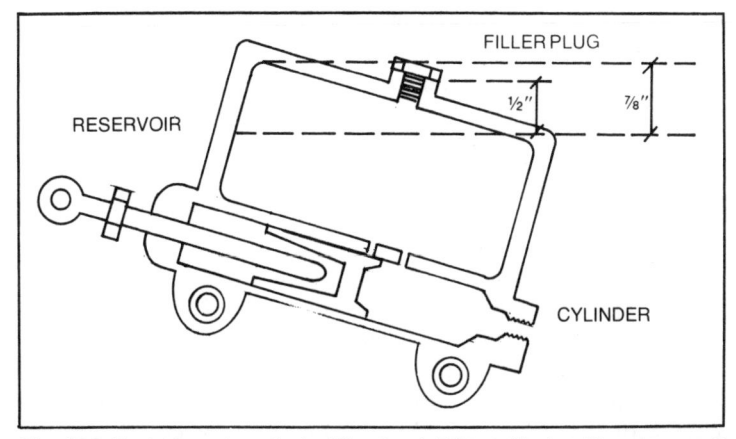

Fig. 15-9. Typical master cylinder filling level. Fill to ½" below filler plug or ⅞" below uppermost interior surface of reservoir.

that you can use instead of investing in expensive new tires. Check with your local auto parts dealer to see which materials he can supply.

## LUBRICATION FOR OLD CARS

There are special greases available for antique cars at premium prices. These special lubricants are supposed to have the same specifications as the grease that was available for the purpose when the car was new. Lubricant technology has made considerable progress since antique cars were new, and you should be able to use modern greases with no problems.

For example, old water pumps had packing glands to seal around the shaft, and a heavy grease was specified. At the time such pumps were manufactured ordinary grease was too water soluble for use in water pumps. Today a variety of greases resist removal by water. Go to your local parts man or to an oil distributor for information on what kind of lubricants are available for the special needs of your car.

Lubrication for some antiques requires an oil can. Some old cars had a rack on the firewall to hold the can, which was required to squirt some oil on exposed parts that had no automatic oil supply from the crankcase, such as rocker arms. The car owner used the oil can every morning and, on long drives, every 50 miles or so.

Some of the old steering gear boxes were bad about leaking the grease out and needed heavy lubricants. For example, in some old cars the gears were exposed. In the Ford Model T, the box was above the steering column. For these special steering gear boxes, get grease that is heavy enough to stay in the box.

Before lubing any point on your car make sure the fitting is clean. Use two rags to clean each fitting, a dirty one to take off the heavy dirt and a clean rag to polish the fitting. Lubing the car without cleaning the fittings will force grit into the joints, producing excessive wear on the bushings. A dirty grease job is probably worse than no grease job.

Early-day car lifts used by service stations for lube jobs raised the car by the frame rather than the wheels. This removed the weight of the car from the suspension system and permitted the grease to enter joints from where it had been squeezed out by running the car or even letting it stand. You can do the same by jacking the car up by the frame and putting supports under the frame at four points.

For a quick grease job, have someone rock the car while you lube it. This shifts the weight off the parts momentarily and lets the grease into the joints.

Some fittings will take grease poorly or not at all. Your first thought may be that the bushing is tight and like new. The opposite condition is more likely. New bushings usually have a groove, like a worm track, for the grease to travel along on the surface of the bushing. As the bushing wears, this groove becomes shallower and shallower until it disappears. When the weight of the car is pressing on such a bushing, the path for the grease is blocked. This is another reason for jacking up old cars for lube jobs.

In the case of some stubborn fittings you may find that even with the load off the bushing the fitting won't take grease. One possibility that should not be overlooked is that the joint has enough grease. One caution: *don't* apply heat to try to get the fitting to take grease. One man did this and expanded the grease already in the fitting which built up enough pressure to send the small ball check valve out through the blown fitting and around the shop like a ricocheting bullet.

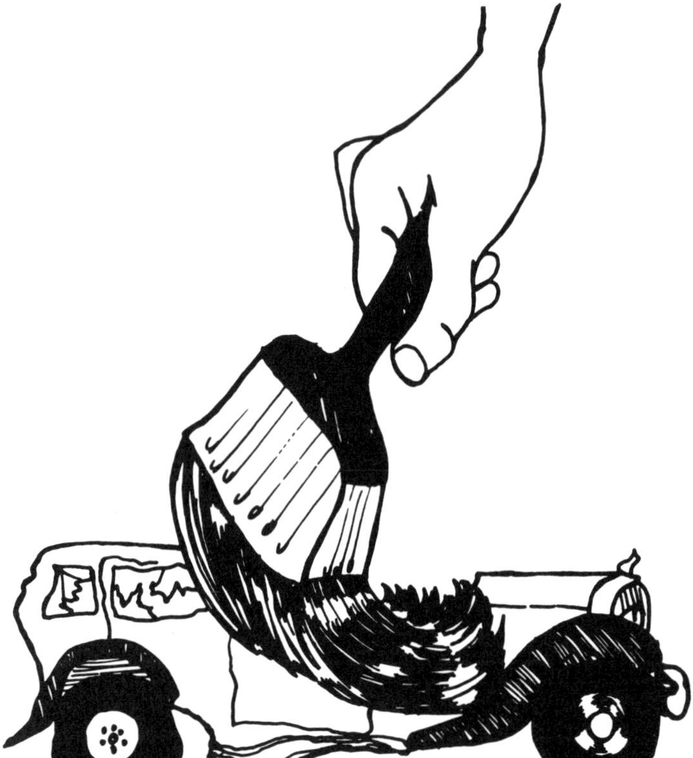

# Chapter 16
# Body Restoration

The first step in body restoration is to know what must be done. It is essential that you know the original shape, color, and materials used in or on the car when it was new. This means that unless you have an *original* car (not a restored one) as a reference, you must move slowly to avoid erasing evidence that can give you valuable information. For example, don't send old disk wheels out to be sandblasted until you have checked them for paint color and know you can match that color. Using the wheels as an example again, even if they have been painted several times, the insides of the wheels will usually have some original paint.

For special jobs that you can't do yourself, check with members of a local car club for recommendations of shops that do good work. Some electroplating shops handle parts to be plated carelessly, and their sloppy work can ruin the appearance of your car. If you see an old car with perfectly smooth bumpers and other chrome work, find out who did the plating.

If the car has plated screws or bolts, it is better to buy new parts rather than to have them replated. The plating is likely to be more expensive on small parts, and it can also change the dimensions of the threads enough so that a nut, for example, won't go on the bolt.

On very old cars, the bright parts may have been nickel or even brass plated. You can usually clean these and coat them with plastic to keep them looking new without frequent polishing.

In body restoration the key word is *patience*. Don't set up a rigid time schedule unless you are prepared to break it. On any car that has the potential for an authentic job, the quality shouldn't be compromised by slavishly sticking to an overly optimistic deadline. Some full restorations have required as much as five years. And many old cars are worth it.

## A SPECIAL PROBLEM WITH BODY BOLTS

Some body parts are bolted into a nut plate, a piece of steel that is permanently fixed to the body or frame but is threaded like a nut. If the bolt was badly rusted to the nut plate, you may have twisted the nut plate loose in trying to remove the bolt. When the plate rips out, it leaves a hole where the plate should be, so there is no receptacle for the screw or bolt.

To fix this kind of damage, you will probably have to make an extra hole to gain access to the area. Make this second hole where it doesn't show, preferably under the body. Braze a nut to a washer, using brass brazing so the heat won't be great enough to damage the threads in the nut. Braze a piece of welding rod to the washer, making the piece of rod long enough for you to reach the location of the broken-out nut plate by reaching through the extra hole you made. Rethread the nut with a tap to make sure the threads are all right. Insert the nut and washer through the hole, holding them by the welding rod handle. Place the nut under the hole where the nut plate was located, where the washer will catch the metal. Have a helper screw the new bolt into the nut while you hold the nut and washer assembly by the welding rod handle. You may have to wiggle the nut to get the bolt started. After you have tightened the bolt, cut off the rod. This trick is useful at any hard-to-reach spot, but especially so on radiators.

## WOOD WORK

If your car is old enough to have any wood parts, inspect them carefully for dry rot. In some cases you can reinforce old wood that is imperfect but not completely rotten. Wood frame doors, for example, can be trued with screw eyes and turnbuckles. Place one screw eye at the upper corner of the lower section, just under the window at the hinged end of the door. Put the other one at the lower corner of the door on the latch end. Then install pieces of wire or cable to each screw eye, making the pieces long enough to reach a turnbuckle. Tighten the turnbuckle until the door is true. The cables and turn buckle will be hidden by the door panel.

Clean all wood parts for careful inspection of the condition of the wood. If you find parts that are weakened, but not rotten, in locations where a turnbuckle is impractical, you can add wood gussets for reinforcement. These should be installed with wood glue. Gussets add considerable strength and slightly more weight than the car had when new. If the gussets show in any way, you would not use them for a show car. But the gussets can be made and added in fraction of the time it takes to renew all the old wood. And you can even use splices to strengthen and save old wood parts.

Wood parts can also be reinforced by fiberglass cloth and fiberglass. Again, you wouldn't do this if your goal is a perfectly authentic restoration. Car buffs frown on the use of fiberglass at *any* point on an old car. Whether to use these short cuts to a reasonably good restoration job is a question that only you can answer after due consideration of the car you are reworking, your time budget, and your personal goals in doing the car.

One problem with wood parts which must be replaced is to find thoroughly seasoned wood. If you go to a lumberyard, buy the boards, and immediately make the parts, they will probably warp and shrink. Although lumber is supposed to have been kiln dried, it behaves like unseasoned wood.

The surest way to get seasoned wood is to buy an oversupply and store it in a dry place for several months or longer. If you want to get started on the job sooner than that, try the local cabinet shops to see if they will sell you some thoroughly seasoned wood. People who work wood as a hobby often find supplies held by someone who has retired from the hobby. In rural areas you can check with owners of old saw mills for clues to a supply. Some farmers in wooded areas have rough-sawed hardwood boards stored in a barn loft. This kind of wood is hard to find but well worth the effort if you are successful.

**DOOR AND GLASS REPAIR**

The pins on old door hinges will usually be well worn and must be replaced. If you cannot find exact replacement pins, look for pin stock of the right diameter. You can heat the end of a piece of pin stock and enlarge it. Other possible substitutes: a rivet or a bolt. You can grind the head to match the appearance of the original part.

The hinges on old car doors are often poorly braced. They often break behind body curvature. If you weld one of these, weld the sheet metal into the hinge to give extra strength.

The glass on many old cars will be flat and easy to replace. If possible, take an old window glass, for example, to a glass shop for use as a pattern in cutting a new glass. On old production cars and antiques even the windshields are flat, although sometimes divided.

## BODY AND FRAME ALIGNMENT

To check the alignment of your car frame, measure the two diagonal lines that connect the four points in any rectangle formed by any of the various matching points on the left and right side of the frame (Fig. 16-1). Typical points to use as reference are those at the four extreme corners of the frame, as well as each body mount. If the frame is true, the members of each diagonal pair will be equal.

Frames should be straightened cold, if possible. If heat is applied, the metal should not be heated above 1200° F., or a deep cherry red color. Old high carbon steel frames will be weakened by excessive heat.

If you have to drill new holes to mount the body on the frame, be careful to locate them so the body will be true with the frame. One 1970 model truck that we know about had a problem with lug bolts when new. The lug bolts on the right front wheel kept breaking, so the owner took the truck back to the dealer who installed bigger bolts. The truck went around a corner, and the bigger bolts broke. A careful inspection of the truck showed that the body was out of line. The truck body was then removed and carefully aligned. End of problem.

When you are ready to replace the body, you may need new body mount parts. Parts men don't keep these in stock, but you can often find an engine mount assembly that will work. These are made up of a pad with a bolt through the pad. Use the old body mount parts as a guide to finding suitable substitute mounts.

## HAMMERING OUT DENTS

If you suspect any rusty metal in the sheet metal, explore the metal with a pick hammer. Strike the metal lightly with the pick end of the hammer. The pick will break through any weak areas that have any significant rust.

Before trying to correct dents in your car's sheet metal, try your skill with a body hammer on some useless metal. The trick is how you swing the hammer. Instead of using your whole arm, use only finger and wrist movements (Fig. 16-2). Make sure the face of the hammer strikes the metal squarely; if you hit the metal with the edge of the hammer, you will stretch it.

As you begin to practice the finger and wrist action with a hammer, it will seem unnatural, but it is necessary to prevent damage to the metal. This wrist action also permits you to get enough power into short swings in close quarters, such as under fenders and behind narrow quarter panels. Remember to hold the hammer loosely with your thumb and forefinger, work it with your other fingers. You should aim for a 90° arc. This method can, with practice, give you great accuracy. It also prevents shock to the arm. There will be some rebound of the hammer from the blow; don't fight it.

The size of the hammer head will control the amount of force applied to a given area. If a square head hammer measures 1" on each edge of the face and you strike with a 50 lb. force, the pressure exerted will be 50 lbs. per square inch. If the hammer head measures a little over 1-3/8" along each edge, the force will be 25 lbs. per square inch. But if you are using a pick hammer with a 1/16" square point, the force will be more than *six tons* per square inch. As you gain experience with metal hammers, you will learn which hammer to select and how much force to use to do the job. Too much force stretches the metal.

The dolly is the companion tool of the sheet metal hammer. A dolly has one surface flat, the opposite side convex. It can be used for direct hammering, where it is placed directly behind the dent, or for indirect hammering, where it is offset (Fig. 16-3).

It is easy to use too much force as a beginner and stretch the metal. When this occurs, you will find that the metal has lost its tendency to return to shape and there appears to be too much metal. This means that the metal is thinner than it was before you started hammering. To restore it, heat several spots red hot. The spots you heat should be about the size of a dime, spaced over the area that you want to shrink.

There are situations where you must intentionally stretch the metal to correct the problem. Old dents are hard to get out because the longer a dent stays in the sheet metal, the more the metal becomes set in that condition. A dent produces stress patterns in metal, similar to those produced by the metal working done at the factory. When you try to remove an old dent, it will try to go back to the dented condition. In such cases you can stretch the sheet metal with a pick hammer, then heat it to shrink it again. You will have to use body filler to get a smooth surface on the metal, but the dent will be gone.

## REPLACING SHEET METAL

If your old car is in bad condition, you may find areas of sheet metal that are too rusty or weak to be corrected. In this situation you must remove some of the metal and replace it with a sound piece. You can usually find appropriate sheet metal from a wrecked car of similar vintage in a salvage yard.

Here is how one typical metal repair job turned out. A 1955 Ford Crown Victoria was rusted out under the trunk lid from fender to fender. The owner went to a junk yard and had the man who ran the yard cut out a section, much larger than needed, from the same model Ford. The section he bought included some of the trunk and part of each fender. He used tin snips to cut away the bad metal from his car, cutting as close as he could get to the welds where the fender joined the body. Then he used a chisel to remove the remaining welds. He removed the piece of old metal and straightened it where the chiseling had bent the metal so it would serve as a pattern. Then he drilled out the spot welds in the new piece of metal and cut it to fit. He had to break loose a brazed area under the tail lights, both on the car and on the new piece. He

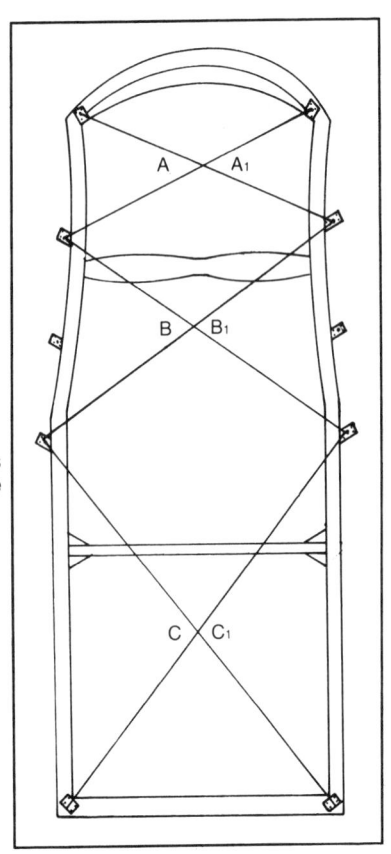

Fig. 16-1. Typical reference points for frame measurements. If the frame is true, $A = A'$, $B = B'$, $C = C'$.

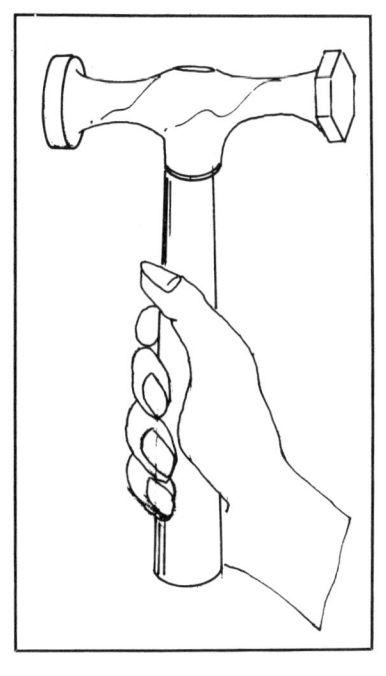

Fig. 16-2. Grip the hammer so that it pivots around your thumb and forefinger. Swing the hammer with a motion of the wrist, not the elbow.

cleaned the piece of metal from the salvage yard and slipped it into place, welding it there. This work was done close to the gas tank, so he filled the tank with gasoline and wrapped it with wet rags to control the temperature around it. Remember: a full tank can cause a fire but isn't as likely to explode as a partially full or empty tank.

## USING A GRINDER

If possible, you should use three grades of grinding disks: a #16, a #24, and a #50. The #16 is good for paint removal because it is coarse enough that the paint doesn't easily clog the disk. A #24 disk can be used to remove paint, but it is better to use for locating low areas on the sheet metal. The #50 disk is used for finish grinding.

Again, when you start to use a grinder for the first time, practice first on some useless metal. The grinder offers a fast method of removing rust and old paint, but you must let the grinder do the work without applying pressure to it. Hold it so the disk makes an angle of about 5° to the sheet metal. Switch on the grinder and it will start to move. Turn your wrist to reverse the direction of travel. Practice this technique of controlling the grinder's direction of movement with your wrist.

When you start to work on your car, let the grinder move across the damaged area, then reverse its direction (Fig. 16-4). Move the grinder onto new metal far enough so that it bites into about 1" of new metal with each pass. As it passes over the metal, watch for dimples, low spots where the paint isn't touched by the disk. Tap these flush with your hammer. Repeat the procedure until the area is as smooth as you can make it. Don't remove any more metal than you have to.

After you have established a good criss-cross pattern with the #24 disk, go to the close coat #50 disk. Try to feather-edge the area with undamaged areas around it. This will save a considerable amount of hand sanding later.

## USING BODY FILLER

Before using any filler on your car, check with the parts house you deal with to see if the filler you are buying is compatible with the primer and paint you are planning to use. Homogenized filler seems to work well, making a softer filling which has fewer pin holes than other fillers. Pin holes present a difficult problem because they require refilling or the use of spot putty.

As with painting, preparation is important. The car surface, the tools, and your hands must be free of grease or oil of any kind. If you are working on a car that has been waxed within recent months, get your jobber to recommend a cleaner. But if the car has a chalked or rusty finish, the cleaner would be a waste of money, and you must use the grinder and sandpaper to prepare if for filler.

In planning to fill an area, make sure that the required depth of filler will be no greater than ¼" at any point. Sand any area not prepared by the grinder with a #60 or #80 grit paper.

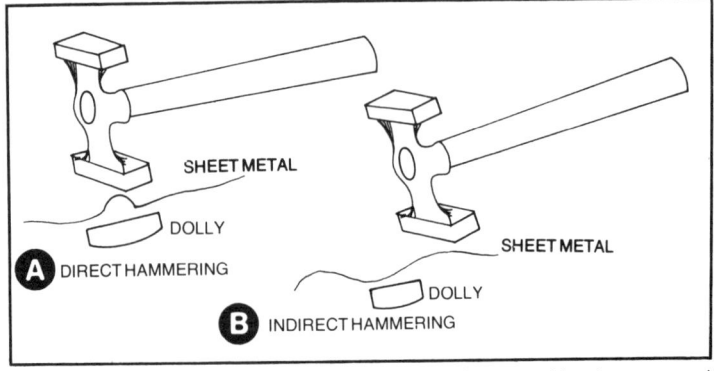

Fig. 16-3. Two methods of removing sheet metal damage with a hammer and dolly.

Fig. 16-4. Using a grinder to knock down the high spots on a weld after repairing a break.

To apply the filler, you will need at least a couple of tools, one about 1″ wide and one about 3″ wide. A piece of old venetian blind makes a good narrow tool; a 3″ putty knife is fine for larger areas (Fig. 16-5). If you need to match the curve of a still larger piece of sheet metal, prepare a piece of narrow flexible wood that will bend to conform to the shape of the metal. You can use this much like a concrete worker uses a straight edge to level fresh concrete, except that the flexible wood will shape itself to the metal.

You will need a mixer board, about a square foot or larger, to mix the filler with its hardener. Make up some practice batches so you can judge how much hardener to add to the filler. If you add too much hardener, the final filler will be easily broken; too little and it will never harden. The hardener is red, so you can judge the mix by the color after you have thoroughly mixed the hardener into the filler. The final hue should be slightly pink, but make sure the color is uniform. Avoid rapid mixing; this will put excess air into the mix which can produce pin holes in the surface of the hardened filler.

Spread a thin layer of filler over the damaged area to assure a secure bond, then add the thickness of filler that you need. Let the fresh filler set while you wipe the applicator clean. Test the filler occasionally with your fingernail. When your nail leaves a mark in

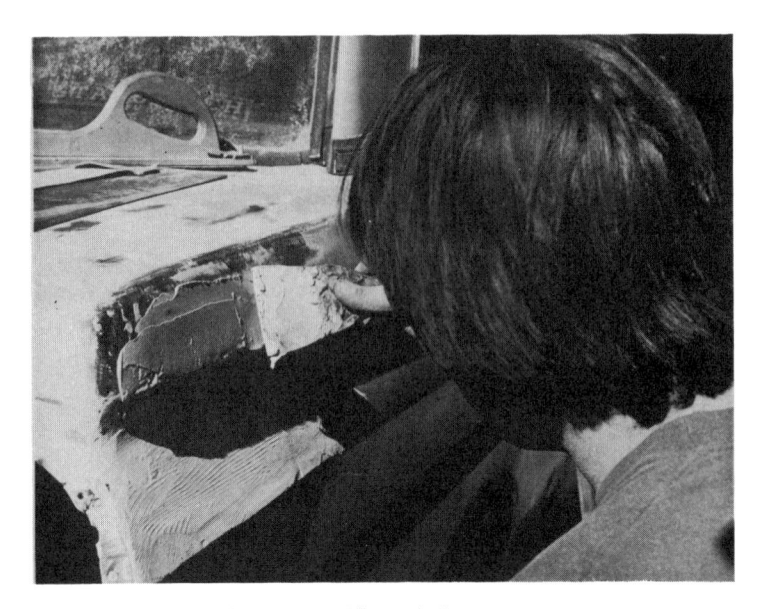

Fig. 16-5. Applying body filler with a 3″ putty knife.

the filler but it doesn't stick to your finger, it is ready for filing. One characteristic that you may not expect but should be aware of, the filler will set faster in the center of the filled area than on the edges. The chemical reaction between the filler and hardener generate heat which promotes setting, and the thicker the filler, the more heat generated and retained by the filler. Where the filler is thin, the sheet metal will conduct the heat out of it, retarding the setting process. If you file too quickly, you may tear the thin edges of filler loose from the metal.

Another precaution: *don't* apply filler to hot sheet metal. Excessive heat will produce gas bubbles and make pin holes. It is impossible to give a rule of thumb about how long the filler will need to set; the time will depend on the temperature of the air and on other factors that will vary from job to job.

When the filler is ready to file, choose a file to fit the contour of your repair work. Files are available in either flat or rounded shapes. Body men call the files most frequently used for this job "cheese graters." Stanley makes a tool called the *Surform* that works well.

Rough file the area down almost to contour, then refill any areas that prove to be too low. The area should be close to perfect before you use sandpaper. When the file hits metal, stop working because it will remove the softer filler much faster than the metal, making a low area. You will probably have to refill low spots several times before you are ready for final sanding.

## SANDING

Again, preparation for sanding must be done carefully. Make sure you use *clean* sandpaper. This means that you must have a clean drawer or other place to store the paper until you are ready to use it. Never set a sanding block or sander on a dirty surface. Even invisible droplets of oil are enough to ruin a paint job because the oil prevents the paint from adhering to the metal. This produces a condition called "fish eye," spots that look like fish eyes. A painting operation must be surgically clean for best results.

If some of the metal is of questionable cleanliness, use a coarse grade of sandpaper on that area first to pick up any grease. Typical areas that should be rough sanded first are those under the car, such as the wheel wells, where road tar or grease may be present.

Inexperienced sanders often use their fingers to hold the paper, but this practice can produce ridges in the final surface that will show. If you are doing the job manually, use a sanding board or a rubber sanding block (Figs. 16-6, 16-7). The rubber block can better form to fit curved metal. In some recesses you can use the heel of your hand.

As you work on each area, move to several locations so the angle of reflected light will be different and you can get a better view of the job. To maintain a proper contour, sand first in one direction and then in a cross direction.

As you sand the car, you may find minor depressions that need filling. Keep a felt tip pen handy to mark these as you see them by drawing a circle or ellipse around the depression. Such areas show up when the sandpaper on a block or board fails to attack the surface in the low spot.

For rough sanding, after filling, use a #36 grit paper until the file marks are removed, then go to a #80 grit paper to finish the contour shaping. When the sanding for an area is done, it should be primed if there will be a delay before the whole car is primed. If you plan to use an enamel paint on the car, you can use small aerosol cans of primer to protect newly sanded metal. Lacquer is hard to find in spray cans. If you have no spray equipment but are planning to rent it for the final coat, you can apply the primer with a brush. Put on a liberal amount so that you won't hit bare metal when you sand the primer.

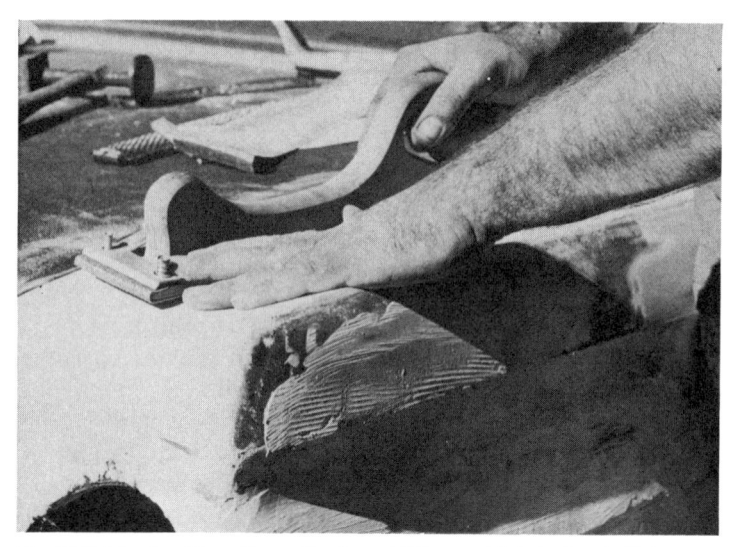

Fig. 16-6. Leveling filler with sanding board. Filler on side to be leveled later.

As you continue with this important step in the restoration of your car, remember that the quality of your paint job depends on how carefully you prepare the surface. Don't hurry this part of the work. However, we do know of *one* quick preparation job that worked out well. Delmer, a man we know, bought a faded maroon 1941 Ford. The paint looked so bad he went immediately to a paint shop to see how much they would charge to paint it black. The painter looked at it and said that it wouldn't do any good to paint it unless all the paint was removed. And *that*, he said, would take a lot of sanding. He told Delmer to get the paint off, then bring it in.

The next day, Delmer showed up at the paint shop with his Ford all bright metal, not a trace of paint. Astonished, the painter said he hadn't expected to see the car for a week or two. And how did Delmer get the paint off so fast? Delmer then told him that he worked at a plant where he had access to a steam bath which washed the old oxidized paint right off. Most paints cannot be removed so easily, but some of the early colors, particularly maroon, oxidized badly when the car was left to the weather.

## MASKING

To mask your car you will need one or two large rolls of masking tape and a pile of old newspapers. Examine the newspapers carefully and use several layers so that the tiny holes made by the presses will be covered by other layers of papers.

When you mask a rubber or chrome part with the tape, make sure the tape does not touch the body. Since a perfect job of masking is extremely difficult, make the tape run just slightly onto the chrome or rubber part. There are two reasons for this. It's easier to get paint off the chrome than to cover a missed place on the body. And if the tape extends onto the body surface, you may pull some body paint when you remove the tape. The paint forms a surface from the body onto the tape, but if the break between the body and the chromed part is also between the body and the tape, this won't happen.

Use newspapers to cover large areas, such as glass or open doors. The door areas must be masked so you can paint the door jambs. To support the newspaper across the open doorway, use strips of tape, criss-crossed to support each other like a spider web.

## SAFETY PRECAUTIONS

Before you start painting your car, give careful attention to making your paint area safe. The area must have adequate

Fig. 16-7. Using the sanding block for final sanding before primer.

ventilation. Many of the paints and thinners you will be using are toxic if inhaled in high concentrations. Check your fire extinguisher to make sure it is in working condition and within easy reach. Don't smoke and don't allow anyone else to smoke while working with paint. Don't plug in or unplug electrical equipment during the work. Make sure any ground wires are in place to avoid static sparks. Clean your area of any loose material that could cause or feed combustion.

These precautions should be extended to adjacent rooms because evaporated thinners can travel, and a mixture of thinner vapor and air is explosive. It can be set off by someone flicking a light switch, operating an electrical motor with brushes that can cause sparks, or by any number of other sources of sparks. Your air compressor should have an outside source for the air to be compressed. Compression of gases raises the temperature, and thinner vapors mixed with air can be ignited by high compression just as fuel is ignited in a diesel engine. Mike knows of one compressor that exploded, knocking the side out of the paint shop.

If the spray gun becomes clogged, don't clear it by holding your hand over the nozzle to make the back pressure blow it out. Mike did this many times, but once (and once was enough), the nozzle didn't clear. Instead it blew paint primer into his eyes. He says this makes impacted teeth seem like a hangnail.

Use a good mask that seals around your nose, so that the air you breathe goes through the filter (Fig. 16-8). Most paint vapor is somewhat toxic. It can cause swelling in the lymph nodes in your neck, and fever that lasts two or three days. The long-term effects may be even worse if you insist on breathing the vapor.

If you happen to use any heat lamps to promote drying, keep the area clean of any refuse that could be ignited or might undergo spontaneous combustion because of the added heat.

## BUYING PAINT

Don't economize on your final coat of paint, but you can make substitutions on your first coats. By buying a color on sale that is close to the final color you want, you can get good coverage at lower cost. Make sure you buy paints that are compatible, using the same brand and type of paint for each coat. Almost any paint supplier will have discontinued colors or batches that are mismatched and on sale. If you don't find this kind of thing at the first dealer you visit, go to another one. Some paint stores sell all their bargain paint to a local body shop that is a steady customer.

Mike once bought 50 gallons of discontinued lacquer at a dollar a gallon. He had to take the whole lot to get the price, but he sold off the black to car dealers to paint under the hoods of their used cars and recovered his cost.

## PAINTING

If you have never painted with a spray gun, make several trial runs on some old sheet metal before you try to paint your car. You must learn the proper distance to hold the gun, which will vary somewhat according to the paint you are using. For example, if you are using metallic paint, the distance must be slightly greater than average because if you apply the paint too thickly, it will be wet enough to permit the metallic particles to sink to the bottom of the paint layer, giving a darker than normal shade. Try to hold the

Fig. 16-8. Wear a mask while painting. Note how hose is carried over shoulder to keep it off fresh paint.

nozzle the same distance from the metal for the whole job. If you don't, the final color will not be uniform in color. One man who painted a car with the doors removed, then painted the doors, found that each door was a slightly different shade because he had been careless about distance. The gun should be held back just far enough so that there is a slight drying action while the paint is in the air. The exact distance will be influenced by the temperature and humidity. If you restore an antique car with black paint, there is not the problem of dark or light shading.

Dress for the part by seeing that you have no clothing that is so loose that it falls onto the fresh paint when you lean over the hood or other part. When painting the top and the hood, you can loop the hose over your shoulder so it won't drag across the painted surface.

Spray the small cracks and recessed areas first, before you go to the large flat areas. If you do the recessed places last, you will have some overspray on the flat surface where it can easily be seen. Such overspray on a large surface will ruin the smooth finish.

Give the primer plenty of time to dry. Modern primers are supposed to dry without excessive shrinking, but the best jobs require time for the primer to properly set. The more time the better. The same is true for the final coats. For a *really* superb finish, paint the car and let it set for a year or more, then paint it again. Block sand it each time. The extra coats of paint will act as a micro-filler, filling even minor imperfections that you may have missed in sanding the car.

After the car is painted, don't touch it for at least a few weeks. Mike once took his 1941 Dodge to an old car meet within a week after painting it. While talking to a friend they leaned against the car. Days later he noticed the imprint of the fabric of their clothing which was easily visible when viewed from certain angles in bright light.

Don't drive the car until it is thoroughly dry. Tar and other road materials can become embedded in the paint, and they are almost impossible to get out. Even filling the gas tank can endanger your new paint job. Gasoline can erase fresh paint, or at least cloud it so that it is permanently marred. Some vintage cars, such as the 1932 to 1934 Fords, are especially bad about gasoline spillage. The best way to solve the problem for these cars, especially if you want to keep the car authentic, is to keep a low tank level.

**INTERIOR**

In preparation for restoring the interior of your car you must decide just how much you will do yourself (Fig. 16-9). It may be more practical to send out the seats to be upholstered, but make sure the upholstery shop knows *exactly* what you want. The seat upholstery usually should match that of the door panels.

On old production cars or antiques the upholstery material will be tacked to a wood frame. For such jobs you will need a pair of scissors, a tack hammer, both a yardstick and a tape measure, and access to a sewing machine. You also must have a large, clean working surface, such as a 4' × 8' sheet of plywood supported at a comfortable level.

If you are redoing a car that originally had leather upholstery, don't substitute vinyl unless you feel the car isn't worth an authentic job. Some low-priced cars once used leather, but if you consider the car worth a full restoration, you shouldn't economize here. And for a high quality leather interior, you will probably want to employ the services of a professional upholsterer. Each decision of this kind must be made with respect to the value of the car. It should have been made at the outset and then reflected throughout the car rather than in just one part.

Before you remove the old upholstery, see if it can be renewed in place. Begin by giving the car a thorough cleaning with a vacuum cleaner. Old leather upholstery that isn't cracked can be cleaned with a weak detergent/lukewarm water solution and wiped immediately with a damp cloth, then a soft, dry cloth. Many of the stains on old broadcloth can be carefully removed. Grease or oil stains should be rubbed with a dull knife blade or a putty knife, then removed with spot remover such as is sold for use on clothing. If the cloth has old mildew stains, soak it with a 10% solution of oxalic acid or a weak solution of white vinegar and water. Leave the solution on the upholstery for about a half minute to a minute, then blot off the solution and use hot and then cold water to remove it. For iron rust, rub with warm suds and rinse with cold water. Paint is more difficult to remove from upholstery, but much of it can be eliminated by scraping the surface of the paint and rubbing it with turpentine or even other solvents, such as lacquer thinner. Repeat this process until the paint is removed, then rub the area with lukewarm suds and rinse with water. If water spots remain from any of these treatments, or if rain has stained the car interior, sponge the entire interior with cold water. Then rub it with a solvent.

If your upholstery fabric is badly stained and you can't remove the stain, there is one final way to renew it without installing new material: dye it to a darker shade. Obviously you would not use this method if you want the car to be restored to its exact original condition, but dyeing will save considerable upholstery work that you may not be prepared to do yourself. Go to your auto parts store and ask for auto fabric dye. Apply the dye with a sponge, using care to make all the fabric in your car the same shade. If one area turns out to be lighter in shade than the rest, go over it again with the sponge. Let the dyed fabric set *thoroughly* before you use the car, or you may find that the color will rub off onto your clothing.

If the nap is pressed flat, use a steam iron on the fabric, then brush immediately. Repeat the process if necessary.

In many old cars the upholstery will be beyond repair, and you must replace it. In that case do one side of the car at a time, leaving the old upholstery on the opposite door panels to guide you. Save the old cloth as you remove it so you can use it as a pattern to cut new material.

**DOOR PANELS**

To recover the door panels, remove the window molding, the arm rests, and hardware. The old screws in the molding may be rusty and need replacement. If they have special heads, you can often find a screw made for modern cars that will have the same dimensions but a different head. Keep the old screws and use them as guides to grind off the heads of the new screws to match the old ones. After grinding, groove the new screws with a hacksaw so they will accept screwdriver blades.

If the upholstery on the door panel is bad, the panel itself will probably be in bad condition. Try to get the old one out in one piece so you can use it as a pattern to cut a new one from ⅛" hardboard. Cover this board with the new material, lapped over the edges and glued to the back of the board. Stretch the material, starting at the middle of each side, then working toward the corners.

For pleated panels you will need a double layer of material, but the backing layer can be made from a cheaper grade. Sew pleats in the covering material, allowing enough fullness for stuffing. Use polyester thread for durability. If you are a stickler for using authentic material even where it doesn't show, stuff the pleats with cotton batting. But polyurethane foam is a better choice for smoothness and resiliency. For a closed pattern, such as a diamond-tufted panel, the stuffing must be sewn between the fabric and the backing in a single operation.

The old spring catches on the door panels are likely to have been broken. For a thorough restoration these should be duplicated. If you are doing only a semi-authentic job, you can use screws to hold the panel on the door. Drill holes through the panel at screw points, spacing these at equal intervals around the panel. It's a good idea to drive nails through at each point first to prevent the drill bit from catching the material and twisting it. Use screws with attractive heads to fasten the new panel to the door. For an even more radical departure from the original appearance, you can install wood grain paneling. For this purpose choose hardboard-backed paneling rather than plywood, which splinters easily.

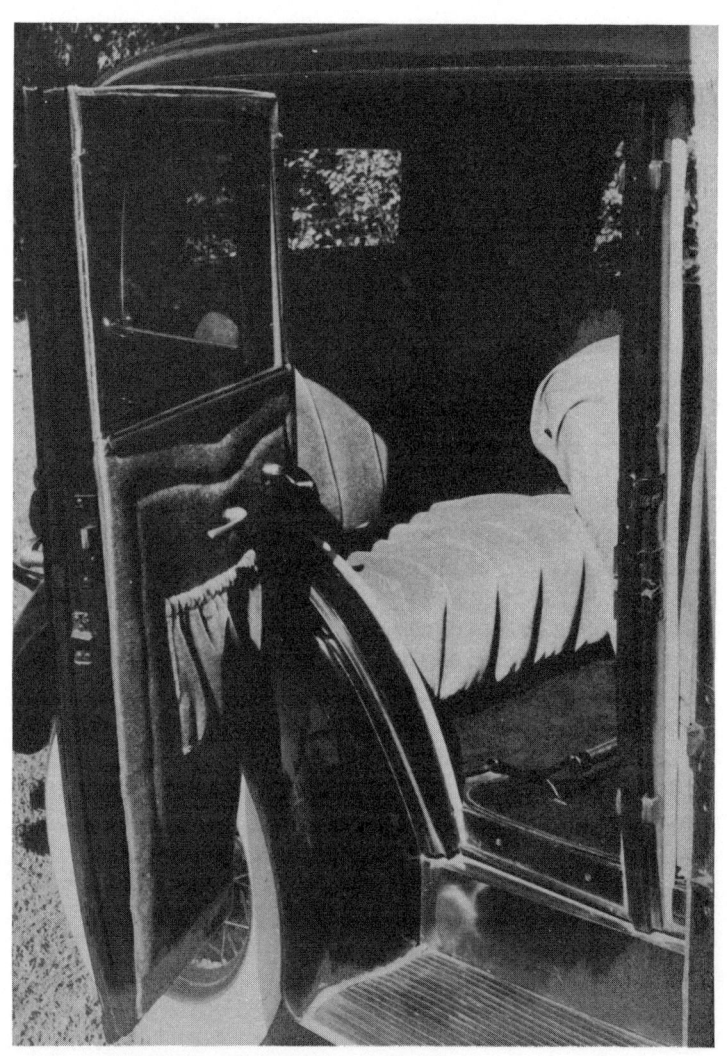

Fig. 16-9. A professional upholstery job.

## SEATS

The seats on most old cars can be easily removed from the car for reupholstery. On some old four-door cars the seats are permanently attached to the door posts, and you must do the job *in* the car. Again, try to remove the material in one piece to use as a pattern. Under the cloth you will find cotton or hair stuffing which may or may not be usable. Make a note of the amount of stuffing installed originally and try to duplicate it.

It's a good idea to spray paint the old springs with a rust inhibiting paint. Unless the springs are broken, you can probably use them as a base for the new upholstery. Obviously, wood frames must be repaired if in bad condition. Again, use braces and splices with a good wood glue to avoid having to rebuild the entire structure.

When you apply the stuffing and covering material, drive in the tacks that hold the cloth lightly at first so you can remove them if necessary to restretch the material.

To install the new fabric, lay the material over the seats and stretch it tightly as you tack it. Again, start at the centers and work toward the edges. Tack the hidden edges, such as the bottoms of the back cushions and the rear edge of the bottom cushions, last. This allows you to do the final stretching without disturbing the appearance of the earlier work and you'll have a smooth job.

For a tufted or pleated upholstery, lay out the backing material over the seat springs and mark it at the edges of the seat structure. These marks can be used as reference marks so that you can center any pattern that you will make in the finished upholstery. For example, try to center the pleats so that if a half pleat shows at one end of the back, a half pleat will also be visible at the other end. This method will produce a more pleasing appearance than just arbitrarily laying out a pattern of pleats and letting them fall where they may. Remember that any pleated or tufted pattern will require more material than a plain upholstery.

## HEADLINER

To remove the headliner, first take off any chrome strips around it. Use care to remove the wires, if present, from the wood strip near the edge. Unless you are careful, you will rip the old, and usually rotten, liner so badly that it can't serve as a pattern.

If the material is split, separate the pieces and lay them out on a new piece of material. Some old headliners are made from several pieces that are sewn together. Single-piece headliners often appear to be pleated, but this appearance is produced by the wire that holds it. If the old headliner was made from multiple pieces, carefully separate each section and use it as a pattern. When replacing badly torn headliners, leave some extra material in each direction for seams.

To install the new headliner, start at the front center, with the wires to the top, then stretch the material to each side from the center. Then go to the rear and stretch the material from front to back in the center. Next, stretch it to each side at the rear. Finally stretch the material along each side, from the center out. When you are through, there will be some excess material which can be trimmed off. Cover the raw edges with the same kind of material used originally. This is often a cloth bead or sometimes a braided rope material.

If your material has a nap, such as corduroy, make sure it all runs the same direction or the shade will not appear uniform after it is installed.

### PANEL DIALS

If the car had been out in the weather for any length of time, the speedometer and other dials will usually be in bad condition. Try cleaning these with a cotton swab dipped in solvent. For dials that need new lettering, you can get stick-on letters and numbers from an art supply store, a printing shop, or a hobby shop. If the old ones are visible, use them to select new figures that will match the style of the old ones.

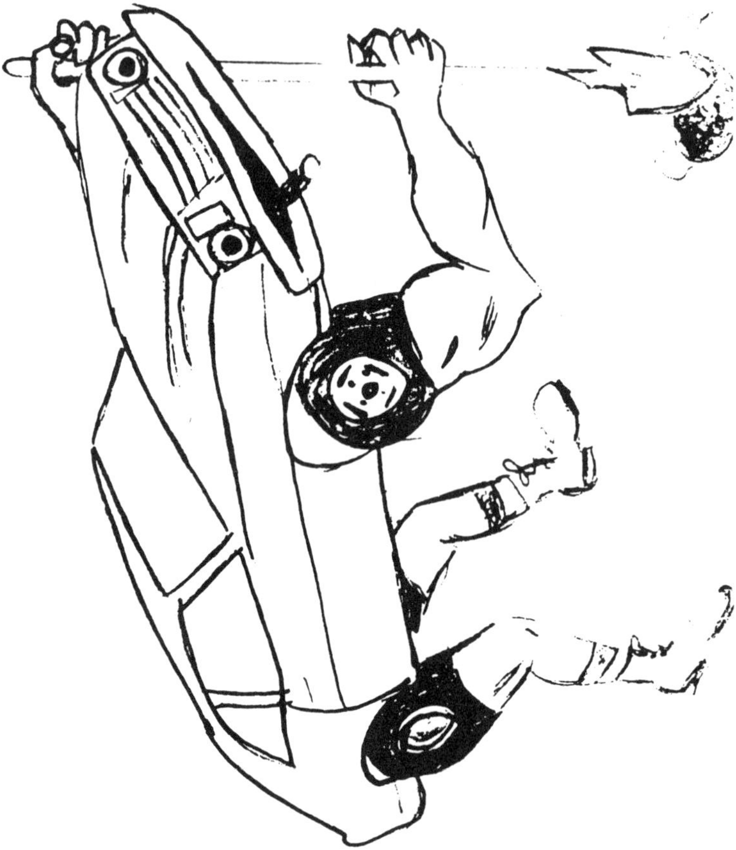

## Chapter 17

## How to Get a

## Work Car Cheap

If you follow the car buying pattern of the typical motorist, you will someday find, in shock, that you have a $100,000 car—but it will be worth maybe several hundred dollars. How? By drifting along with the buy-new-and-trade-in habit that has hooked most Americans. In earlier times, during the 1920's for example, people who bought quality cars expected to drive them for at least several years, maybe 10 or more. In those years a high-priced car might show little styling change from year to year, and Packard advertised that an owner need make no apology for its car, even after a decade. Later, as the auto stylists became more important to the industry, people became more conscious of the year the car was made than of its pedigree. And so the seeds were sown for the annual model change and the three year trade-in.

Some car buyers, even those who trade often, consider their car an investment and their monthly car payments a kind of forced savings plan. The problem with that kind of reasoning is that the car usually runs down before the payments, at least in value. Most drivers never face up to their biggest car cost, depreciation.

### THE OLD CAR GET AWAY

If you have an average or better ability to use your hands, you can let someone else take the brutal depreciation, then buy. The prudent car buyer will find a car that is good enough for his purposes but enough out of demand to be cheap. It will be old enough to have suffered severe depreciation, but new enough that few collectors will be interested in it. In this chapter we will give you a complete procedure of how one low-priced car was reworked to make a very successful work car. In fact, this one turned out so well that it would be acceptable as a first car unless you need the image that some people associate with a late model car.

The procedures detailed in this chapter will obviously show repetition of procedures mentioned earlier for vintage cars, but here the emphasis is how to rework a modern compact instead of a 1930s car. And instead of restoring the car to its original condition, we will set a more practical goal. We want a working car that runs well and gives a decent appearance. This means that we will not hesitate to make changes in original specifications if the change appears to make the car more attractive, more useful, or, especially, if the change costs less than an exact replacement.

The idea of a cheap work car is one that Mike has exploited several times. Recently he decided that his old work car had just about had it, and, with the price of gas up every week, he didn't want to rebuild its big V-8 engine. He started looking around one day, trying to find a suitable replacement, when an unbelievable coincidence got him a car much more quickly than he expected.

## MIKE'S STORY

I was sitting on my front porch, wondering where to look next, when my neighbor's son came by. He said he was moving out of state and needed some money. He had a 1965 Falcon that he would sell for $100 (Fig. 17-1). One advantage of a Falcon is that its production was great enough to make spare parts easy to get. I asked about the car's general condition, and he said it would run.

When we got to the car, he hit the key and it started immediately. But there was a miss. He gave me a ride around the block, and I could see that it was underpowered. The miss could, of course, do that. I got out and raised the hood.

"The battery doesn't go with the car. It's borrowed," he said.

A light rain was falling, so we got into the car to talk trade. I opened the glove compartment and saw the title. It showed August 17, over two months earlier, as the date it was notarized. The transfer had never been completed, so the car was unregistered. In our state you have only 30 days to register a car without penalty. It's always a good idea to check state law on this to avoid unnecessary charges. I told him there would probably be a penalty when I tried to register the car.

"I don't think so."

"O.K. You make the title good, and I'll give you $100."

Fig. 17-1. This rear-end view shows general appearance of car when purchased.

He grinned and took the money. I took the car to my garage and started pulling spark plug wires out of the distributor cap, one at a time. When I got to the wire from cylinder #5, the engine ran just as well with the wire out as in. I removed the spark plug and ran a compression check on that cylinder. Fifteen pounds per square inch. Maybe the adjustment on the valves was too tight. I backed off the nuts and tried again. Wishful thinking. I could see the rocker arms move, so the valves weren't stuck. The engine had a burnt valve.

So, with one cylinder playing dead, I faced a decision. I could grind the valves, or I could drive a car that would lose speed every time I went into a heavy fog. Not much of a choice, so I got out my tools.

## ENGINE DISASSEMBLY

I drained the cooling system and took off the hoses. Then I crawled under the car and unbolted the exhaust pipe from the manifold and took it down. I removed the air cleaner from the carburetor and disconnected the accelerator rod and distributor vacuum line at the carburetor. Next, I disconnected the fuel line at the fuel filter hose. I removed the heater hose lines at the carburetor and the fuel line at the fuel pump. I removed the last two lines together. I removed the spark plug wires and the temperature sending wire at the unit, then the crankcase ventilation system. I backed off the rest of the head bolts and lifted off the head.

With the head off, the trouble was easy to see. The exhaust valve in number 5 cylinder was cooked. When I removed the exhaust manifold, in preparation for having the valves ground, I noticed that some of the bolts had not been tightened. This convinced me that someone had done some sloppy work indeed and there was a good chance that the head hadn't been torqued right. If true, the head was probably warped. I took the head to a machine shop, and the man there confirmed my suspicion. I told him to resurface the head when they ground the valves.

After giving the engine some thought I decided to do a complete overhaul. I examined the cylinder walls and found that they were ridged, so I cut the ridges out with a ridge reamer. Then I used a steel scraper to clean the top surface of the block. It's important to remove *all* traces of gasket or any other material. I cleaned the block and cut the cylinder ridges with pistons in the block so that metal particles couldn't fall down onto the crankshaft.

Next, I removed the pan bolts. Before I could get the pan down, I had to disconnect a tie rod at one end. After removing the pan, I took out the oil pump and put it in the vise. I pulled the screen and cover off so I could inspect the gears. Instead of being mirror smooth, like a new one, the gears were marked and lined, showing that they had lost their hard facing. Some grit had probably run through this pump. Even minor scuffing of oil pump gears can send metal filings through the whole engine, reducing it to a pile of junk. I decided to put in a new oil pump.

I removed the rods next, checking to see that they were numbered. I took off the rod cap of each one and set them in a row on a clean cloth on my workbench. Then I placed my thumbs on each bolt of the rod and pushed the rod upward, making sure the bolts didn't touch the crankshaft. I handled only one rod and piston at a time to avoid a mixup.

When I got all the piston and rod assemblies out of the block, I replaced the rod caps and set them back on a clean area of the bench. Then I put the rod from the first cylinder in the vise so I could remove the old rings from the piston. I used a scraper to remove the carbon build-up from the top of the piston, being careful not to scratch the piston. Then I got my ring groove cleaning tool and removed the carbon from the ring grooves. I redrilled the oil return holes behind the oil ring, using a drill bit the same size as the original hole. Then I buffed off the piston above the skirt with a wire brush wheel on a drill, rinsed the piston with solvent, and blew it dry. I followed this procedure on each piston, setting each one back on the clean space on my workbench as I finished it.

## NEW RINGS

I got out the package of rings and read all of the printed information on the package. I installed the oil ring, then the compression rings in order up the piston. I checked the position of the ring gaps to see that they were 180° apart and 90° from the ends of the wrist pins; then I poured oil on the piston and smeared it over the surface. I carefully placed my ring compressor over the rings and tightened it. I set the piston on the clean space on my bench, upside down, so I could remove the rod cap. I cleaned the rod cap with a clean cloth and got out the new insert bearings for the rods, installed them, and carefully spread a thin layer of grease over the inner surface of the bearings.

I took the first piston assembly to the engine, and, after checking to see that the crankshaft journal for that cylinder was at the bottom of its stoke, I placed the piston into the cylinder. Then I got under the car and guided the rod bolts past the crankshaft journal while a helper bumped the piston down with a hammer handle.

We continued this procedure until all the pistons were in the cylinders and the rod caps installed. We checked each piston to see that the notch on it went to the front and each rod bearing to see that the tangs on each half were on the same side of the bearing. I postponed torquing the rods until all were installed.

The new oil pump was installed next. Then I applied a sealer to the new pan gasket and stuck it in place, letting the sealer hold it while I replaced the pan.

The machine shop had ground the valves and resurfaced the head. I applied a coating of sealer to both sides of the head gasket and set it in place. Then I installed the head, torquing the head bolts in sequence, going to about ½ torque, then ¾ torque, and finally to full torque. Then I replaced the parts I had removed to work on the engine.

After installing the used carburetor I had bought to replace the damaged one that came with the car, and replacing other parts, I was ready to test the engine. It ran just fine.

## BODY CONDITION

After getting the car in good mechanical condition, it was time to think about how it looked. It wasn't good. The more I looked at it, the worse it appeared. The worst problem was a poor paint job.

The old paint had poor adhesion and was peeling in large patches all over the car. This meant that it would have to be sanded off.

At first look the body didn't show great damage, but a closer look showed plenty of problems. Someone had botched an attempt to straighten a dent in the right rear. The tail light set at an angle to the body line, showing the body was even worse than it looked at first glance. The fender there had a buckle in its top. The trunk lid had a bulge in its top and a dent in its rear. The hood had a series of dents and body putty was falling out of a depression in the right front fender. Standing back, you could see numerous door dings all over the car.

I decided to start on the trunk and right tail light area. When I examined the trunk lid more closely, I found two old dents that had been filled with fiberglass instead of being pounded out. Whoever had done the filling had also ground away too much metal, leaving the metal weak on the high points where I needed it strong and strong in the creases where I would have preferred it to be weak. These long-neglected dents gave an illustration of a habit of metal to set if a dent is left uncorrected too long. When sheet metal is formed under great pressure by presses, the metal assumes stress patterns which resist change. If dented, the metal will easily go back to its original shape. But if the dent is permitted to stay in the metal, the new dent produces new stress patterns. The longer it stays in the metal, the more the metal will resist correction. When you try to remove an old dent, it will try to return to the dented condition.

## A TRIP TO THE SALVAGE YARD

After checking the trunk lid, I decided to look for a less damaged one in a salvage yard. Trunk lids are not particularly expensive, and this is one easy-to-replace part that can save a considerable amount of pounding and grinding. Also, I didn't trust the strength of the old one where the previous body worker had ground away too much steel. On a trip to a local salvage yard I found several 1965 Falcons. I checked every trunk lid carefully, sighting along the rear edges to see if there were any wavering that would indicate previous damage. I chose one that checked straight and appeared to have the original paint.

While at the salvage yard, I noticed a Falcon Futura that had a perfectly good strip of chrome that extended across the rear of the car between the trunk and the bumper. My car wasn't a Futura and had no such strip, but it was damaged in that area. Since I was fixing up a work car instead of restoring a classic, I decided to get the chrome strip and save some work. I could simply bump out the worst of the damage with a heavy hammer, then cover it.

The "new" trunk lid gave one additional advantage. The rear of the car had obviously had considerable damage, and the earlier repair work had been poorly done. Looking at the car with the original trunk lid on it, I couldn't be sure just how far the whole rear body was out of shape. When I installed the undamaged trunk lid, I had a gauge to measure the alignment of the other rear body parts (Fig. 17-2). I could see immediately that the rear fenders had an arch, caused by a rear end collision, that placed the fender about ¾" above the trunk lid at the center of the arch. And, at the rear, the trunk lid extended beyond the lower parts of the rear fenders. The right tail light was the most out of line part on the whole car. It was aligned with the sheet metal around it, confirming that the whole fender was out of shape.

## SHEET METAL WORK

I opened the trunk lid and placed the base plate of a bumper jack against the inner wheel well and jacked the lifting bracket out until it engaged the lowest point of the damage that it would reach (Fig. 17-3). I applied pressure, a little at a time, as I used a body hammer to tap down high points on the exterior. This procedure relieved stress as the damaged section was jacked out. In hammering down the high points, I was careful to deliver the hammer blows by finger and wrist movements only. Using the whole arm in an uncontrolled swing can damage light sheet metal. I was also careful to see that the face of the hammer struck the metal squarely instead of the hammer edge which would have stretched the sheet metal.

After I jacked out the major part of the damage, and had the rear fenders almost matching the shape of the trunk lid, it was time to use the dolly along with the hammer. I wasn't able to see the dolly, of course, as I held it inside the trunk under the fender area where I hammered.

In jacking out the rear fenders, some new problems came up. First, the shape of the fenders were over—corrected in places, making the top of the fender lower, instead of higher, than the trunk lid. These depressions had to be bumped out again. Also, the jacking broke some of the spot welds that held the body parts together, so I had to reweld the parts.

Because of previous damage and hammering on the fenders, the metal was extremely weak in places. It moved so easily that I had to be careful not to bend it too far. Luckily, this thinner metal was high on the fenders where rust is no great problem. Because of this I did not consider replacing it, but pushed it toward the inside of the trunk and put filler over it. This made the work go slowly because the sanding would continually reveal low places that would require more filling.

## GRINDING AND FILLING

When I had straightened the sheet metal as much as I could with the jack and the hammering, I got out my grinder (Fig. 17-4). The grinder removed the old paint and the excess filler much more quickly than I could have removed it by sanding. When I saw dimples or low spots where the grinder left spots of paint, I used my hammer to tap them flush.

Fig. 17-2. When "new" trunk lid was installed, it projected beyond rear fender area, showing how much body had been deformed.

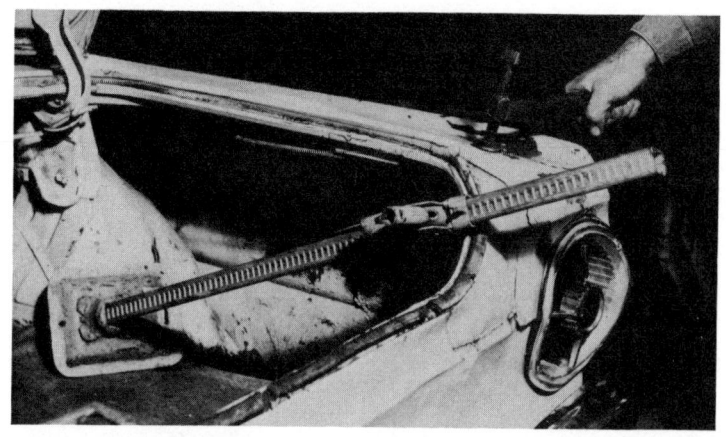

Fig. 17-3. Hammering down high points while straightening body with bumper jack.

When using the grinder I started with a #16 open coat disk, then I went to a #24 close coat disk. The #16 disk permitted me to remove more paint before the disk was clogged, but the #24 was better for locating low spots. After I established a good criss-cross pattern with a #24 disk, I chose a #50 grit disk for finish grinding. On vertical surfaces I was careful not to push the grinder just as I had avoided pressing down on it on the horizontal section.

I had to use filler on several parts of the rear fenders (Fig. 17-5). I sanded the area with #60 grit paper to prepare the surface. Then I mixed the filler on my mixing board and applied it. I used a piece of old venetian blind as an applicator on small areas, a 3″ putty knife for larger ones. I used extra pressure at cracks and holes to force the mixture down into them. After applying the filler I checked it every few minutes until my fingernail made a slight impression in it. Then I got my cheese grater file to remove the excess filler. After it hardened completely, I sanded it.

I found some rust on the left rear quarter panel. Such spots would bleed through the paint in time, so I decided to remove these. I used a torch to remove the metal, causing distortion. You can use a saber saw with a metal-cutting blade or tin snips to remove metal and an electric welder to repair the holes. I explored the area with my pick hammer for other weak places. At places where the metal was weak in areas which would be subject to rust, I welded some new metal into the section. Then I ground it down even with the contour lines of the car. To smooth it, I filled over those spots with body putty.

To try to discourage further rusting, I used an air hose to blow the dust out of the space between the inner and outer fender in the area where the rust spots had formed. Then I poured paint down into these inaccessible places. Primer would probably be a better choice for this kind of job if primer is available when needed.

## THE REST OF THE BODY

I worked forward along the left side of the car, using a pick hammer to probe for rusty or weak areas in the lower parts of the body. Surprisingly, these seemed to be good, but at the left door I found a problem. The car had evidently been in a front end collision, too. The door was greenish-blue under its surface paint. The hood also had that color, but the rest of the car, except for a formerly red rear fender, had been white. The left door did not make a perfect fit with the body. The crack at the back of the door, when shut, was too narrow. But the door worked well, so I decided

Fig. 17-4. Using grinder to remove high points on weld after repairing fender.

Fig. 17-5. After jacking body out and after filling, grinding, and sanding, the body matched the shape of the trunk lid.

to leave it. A correction would have required considerable body changes just to remedy the width of a crack which I didn't consider important. Decisions on a work car can sometimes be made on a more practical basis than those affecting the restoration of a vintage car that you will want to show.

    I found that the lower ridge line on the door didn't line up with that of the body. The ridge had been filled, but inadequately, so I had to fill again and build up the line until it was flush with that of the body. The tops of the front fenders had numerous tool dents from people working on the engine, requiring extra sanding and working. A mirror had evidently been jerked off the door, leaving two screw holes that were enlarged by the loss of the mirror. I dented these holes with a pick hammer so I could fill and finish them off to match the sheet metal around them. The left front edge of the hood had a crack in it. As I ground away a large amount of body putty, I found why it had been cracked. The hood in that area was under tension so that each movement when the hood was opened or closed caused it to flex. Pressing on any point caused this flexing or popping. I tried to shrink the area with a torch, but that only enlarged the affected area. So I hit the high points with the pick hammer to stretch the metal inward, severely re-damaging the part. This removed the tension which had caused it to pop out of shape at every movement. I filled over this area, which required more putty than I would have liked but which solved the problem without finding another hood.

There was a gap at the right front headlight where a hunk of putty had fallen out. I removed the old putty and found that the previous work here was really bad. Inadequate preparation had allowed the metal to continue rusting until it was worthless. I cut the worst section out with my torch. Then I selected a piece of 3/16" metal rod and formed it to match the contour on the left front fender, then reversed it so it would fit the right fender. I tack welded it in place, then added metal to this rod to form the new body line. I filled the rough places with body filler.

**SANDING**

When I started to do some of the final sanding on the car, I found that my old sander was causing a familiar problem that can ruin a paint job. It was depositing a thin film of grease at intervals over the metal. Even though some of these spots were invisible after sanding, they would prevent the paint from adhering to the metal. I went out and bought a new sander.

My new sander had a choice of straight line or orbital movements. I found that the straight line movement produced ridges in some areas where I couldn't move the tool adequately to make the sanding pattern overlap. When I got to the inside of the door jambs, I found a grease build-up, so I used solvent to remove the worst. Then I used a piece of rough sandpaper to pick up the remaining grease and followed that with other pieces of sandpaper until the dust from sanding was dry. Such places must usually be sanded by hand.

I also used old pieces of sandpaper to remove grease and road tar around the wheel wells; I evidently didn't get all of it because while I was later working on the muffler, I noticed a place under on one wheel well where the paint had flaked off. No serious defect, but a clear indication of what happens when you leave *any* foreign material and try to paint over it. It reminds me of the saying, "Why is there never enough time to do a job right but always enough time to do it over?"

As I worked on the car, I decided that because of the many small dents I would let the old paint serve as filler where possible. This permitted me to finish the job much more quickly than if I had removed all the paint and meticulously corrected each tiny imperfection. My goal was to produce a car with an overall good appearance, not necessarily as good as new. The condition of the body was one reason I was able to buy the car for $100. The finished car would be sound, but not perfect. The decision to let the paint work as filler saved tremendous time on the top because it meant that I didn't have to remove the headliner in order to do a perfect job of hammering out the dents.

## ANOTHER TRIP TO THE SALVAGE YARD

At the front of the car I found that the grille was too badly damaged to be useful. While at the salvage yard I had looked for a grille but couldn't find one. The wide aluminum grille on this model is evidently easily damaged, and there were few good grilles of any kind in the yards I visited, even though one had about 40 acres of cars. I carefully measured the space available for a grille, about 11" x 43". A smaller grille could be used, but none larger than that. A smaller grille with an obvious center line, requiring it to be lined up with headlights or other parts, might not fit. So I decided to look for a plain grille that could be used without requiring some special alignment. The bumpers on the Falcon were also damaged, so I decided to replace them if I could find some cheap but good bumpers.

Armed with a tape measure and a crude drawing of the front and rear of the car, complete with noted measurements, I returned to the salvage yards. At one yard I found a 1973 Rambler Ambassador with a grille that measured about 40" wide. According to my drawing this would leave a space of about 1½" between the ends of the grille and the headlights. The more I looked at the Ambassador grille, the better it looked, so I removed it (Fig. 17-6). I couldn't find a 68" bumper at the first yard; most bumpers on late model small cars were too small, those on full size cars too large. I finally found a front bumper on a 1965 Rambler and a rear bumper on a 1977 Mercury Monarch with rubber stops that would fit. The headlights on the Falcon were damaged too, so while I was out, I found a couple of square headlight rims from a 1976 Volare. They seemed to go well with the Ambassador grille.

Back at the shop it looked as though the headlights I had obtained were not right for the Falcon and the grille. There was too much space between the grille and the light rims, so I considered putting parking lights there. This idea was dropped for two reasons; I couldn't find any salvage lights that would fit, and the Rambler bumper had parking lights already installed in it. I gave up on the higher placement for parking lights and went to a welding shop to get material to make a frame for each headlight. I bought a 10' length of 1" × 2" × 1/8" rectangular tubing and a 10' length of 1" × 1/8" flat steel. From these materials I cut and tried until I had pieces that could be welded into a frame that fit the contours of the Falcon, the grille, and the headlight rims.

I found that the holes in the Rambler bumper were placed just right for the Falcon after I had reversed the mounting brackets on the Falcon. At the rear, the holes on the Monarch bumper didn't line up, so I had to do some measuring to locate new holes. I measured the width of the rear of the car, marked the center point on the new bumper, then used a square to place the holes so the bumper would be centered on the car. To get the bumper to set true in the horizintal plane, I had to use spacers on the bottom edge of the mounts. The Monarch bumper was a double bumper with a steel insert, as decreed by the Feds, to give extra impact protection. This extra steel aded about 50 pounds of weight that I didn't want, so I removed it.

If you rework a car for daily use, such as this, you may not want to go to the extra trouble of fitting salvage parts from other kinds of cars, but it *is* one way to keep the final cost low. Obviously it requires more time than just bolting on the right replacement parts. But it can give your car a special custom look.

Modern cars are often harder to rework than old cars because even a slight distortion which wouldn't be noticed on a curved surface will show up on a large flat area. One problem of this kind occurred on the Falcon's damaged hood. After knocking off the old putty and using my pick hammer to stretch the metal to remove the tension on it, it was necessary to fill a large area with a thin coat of filler. The problem was how to produce a smooth surface on the filler that would conform to the very slightly curved form of the hood. Since the area was almost flat, any distortion would show. I found a strip of pine of about ½ inch cross section and long enough to reach across the filled area. The strip was stiff enough to hold its shape but flexible enough to assume the slight curve of the hood. I applied the filler with my putty knife, then dragged the wood strip

Fig. 17-6. A salvage yard 1973 AMC Ambassador furnished a suitable, though non-stock, grille.

over the filler much the way a concrete worker uses a straight edge to level a concrete floor. The strip, about a foot and half long, quickly formed the filler to fit the shape of the hood. I could never have gotten the same degree of accuracy with my 3" putty knife.

## INTERIOR METAL

When I got to the interior of the car, I found that it was as bad as the exterior, maybe worse. The seats looked like someone had slashed them with a razor, then patched them with plastic tape to hold them together. They also sagged. The carpet was worn, loose, and filthy. I had noticed all this when I bought the car, but I also noticed that the door panels and headliner were all good. But the worst damage was in the floor. On the driver's side the sheet metal was riddled with rust, and at one point there was a gaping hole (Fig. 17-7). I removed the mats, the carpet, and the underlayment to inspect the damage. Then I removed the seats. I cut out the weak and rusty metal with a torch and welded a 12" × 18" flat section of fender from a junked car into that part of the floor. I also had to make several repairs to the right front floor and to the right rear. Then I drilled some holes to drain any water that might accumulate in the floor. I poured some paint primer over the surface to discourage further rusting (Fig. 17-8). Then I went to a carpet store and bought a remnant of home carpet large enough to cover the floor. I also got a pad to go under the carpet. I had to cut and seam the carpet to make it fit over the transmission hump.

## PAINTING

When I painted the car, I primed the door jambs first. If you work in a confined area, as I did, you may have some trouble with runs when painting some restricted areas. Some overspray is inevitable, one reason for spraying door jambs *first*. I always spray recessed areas before spraying large flat surfaces so there will be no overspray on the flat surface to ruin the finish.

I waited two weeks after priming the Falcon before spraying it with the final color. The extra time gave the primer time to shrink. Some paint manufacturers use additives in the primer which are supposed to prevent shrinking, but my experience has proved to me that allowing time to elapse between priming and final painting does the best job. Even with the two weeks I allowed, I can see places where the paint job shows that my sanding hit bare metal (Fig. 17-9). You have to inspect carefully to see them, but they are there. If I had wanted to do a super job, I would paint the car and let the paint set for a year or two, then sand it again, using the old paint as a filler. Then I would paint it again.

## WHEELS AND TIRES

The tires on the Falcon were in bad condition, so I didn't bother to cover them with any kind of wheel cover or masking material. The car had 13" wheels, and I wanted to go to a larger wheel. I found two 14" Mustang wheels and immediately installed these on the rear. When I find two more, I will put them on the front and have 14" wheels all around. The rear wheels cost $20 with fairly good tires installed on them. These tires, E70 × 14", are significantly larger in diameter than the original equipment tires. They make the speedometer inaccurate, but there are some worthwhile compensations for that minor disadvantage. On the highway the car runs as if it is in overdrive, the engine purring along at low speed. This will make for good highway gas mileage but at some loss of acceleration from stop lights. At the price of fuel, I can accept second place in the race to the next stop sign. On my next trip along a turnpike I will use the mile markers to calculate a correction factor for my speedometer. While using a larger wheel is good for economy, it shouldn't be overdone or the engine will be overtaxed, and that is bad for both gas mileage and durability.

Used tires can be an attractive alternative to buying new tires if the price is right. They should offer significant savings over new tires. Sometimes you can find a high quality used tire, such as a

Fig. 17-7. The condition of the floor in driver's area. Note hole near door.

radial, that will have many thousands of miles left. Some cheap new tires may not last over 12,000 to 15,000 miles. So you may get better value from premium used tires or, if you prefer new tires, by investing a little more money to get a better tire.

Another possibility for a work car is recapped tires. One problem with some recaps is that the original carcass may have had a puncture that will permit air to seep through under the cap. This kind of flaw means trouble—usually a lump in the tire and then a blowout. One recapper told us that he expects to lose at least one recap in every ten. There are many other possible problems with recapped tires. I once put four recapped tires on a car and had the two on the rear fail almost immediately. The recapper replaced those under protest. Then, after two thousand miles, the tread on one of the front tires had worn out while the other tire looked brand new. The recapper told me they couldn't replace the tire because they judge the age of the tire by the tread and in this case the tread was gone. Examination showed that the problem was in the tire, not the front end of the car nor in improper inflation because both front tires had received identical treatment. Much later I learned the reason for the rapid wear on the one front tire: the recapper had not used enough heat on the tire that wore out, leaving the rubber too soft.

Some northern recappers use steel shavings, such as cuttings from a lathe, in the rubber applied to recaps. On other tires, wood shavings or pieces of cork are sometimes used, leaving hard lumps

Fig. 17-8. Floor after welding in sheet metal and priming it.

of charcoal-like material. These additives are useful to provide better traction on ice, the steel bits for rear tires and the charcoal pieces for front tires.

## UPHOLSTERY

As I examined the seats that came out of the Falcon, I decided that they probably were not original equipment because they had head rests. They could be reworked, but considering the cost of

Fig. 17-9. Final sanding before painting. Note use of old paint as filler.

Fig. 17-10. The finished work car.

materials and the time it would take, I decided to look for something better at the salvage yard. I measured the interior of the car from door to door and took my trusty tape measure with me. I

Table 17-1. Cost Of Work Restoration. Note That Although The Car Is A 1965 Model, It Is Now In Top Condition, Both Mechanically And In Appearance. For A Reliable Car The Cost Seems Modest, Even Considering The Labor Time.

| | | |
|---|---|---|
| Initial cost | | $100.00 |
| Engine Parts | | |
| Chrome-moly rings, rod inserts, oil pump, head and pan gaskets, valve seals, 2 valves, used carburetor, oil filter, thermostat, distributor wire. | | $124.00 |
| Machine Shop Labor | | |
| Grind valves, knurl valve guides, resurface head. | | $30.00 |
| Salvage Parts for Body | | |
| Seats from 1976 Chevy Monte Carlo | $50.00 | |
| Trunk Lid | 10.00 | |
| Bumpers and grille | 17.50 | |
| 2 Used 14" wheels with tires | 20.63 | |
| Carpet remnant and pad | 27.50 | |
| | | $125.63 |
| Materials for Body Work | | |
| Grinding disks, sandpaper, hacksaw blades, body filler. | | $57.11 |
| Paint | | |
| Primer, sealer, thinner, sale paint, gallon can for mixing, | $79.95 48.90 | |
| 1 gallon finish paint | | $128.85 |
| Total Cost | | $565.85 |

325

knew that even large cars sometimes have seats that can fit into compacts, so I checked every car I approached to see if the seats were good. A 1976 Chevrolet Monte Carlo had the best looking set of seats in the yard. In fact they were like new. I ran my tape measure across them and found that they were 2" *narrower* than those I removed from the Falcon.

The man at the salvage yard tried to talk me out of the seats when I told him I was going to put them in a Falcon. "They won't go in that size car," he said. I showed him my tape measure, but he still wouldn't believe me. Finally he agreed to sell the seats for $50. Considering the quality of the material and its condition, it was a reasonable price.

The brackets would not fit the Falcon floor board, so I adapted the Falcon bracket to the Chevrolet seat. That made the seat fit the holes in the floorboard. The rear seats didn't quite reach to the door panels. The extra space can be filled several ways. An arm rest or a fabric-covered block of wood are two obvious methods of making seats that are too narrow look right.

The new seats completed my work on the Falcon (Fig. 17-10). The car now provides reliable transportation, and the front end is distinctive enough that a man stopped my wife and asked her what model car she was driving. I guess it's a '65, '73, '76, '77 Ambassador Monarch Volare Falcon.

Table 17-1 shows just how little this reliable transportation cost me.

# Chapter 18
# An Encouraging Word

When you find that a certain part is unavailable for the make and year of the car you are restoring, don't panic. Throughout automotive history most car makers have been assemblers rather than integrated manufacturers, simply buying the parts needed from a parts maker who also supplied parts for other cars. Such standard items as Borg-Warner transmissions and Continental engines have appeared in many different vehicles.

This historic situation means that there is a good chance that some part that seems totally unrelated just might fit *your* car. For example, who would have thought that an Oldsmobile camshaft bearing could be cut to fit the connecting rod of a Cushman pick-up? Or, slightly less fantastic but still surprising, that a kingpin made for a Jeep would have the exact dimensions of a broken one from an old International truck? These exchanges, just two of several mentioned in this book, show why you should never give up looking for a replacement part.

One of your biggest problems in adapting unrelated parts lies not with parts availability, but with the humans who sell the parts. The typical parts clerk will look at a part and, if it is not listed in the catalogs, will say it's not available. If you can find a sympathetic parts clerk who will permit you to compare pictures or actual parts, you are halfway home. Car restoration is a hobby that requires some imaginative problem solving and a lot of perseverance.

# Appendix

# Appendix
# National Clubs
# And Publications

The following clubs are each dedicated to the preservation of many makes of early cars. There are many other clubs dedicated to specific makes.

| Club | Official Publication |
|---|---|
| Antique Automobile Club of America<br>501 W. Governor Road<br>Hershey, PA 17033 | *Antique Automobile* |
| Classic Car Club of America<br>P. O. Box 443<br>Madison, N. J. 07940 | *The Classic Car* |
| Contemporary Historical Vehicle Ass'n.<br>Box 40<br>Antioch, Tenn. 37013 | *Action Era Vehicle* |
| Horseless Carriage Club of America<br>9031 E. Florence Ave.<br>Downey, CA 90240 | *Horseless Carriage Gazette* |
| Mid-America Old Time Automobile Ass'n.<br>920 Eisenhower St.<br>Tupelo, Mississippi 38801 | *Antique Car Times* |

## Club

The Veteran Motor Car Club of America
105 Elm St.
Andover, Massachusetts 01810

## Publication of Special Interest to Car Collectors

Old Cars Price Guide
Krause Publications, Inc.
700 E. State St.
Iola, Wisconsin 54945

## Official Publication

*The Bulb Horn*

Offers a guide to market activity and going prices for many kinds and models of old cars.

# Index

## A
| | |
|---|---|
| Air Compressor | 131 |
| Air cooled engines | 246 |
| Ammeter | 202 |
| Antique car | 26, 44, 72 |
| Antique Chevrolets | 52 |
| Austin Healey Big Eye Sprite | 93 |
| Automobiles, high wheeler | 43 |

## B
| | |
|---|---|
| Battery | 208 |
|     charger | 132 |
|     hydrometer | 132 |
| Bearings, in old engines | 173 |
| Body alignment | 268 |
|     bolts | 286 |
|     condition | 311 |
|     filler tools | 292 |
|     filler, using | 134 |
|     models | 29 |
|     removal | 146 |
|     sling | 135 |
| Bolts | 129 |
| Brake lining replacement | 280 |
| Brakes, hydraulic | 279 |
|     mechanical | 276 |
| Brass era cars | 49 |
| Buick Special, 1961-63 | 34 |
| Bushings, replacement | 266 |

## C
| | |
|---|---|
| Cables | 211 |
| Cabriolet | 30 |
| Carburetors | 194 |
| Cadillac | 65 |
| Carbon removal | 163 |
| Cars, checking the condition | 107 |
|     choice | 31 |
|     classes | 26 |
|     clubs | 14, 101 |
|     collecting | 32 |
|     dealers | 105 |
|     how to find one | 99 |
|     learning its history | 13 |
|     moving | 111 |
|     value | 12 |
| C-clamps | 129 |
| Chains | 129 |
| Chevrolets, antique | 52 |
|     production cars | 78 |
| Classic car | 26, 57 |
| Clutch | 250 |
|     removal | 251 |
| Coach | 30 |
| Contrary opinion | 32 |
| Convertible sedan | 30 |
| Coolants | 233 |
| Coupe | 30 |
| Cracked block | 242 |
| Cracked head | 242 |
| Cylinder damage | 169 |
|     hone | 133 |

## D
| | |
|---|---|
| Dash gauge problems | 220 |
| Dealers, car | 105 |

333

| | |
|---|---|
| Dents, hammering out | 288 |
| Differentials | 258 |
| Disassembly, preparation | 139 |
| Disc grinder | 135 |
| Doble steamer | 47 |
| Door panels | 302 |
| Door repair | 287 |
| Drill, electric | 130 |
| Driver tools | 255 |
| Drive shaft | 127 |
| Duesenberg | 65 |

### E

| | |
|---|---|
| Electric cars | 44 |
| Electrical meters | 132 |
| Electrical system, basics | 199 |
| Electrical system tools | 132 |
| Engines, cleaning | 162 |
| diagnosis | 158 |
| disassembly | 309 |
| disassembly procedure | 166 |
| frozen | 164 |
| kinds | 153 |
| lift | 132 |
| materials used in | 155 |
| pulling | 142 |
| swaps | 182 |

### F

| | |
|---|---|
| Fan belts | 235 |
| Feeler gauge | 131 |
| Fender covers | 129 |
| Fiat | 96 |
| Filling | 314 |
| Flaring tool | 131 |
| Flywheel | 250 |
| Ford Model T | 50 |
| Fords | 75 |
| Foreign cars | 93 |
| Four-door hardtop | 30 |
| Frame alignment | 288 |
| Front end design | 265 |
| inspection | 266 |
| Frozen engines | 164 |
| Fuel pumps | 192 |
| Fuels | 196 |
| Funnels | 131 |

### G

| | |
|---|---|
| Gaskets | 180 |
| installation | 181 |
| Gas lines | 189 |
| Gas tank | 188 |
| Gear oil pump | 130 |
| Generators | 212 |
| Glass repair | 287 |
| Grinder | 291 |
| Grinding | 314 |

### H

| | |
|---|---|
| Hammering out dents | 288 |
| Hammers | 126 |
| Handy retriever | 131 |
| Headliner | 304 |
| Heating problems | 243 |
| High tension wiring problems | 225 |
| High wheeler automobiles | 43 |
| Hoses | 235 |
| Hot rodding | 10 |
| Hydraulic brakes | 279 |
| jack | 131 |
| valve lifters | 180 |

### I

| | |
|---|---|
| Ignition circuit | 222 |
| pliers | 132 |
| Imperial sedan | 30 |
| Interior metal | 321 |
| strip down | 145 |
| Investments | 12 |

### J

| | |
|---|---|
| Jack stands | 131 |
| Jaguar | 95 |

### K

| | |
|---|---|
| Kingpins, replacement | 266 |

### L

| | |
|---|---|
| Landau | 30 |
| Lathe | 133 |
| Leak detection | 240 |
| Legal considerations | 108 |
| Lighting | 122 |
| Lights | 217 |
| Lincoln | 66 |
| Line cutter | 131 |
| Lubrication | 281 |
| Luxury cars, 1960-75 | 36 |

### M

| | |
|---|---|
| Magazines, source of information | |
| to find a car | 104 |
| Magnesium | 155 |
| Masking | 296 |
| Mechanical brakes | 276 |
| Mercer | 64 |
| Mercury | 77 |
| MG sports car | 92 |
| Models, out-of-favor | 32 |
| Muscle cars, beginning to move | 36 |
| 1960-70 | 35 |

## N

| | |
|---|---|
| Nameplates, collecting | 15 |
| Newspapers, source of information to find a car | 104 |
| Notarized bill of sale | 110 |
| Nuts | 129 |

## O

| | |
|---|---|
| Oil cans | 130 |
| Oil pressure gauge | 133 |
| Olds F-85, 1961-63 | 34 |

## P

| | |
|---|---|
| Packard | 58-63 |
| Paint | 298 |
| Painting | 322 |
| Parts, locating | 116 |
| Phaeton | 30 |
| Pilot shaft | 133 |
| Piston ring compressor | 133 |
| Planetary transmission | 249 |
| Pliers | 129 |
| Plymouth | 74 |
| Pontiac Tempest, 1961-63 | 33 |
| Practical restoration | 15 |
| Press fit, how to make | 270 |
| Price | 108 |
| Production car | 28, 71, 79-80 |
| Public sales | 103 |

## R

| | |
|---|---|
| Radiator | 238 |
| Radiator caps, collecting | 15 |
| Ramps | 131 |
| Ratchets | 127 |
| Rear axle diagnosis | 260 |
| Rear end removal | 262 |
| Rear lead springs, servicing | 271 |
| Renault | 89-92 |
| Restoring | 10 |
| Ring installation | 170 |
| Rings, new | 311 |
| Roadster | 30 |

## S

| | |
|---|---|
| Saab | 95 |
| Safety precautions | 297 |
| Sales, public | 103 |
| Sand blaster | 135 |
| Sanding | 295, 318 |
| Screwdrivers | 125 |
| Seats | 304 |
| Sedan | 30 |
| Sheet metal, replacing | 289 |
| work | 313 |
| Shock absorbers | 274 |
| Shop fixtures | 123 |
| Shop tools, for general use | 124 |
| Shorts, how to find | 206 |
| Shows | 14 |
| Small metal cutting tools | 135 |
| Sockets, set of | 127 |
| Spark plugs | 226 |
| Sport coupe | 30 |
| Stanley steamer | 46 |
| Starters | 216 |
| Steam cars | 44 |
| Steam engines | 46 |
| Steering linkage | 269 |
| Strip down, final | 149 |
| interior | 145 |
| procedures | 141 |
| Stud extractor | 133 |
| Stutz | 63-64 |
| Swap meets | 14 |

## T

| | |
|---|---|
| Temperature gauges | 245 |
| Test light | 205 |
| Thermosiphon | 231 |
| Thermostat | 232 |
| Threading tools | 130 |
| Timing light | 133 |
| Tire gauge | 131 |
| Tires | 280, 322 |
| Title laws | 110 |
| Tool catalog | 125 |
| for body work | 134 |
| purchasing | 121 |
| Torque converter | 249 |
| Touring car | 30 |
| Town car | 30 |
| Trailers | 113 |
| Transmission | 252 |
| trouble diagnoses | 253 |
| Triumph sports cars | 94 |
| Troubleshooting | 200 |
| with meters | 202 |
| Trucks | 29 |
| for car hauling | 115 |
| Two-door hardtop | 30 |

## U

| | |
|---|---|
| Universal joints | 255 |
| Upholstery | 324 |

## V

| | |
|---|---|
| Vacuum gauge | 132 |
| tanks | 190 |
| Valves | 177 |
| arrangements | 154 |
| lapping tool | 132 |

| | | | |
|---|---|---|---|
| Volkswagen | 85-89 | Welding equipment | 136 |
| Voltage regulation | 214 | Wheels | 322 |
| Volt-ohmmeter | 202 | Wills Sainte Claire | 67 |
| Volvo PV-444 | 96 | Willys-Knight | 54 |
| | | Wood blocks | 131 |
| **W** | | Wood work | 286 |
| Wash vat | 130 | Workshop | 122 |
| Water pump | 238 | Wrenches | 126 |